# SAT

CORE VOCAB 3000 plus

# SAT

## CORE VOCAB

### 3000 plus

KEITH KYUNG

재밌는거폭

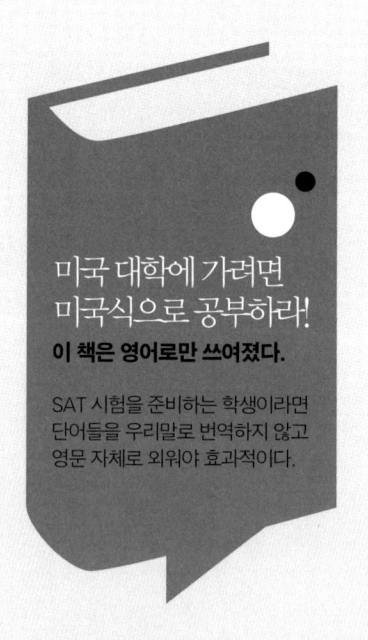

미국 대학에 가려면
미국식으로 공부하라!
**이 책은 영어로만 쓰여졌다.**

SAT 시험을 준비하는 학생이라면
단어들을 우리말로 번역하지 않고
영문 자체로 외워야 효과적이다.

이 책에 담긴 어휘들은 저자 KEITH KYUNG이
여러 해 동안 SAT를 가르치면서 그 경험을 바탕으로 정리한 핵심 리스트이다.
SAT 응시생들이 이 책을 활용한다면
**단어의 비밀병기를 가지는 것과 같다!**

# Preface

Along with the announcement of the latest changes to the SAT, the word was out that its vocabulary level will be significantly simplified. Many college-bound students were elated by the news. However, as someone deeply involved in the world of SAT education, I thought that it would be a bit premature to breathe a sigh of relief. I was right: the structures and question formats did reveal some major changes, but the fundamentals did not. Sure, the prompts no longer require test takers to identify the correct answer among a slew of words we hardly use, but this does not mean that students no longer need to learn them. The questions themselves do look simpler now, but the difficulty level of the language contained in the passages is still pretty much the same. In other words, the need to understand what a given passage is saying before answering its corresponding questions largely remains unchanged. In a nutshell, test takers still cannot avoid learning many of the so-called traditional SAT words.

Another important thing to note is that it is very difficult to discount the words that are considered archaic. Yes, we hardly ever use them now, but they are still well alive and kicking on the SAT. Again, the test may have gone through a major overhaul, but the verbal passage sources from which the test writers draw have not. You cannot blame College Board for that because, unless all of our educational institutions decide to drop teaching classic literature or treatises of America's forefathers and enfranchisement advocates altogether, the fancy, old-fashioned language will always be a regular on the SAT. Some of our most talented and influential writers of the past few centuries were rather fond of using them, perhaps partly for effect but likely because the concept of what is really archaic and what is not was not as sensitive or clear as it is today. Think Austen, Jefferson, or Du Bois, and you get the picture.

The old sentence completion section was especially notorious for testing obscure vocabulary, and the SAT people thought that it was time to get rid of it. In its place, the vocabulary in context is stressed throughout the verbal section. This pretty much means that it is now more important than ever before to know the diverse meanings of a given word. Many words in English have multiple meanings, and the list expands even further when their word classes change. Knowing the variations of the so-called SAT words, therefore, will definitely benefit the test takers.

Some of the words in this book may indeed appear a bit too difficult, obscure, or even archaic. The definitions provided for many of the words on the list may have a few too many meanings attached to them for the reader's liking. However, this book was written while keeping the aforementioned realities in mind. The provided list is the culmination of words painstakingly collected into my personal there-is-that-word-again notes throughout my countless years of teaching the SAT. I have every confidence that prospective SAT test takers will excel on the verbal section once they master the words that are included in this book.

# Abbreviation Key

| | |
|---|---|
| **n** | Noun |
| **v** | Verb |
| **adj** | Adjective |
| **adv** | Adverb |
| **pron** | Pronoun |
| **prep** | Preposition |
| **conj** | Conjunction |
| **interj** | Interjection |
| **fem** | Feminine |
| **alt** | Alternative |
| **pl** | Plural * |

* This book only indicates irregular forms.
Simply adding "s" after the word, in most cases, is also considered acceptable.

# Book Structure

This book 'does not contain any miraculous memorizing tips or neat exercises. Rather, it is straightforward, simply listing words that appear quite commonly on the SAT. Hardcore memorization, unfortunately, is still necessary for the SAT test, and this book aims to be an indispensable tool that can help guide students toward realizing their desired scores.

The words are grouped into sixty-four sets, with fifty words making up each set (or List). Setting up a daily regimen is up to the students, such as half of each set per day, a full set, or even two per day for the more go-getting students.

The words in the book are divided into three parts.

The first one contains words that are challenging or that are relatively "easier" but just too important to ignore. The latter is added to make sure that students really know them. Because our experiences in life are different, words that seem easy to some may not be so obvious to others. It is not a matter of intelligence. This primary group includes:

- Synonyms or related words: They are added to help readers have a better understanding of a given word instead of offering counterparts that are too difficult. An obscure alternative often ends up becoming a distraction rather than something beneficial. Note that they are NOT always direct synonyms. Also, in some rare instances, a seemingly difficult synonym will appear because of a lack of a more precise, simpler, or better word.

- Variations, derived, or related terms: Far too many times, I have seen students knowing a certain word but not knowing its variations. This is perhaps because syllables, intonations, and inflections change, sometimes quite drastically, as a given word goes through the transformation. A student, for example, might know the word "incline" but might not associate it with its noun form "inclination." The variations are thus provided so as to help the readers become more aware of the different forms that a given vocabulary could take. This book thus tries to steer away, whenever possible, from indicating simple but legitimate variations, such as just adding "ness" to an adjective or "ive" or "ble" to a noun to make a word into other parts of speech. Doing so would defeat the purpose.

The second group does away with synonyms, variations, etc., as they are relatively easier words. It, however, should be noted that they are certainly not any less important. They commonly appear on the SAT, and they are included to make sure that readers learn (if have not already) or review (if already familiar) them.

The last group includes a collection of commonly confused words. Some are simple, everyday English words, while others may prove to be a bit more challenging. The SAT test sometimes uses this scheme to throw students off, often proving to be an Achilles heel for many highly ambitious test takers. It is imperative to master these words.

# Contents

A Comprehensive Collection of Must-know SAT Words

# vocabulary

Part 1

# List 1

## 01 **actuate** v.
**actuation (n.)**
activate, motivate
to cause a device to operate or someone to act in a specific way

## 02 **affectation** n.
**affect (v.)**
pretense, show
an act or speech that is not natural or real

## 03 **antics** n.
prank, nonsense
silly, playful, or strange behavior

## 04 **antiquarian** n.
**antiquary (alt.)**
collector, dealer
a person who is knowledgeable of (or one who collects) antiques or rare items

## 05 **apparition** n.
**apparitional (adj.)**
illusion, phantom
a stunning or unexpected sight or appearance; a ghostlike appearance or ghost

## 06 **aristocracy** n.
**aristocrat (n.), aristocratic (adj.)**
nobility, ruling class
a privileged upper class with wealth and social standings, or a government ruled by such a class

## 07 . **avocation** n.

diversion, recreation

a secondary job or occupation that one pursues for enjoyment; a hobby

---

## 08 **benediction** n.

**benedictory (adj.)**

benison, grace

a prayer asking for God's guidance and blessing

---

## 09 **betrothal** n.

**betroth (v.), betrothed (adj.)**

engagement, vow

formal agreement for a future marriage

---

## 10 **brigand** n.

**brigandage (n.)**

outlaw, robber

a bandit (usually moving around in forests or mountain areas) who engages in robbery by attacking people

---

## . 11 **burnish** v.

brighten, rub down

to polish and make something smooth or shiny by rubbing

---

## 12 **burrow** v.

excavate, hollow out

to dig a hole or make a tunnel in order to hide or live in it

---

## 13 **capitalize** v.

**capitalization (n.)**

take advantage of; finance

to seize an opportunity or gain advantage; to supply, acquire, or convert into money or resources

---

## 14 **capricious** adj.

**caprice (n.)**

⸕ fickle, unpredictable

given to sudden or impulsive changes in attitude, mood, or behavior

---

## 15 **castigate** v.

**castigation (n.), castigatory (adj.)**

⸕ scold, chastise

to criticize or blame severely

---

## 16 **conflagration** n.

**conflagrate (v.), conflagrant (adj.)**

⸕ blaze, inferno; conflict, hostilities

a huge, destructive fire; a large-scale armed clash or war

---

## 17 **conjugal** adj.

**conjugality (n.)**

⸕ marital, nuptial

relating to marriage, a married couple, or the couple's relationship

---

## 18 **dastardly** adj.

**dastard (n.)**

⸕ cowardly, spineless; backstabbing, evil

lacking bravery; marked by deception and cruelty

---

## 19 **denomination** n.

**denominate (v.)**

⸕ designation; worth; sect

an act or way of naming or classifying things; a unit or value of money, weight, stamp, etc.; an independent branch of the Christian Church

---

## 20 **disclaimer** n.

**disclaim (v.)**

⸕ denial, repudiation; surrender, waiver

a statement denying responsibility, legal claim, opinions, etc.; an act of giving up or refusing a title, interest, estate, trust, etc.

### 21  **dutiable** adj.

**duty (n.)**

taxable

liable or subject to taxation

---

### 22  **efface** v.

**effacement (n.), effaceable (adj.)**

blot out, wipe off; lie low, keep quiet

to erase or make less distinct (as if by rubbing away a surface); to make oneself unnoticeable

---

### 23  **embodiment** n.

**embody (v.)**

actualization, realization

a physical or visible form of something that is abstract (such as idea, theory, quality, etc.)

---

### 24  **exculpate** v.

**exculpation (n.)**

absolve, acquit

to clear or free from blame or guilt

---

### 25  **façade** n.

exterior; pretense

the front or face of a building; a false, outer appearance

---

### 26  **foray** n.

raid, pillage; venture, experiment

a sudden or irregular attack for spoils; a brief attempt to try a new or different area or field

---

### 27  **fumigate** v.

**fumigation (n.)**

purify, sanitize

to apply certain fumes to disinfect or destroy pests or vermin

## 28 **gestation** n.

**gestate (v.)**

⌐ pregnancy, incubation; evolution, formation

the act, process, or period of carrying the unborn in the womb; the process of development of a plan, idea, etc.

## 29 **hibernal** adj.

**hibernate (v.)**

⌐ wintry, brumal

of or relating to winter

## 30 **immaterial** adj.

**immateriality (n.), immaterialize (v.)**

⌐ unimportant, inconsequential; formless, spiritual

enough to be considered irrelevant under the circumstances; having no matter or material body

## 31 **impecunious** adj.

**impecuniosity (n.)**

⌐ poor, penniless

lacking money

## 32 **indigent** adj.

**indigence (n.)**

⌐ poverty-stricken, impoverished

poor or in need

## 33 **indignation** n.

**indignant (adj.)**

⌐ resentment, bitterness

anger or disgust caused by something perceived as unjust or mean

## 34 **indiscriminately** adv.

**indiscriminate (adj.)**

⌐ unsystematically; freely

in a manner that is random or without careful judgment; in a way that is not restrained or restricted

## 35 **inert** adj.

**inertness (n.)**

🗨 stationary; sluggish

without the strength to move; extremely slow to act or move; having no active chemical or biological properties

---

## 36 **introspection** n.

**introspect (v.)**

🗨 self-examination, contemplation

the act or process of inspecting one's own thoughts and feelings

---

## 37 **lithe** adj.

🗨 flexible, supple

easily bent, or agile and graceful

---

## 38 **Machiavellian** adj.

**Machiavellianism (n.)**

🗨 ruthless, unethical

sneaky, cunning, or scheming, especially in politics

---

## 39 **metallurgy** n.

**metallurgical (adj.)**

the science and technology concerning metals

---

## 40 **multifarious** adj.

🗨 multiple, manifold

diverse, or of various kinds

---

## 41 **obsequious** adj.

🗨 fawning, groveling

excessively eager to please or obey

---

## 42 **oscillate** v.

oscillation (n.), oscillatory (adj.)

swing; waver

to move back and forth at a regular speed or rhythm; to change back and forth indecisively between conflicting ideas or opinions

## 43 **proclivity** n.

disposition, leaning

a tendency or inclination toward a particular thing

## 44 **quagmire** n.

quicksand, bog; plight, bind

a soft, swampy ground; a difficult or troubled situation

## 45 **specious** adj.

misleading, unsound

seemingly but deceptively logical, plausible, or attractive

## 46 **stodgy** adj.

filling; bulky; boring; unattractive; outmoded

rich and heavy (as in food); heavily built as to hinder movement; dull or uninteresting; drab or shabby; very old-fashioned

## 47 **verbatim** adv./adj.

word for word, directly

in or following exactly the same words

## 48 **veritable** adj.

genuine, complete

true, real, and not imaginary (used especially to emphasize the appropriateness of a metaphor)

## 49 **virtuoso** n.

virtuosic (adj.), virtuosity (n.)

maestro, artist; expert, master

one excelling in or having a fondness for the fine arts; a person of exceptional skill in a field

50 **woe** n./interj.

**woeful** (adj.)

agony, distress; alas, ay

(a cause or condition of) great grief, suffering, or misfortune; an exclamation to express misery or grief

*⌐* = Synonyms, related words

## 01 **abet** v.

**abetment (n.)**

*⌐* aid, support

to help or encourage someone to do something undesirable

## 02 **absolve** v.

**absolution (n.)**

*⌐* release, pardon

to set someone free from guilt, debt, or obligation

## 03 **accommodate** v.

**accommodation (n.), accommodating (adj.)**

*⌐* board, take in; oblige, cooperate

to provide housing; to provide with something desired or to do a favor

## 04 **ardor** n.

**ardent (adj.), ardently (adj.)**

*⌐* passion, devotion

an intense warmth of feeling, or great eagerness or strong desire

## 05 **aspersion** n.

**asperse (v.)**

*⌐* smear, defamation

an attack on somebody's name or reputation through false rumors

## 06 **astringent** adj.

*⌐* contracting; harsh

causing a tightening of body tissues; sharp, bitter, or severe in taste, manner, or style

## 07 **augment** v.

**augmentation** (n.), **augmentative** (adj.)

enhance, strengthen

to make something bigger or stronger, or to increase or supplement

---

## 08 **avant-garde** adj.

cutting-edge, progressive

promoting or favoring new techniques or experimentations, especially in the arts

---

## 09 **clamor** n.

**clamorous** (adj.), **clamorously** (adv.)

outcry, protest; commotion, racket

a strong, public demand or expression; a confused or continued noise

---

## 10 **commission** n./v.

committee; percentage; carrying out; authorize; request

person(s) chosen to perform a task; an agent's fee; an act of committing; to give power to; to make an order for something to be done or made

---

## 11 **consign** v.

**consignment** (n.)

delegate; demote

to hand over or deliver to another person's care, control, or custody; to assign to an unpleasant place

---

## 12 **contraband** n.

black marketeering, bootleg; fugitive

illegal trade or smuggled goods; a black slave who escaped to the Union during the Civil War

---

## 13 **conversant** adj.

**conversance** (n.)

well versed in, acquainted

having knowledge about something, mainly by studying or through experience

## 14 **dictum** n.

declaration, proclamation; saying, proverb

a noteworthy or formal statement of an opinion or principle; an observation or statement regarded as a general truth

## 15 **dishabille** n.

**deshabille (alt.)**

bareness, dishevelment

the state of being only partly clothed or dressed in a casual or careless manner

## 16 **diurnal** adj.

non-nocturnal; day-to-day, daily

relating to or active mainly in daytime; happening every day

## 17 **ethnocentric** adj.

**ethnocentrism (n.)**

evaluating or judging another culture based on standards of one's own culture

## 18 **euphonious** adj.

**euphony (n.)**

harmonious, melodious

having a sound that is pleasing to the ear

## 19 **fulsome** adj.

overdone; bountiful, unsparing

excessively flattering or lavish to the point of being offensive, insincere, or in bad taste; generous, abundant, full, or mature

## 20 **guile** n.

craftiness, deceptiveness

cleverness marked by deceit and cunning

## 21 **hone** v.

grind; master; strengthen

to sharpen (a blade); to refine a certain skill; to make more intense, firm, or effective

vocabulary

## 22 **impulse** n.

**impulsive** (adj.)

urge; incentive; wave

a sudden, strong desire to act; a motivating force; a pulse or abrupt current of electrical energy

---

## 23 **incapacitate** v.

**incapacitation** (n.)

suspend, prohibit; paralyze, disable

to disqualify or make legally ineligible; to make incapable or unfit

---

## 24 **inept** adj.

**ineptitude** (n.)

unskillful; ridiculous

clumsy or having no competence; foolish or absurd

---

## 25 **instigate** v.

**instigation** (n.)

initiate, launch; provoke, prompt

to bring about or set in motion; to incite or urge on

---

## 26 **iridescence** n.

**iridescent** (adj.)

luster

a display of shining, rainbowlike colors that appear to change as the angle of view changes; a brilliant or enchanting quality or effect

---

## 27 **jabber** v.

chatter, prattle

to speak rapidly and excitedly without making much sense

---

## 28 **lacerate** v.

**laceration** (n.)

slash, rip; distress, torment

to tear, cut deep, or wound (a skin); to criticize harshly or hurt (a person's feelings)

---

vocabulary

## 29 lackluster adj.

colorless, dark; listless, spiritless; common, ordinary

lacking shine or brightness; lacking energy or conviction; mediocre or uninspiring

## 30 laggard n.

lag (n./v.)

loiterer, straggler

a person who is slow or who is always falling behind others

## 31 luminosity n.

luminous (adj.)

brilliance, glow; power, intensity

radiance or brightness of something; the natural brightness or energy of a celestial object

## 32 marginalize v.

marginalization (n.)

lower, relegate

to place someone or something in a weak or unimportant position within a group or society

## 33 moderate adj./v.

moderation (n.)

centrist; temperate; fair; reduce; mediate

not having extreme political or religious views; restrained or calm; having average amount, effect, scope, etc.; to make less intense; to preside over

## 34 monologue n.

soliloquy, address

a long or dramatic speech (in a play, movie, verse, prose, etc.) by a single speaker

## 35 mortify v.

mortification (n.)

shame; subdue, control

to make one feel embarrassed or humiliated; to punish or suppress one's body, needs, desires, appetites, etc., by self-inflicted pain or self-denial

vocabulary

## 36 **omnivorous** adj.

**omnivore (n.)**

all-consuming

eating both animal and vegetable substances; madly or excitedly utilizing or taking in everything

## 37 **pagan** n.

**paganism (n.)**

infidel, heathen

a person without religion or religious belief

## 38 **pariah** n.

outcast, outsider

a person who is rejected, despised, or in exile; a member of a low social caste in India

## 39 **parity** n.

equivalence, par

the quality or state of being equal in power, strength, rank, value, etc.; the fact or condition of having borne offspring

## 40 **pedestrian** adj./n.

boring, tedious; walking, stroller

not interesting or inspiring; (a person) going on foot

## 41 **perpetual** adj.

**perpetuity (n.)**

continual, eternal

occurring repeatedly or lasting forever

## 42 **pertinent** adj.

**pertinence (n.)**

relevant, appropriate

relating to or having a clear connection with a particular subject or matter

### 43 **prescient** adj.

**prescience** (n.)

⌂ visionary, foreseeing

possessing the ability to predict future events

---

### 44 **proprietor** n.

**proprietorship** (n.)

⌂ holder, landlord

a person who owns a business or property

---

### 45 **provocation** n.

**provoke** (v.), **provocative** (adj.)

⌂ instigation, excitement

the act of inciting or annoying, or something that stimulates

---

### 46 **remedial** adj.

**remedy** (n.)

⌂ healing, medicinal; corrective, reformative

intended as a treatment or cure; concerned with teaching methods for students who have difficulty learning

---

### 47 **sacrilege** n.

**sacrilegious** (adj.)

⌂ blasphemy, desecration

disrespect or violation of something held sacred

---

### 48 **stripling** n.

⌂ lad, boy

a young man

---

### 49 **truncheon** n.

⌂ club, rod

a short, thick stick used as a weapon by a police officer, or a baton or staff symbolizing authority

## 50 **vicarious** adj.

**indirect; delegated**

participating through the experience of another; entrusted to handle the affairs of another

---

# List 3

## 01 **alliteration** n.

**alliterate (v.), alliterative (adj.)**

rhythm, recurrence

the repetition of the same letter or sound in adjacent words or syllables

## 02 **annuity** n.

**annuitize (v.)**

pension, allowance

a payment given out (or the right to collect a fixed sum of money) regularly over a defined period

## 03 **assimilate** v.

**assimilation (n.), assimilative (adj.)**

comprehend; blend in; digest

to absorb and fully understand information, ideas, or culture; to become part of a culture or group; to absorb nutrients into the body

## 04 **assuage** v.

relieve, soothe

to lessen (as in pain or stress), calm (as in anger), or satisfy (as in thirst or hunger)

## 05 **auspicious** adj.

**auspice (n.)**

promising; fortunate

pointing to a bright future; favored by luck

## 06 **avalanche** n.

snowslide; barrage

a mass of snow, ice, or rock falling suddenly and rapidly down a mountain; a sudden, overwhelming development, situation, or rush of something

Part 1

vocabulary

## 07 **bawl** v.

🖙 holler; wail

to shout or call out without restraint; to cry or weep loudly

---

## 08 **cardinal** adj./n.

🖙 fundamental; grave; scarlet

of greatest importance; very serious; bright red color; a Roman Catholic official; a bird belonging to the family Thraupidae

---

## 09 **chimera** n.

**chimerical (adj.)**

🖙 delusion, pipe dream; hybrid

an unrealistic dream or illusion; any imaginary creature having body parts of different animals; an organism made up of various genetic cells

---

## 10 **collateral** n./adj.

🖙 guarantee; accompanying; side by side; roundabout; related

a security promised for paying back a loan; acting as a secondary; parallel; indirect; having the same ancestors but of a different line

---

## 11 **corpulent** adj.

**corpulence (n.)**

🖙 bulky, obese

large in body or overweight

---

## 12 **cynicism** n.

**cynical (adj.), cynic (n.)**

🖙 mistrust, suspicion; pessimism, despair

a distrustful attitude or emotion (from a belief that people are generally selfish); the tendency of being doubtful about a situation or the future

---

## 13 **diffident** adj.

**diffidence (n.)**

🖙 modest, timid

shy or lacking self-confidence

---

## 14 **dilate** v.

**dilation (n.)**

enlarge, swell; elaborate, develop

to make bigger, become wider, or expand; to comment or write at length

## 15 **divination** n.

**divinatory (adj.)**

fortune-telling; intuition

the art or practice of predicting the future; exceptional perception or insight

## 16 **educe** v.

**educible (adj.)**

bring forth, give rise to; derive, conclude

to develop or draw out (as in potential); to infer or extract from data, information, etc.

## 17 **effulgent** adj.

**effulgence (n.)**

dazzling, beaming

shining radiantly or brilliantly

## 18 **epitome** n.

**epitomize (v.)**

exemplar, embodiment; abstract, synopsis

a typical or best example of something; a brief summary of a text

## 19 **expound** v.

detail; spell out; announce

to present and explain something point by point; to explain, interpret, or clarify; to comment or make a statement, usually one that is long

## 20 **hegemony** n.

**hegemon (n.), hegemonic (adj.)**

supremacy, domination

influence or dominance over another

vocabulary

## 21 **histrionic** adj.

**histrionics (n.)**

exaggerated; theatrical

excessively or needlessly dramatic or affected; of or relating to the nature of acting, actors, or the theater

---

## 22 **incinerate** v.

**incineration (n.), incinerator (n.)**

torch, reduce to ashes

to destroy by burning

---

## 23 **irascible** adj.

**irascibility (n.)**

cranky, irritable

quick-tempered or easily angered

---

## 24 **jurisprudence** n.

**jurisprudent (adj.)**

body of law

the theory, science, philosophy, or study of law; a legal system or a division of law

---

## 25 **kudos** n.

cheers, applause; prestige, reputation

praise or credit received for an achievement; fame gained from an achievement

---

## 26 **lexicon** n.

**lexicography (n.), lexicology (n.)**

wordbook; word stock; record

a dictionary of a language; the vocabulary specific to a person, group, or certain subject; an inventory or listing

---

## 27 **lucrative** adj.

moneymaking, gainful

producing a surplus or profit

## 28 **maleficent** adj.

maleficence (n.)

menacing, wicked

harmful or evil

## 29 **matron** n.

headmistress, dowager

a woman in charge of an establishment, or a married woman or widow marked by dignified manner or maturity

## 30 **maven** n.

authority, specialist

an expert in a particular field

## 31 **mawkish** adj.

sentimental; nauseating

exaggeratedly or falsely emotional; having an unpleasant flavor or taste

## 32 **mercantile** adj.

mercantilism (n.)

commercial, business

relating to trade, commerce, or merchants

## 33 **misgiving** n.

misgive (v.)

uneasiness, distrust

a feeling of doubt, fear, or suspicion, especially about a future event

## 34 **necropolis** n.

burial ground, graveyard

a cemetery, especially one elaborately built in an ancient city

## 35 **neophyte** n.

proselyte; beginner

a new convert to a religion or cause; someone who is new to a particular subject or activity

### 36 **ordain** v.

**ordainment (n.)**

anoint; decree; predestine

to make someone a priest or minister; to issue an order or command officially; to determine (the fate or destiny) in advance

---

### 37 **palpable** adj.

**palpability (n.)**

tangible, touchable; noticeable, apparent

able to be felt or handled; obvious or easily perceptible

---

### 38 **platform** n.

stage; manifesto

a raised floor or level surface; a declaration of policies or principles; an operating system for computer or other device; a thick-soled shoe

---

### 39 **polyglot** adj./n.

**polyglottal (adj., alt.)**

multilingual; diverse

(a person) knowing or using multiple languages; (a book, region, etc.) written in or containing various languages or linguistic groups

---

### 40 **proliferation** n.

**proliferate (v.)**

multiplication, generation; mass, multitude

rapid increase in numbers or growth of cells, parts, or offspring; a great number of something

---

### 41 **rapt** adj.

captivated; elated

completely fascinated or absorbed; filled with intense joy and delight; transported into the air, or carried away to heaven

---

### 42 **redress** v.

correct, rectify

to compensate, or to set right a wrong

---

### 43 **retrench** v.

**retrenchment (n.)**

curtail; delete, cut out

to reduce in quality or extent, especially costs or spending; to remove or omit

---

### 44 **seminal** adj.

spermatic; original; crucial

of or relating to seed, semen, or reproduction; influencing or contributing to later development; of fundamental or pivotal importance

---

### 45 **somnolent** adj.

**somnolence (n.)**

dozy, languid

drowsy or sleepy, or suggestive of or inducing drowsiness

---

### 46 **sprightly** adj.

active, vigorous

spirited, energetic, or zesty

---

### 47 **sublimate** v.

**sublimation (n.)**

refine, redirect

to divert or change an expression or desire into one that is more socially acceptable; to change directly from solid to gas state

---

### 48 **temperance** n.

**temperate (adj.)**

sobriety, abstinence; control, discipline

the fact or practice of drinking little or no alcohol; self-restraint in conduct, thought, or expression

---

### 49 **truncate** v./adj.

**truncation (n.)**

trim, abridge; flattened, blunt

to shorten by cutting off; having a square, broad, or even end

---

## 50 **wrought** adj.

hammered; fashioned; decorated; manufactured

beaten into shape; formed into shape by artistry or hard effort; elaborately adorned or ornamented; processed or prepared for use

vocabulary

# List 4

✐ = Synonyms, related words

## 01 **aboriginal** adj.

**aborigine (n.)**

✐ native, indigenous

the earliest to exist in a land according to historical or scientific records

## 02 **acquiesce** v.

**acquiescence (n.), acquiescent (adj.)**

✐ consent, submit

to accept by silence or not deciding to object

## 03 **adamant** adj.

✐ firm, resolute

unwilling to be persuaded

## 04 **ambulatory** adj./n.

**ambulate (v.), ambulation (n.)**

✐ wandering; adjustable; walkway

able to walk; relating or adapted to walking; not fixed or stationary; capable of being legally altered; a place intended for walking

## 05 **antilogy** n.

✐ contrast, opposition

a contradiction in terms or ideas that are related

## 06 **aphorism** n.

**aphorist (n.), aphoristic (adj.)**

✐ adage, maxim

a short saying that expresses a wise observation or general truth

Part 1

vocabulary

## 07 **appropriation** n.

**appropriate (v.), appropriable (adj.)**

takeover; funding

an act of taking something exclusively or without having the right; funds set aside for a specific use

---

## 08 **askance** adv.

suspiciously; sideways

with (an attitude or look of) mistrust or disapproval; with a sidelong glance

---

## 09 **beau** n.

**beaux (pl.)**

beloved; dandy

a boyfriend or male lover of a woman; a man having a reputation for dressing well and good manners

---

## 10 **bedeck** v.

**bedecked (adj.)**

adorn, embellish

to decorate, cover, or clothe with fine things

---

## 11 **beneficiary** n.

recipient; inheritor

a person receiving some sort of help or benefit; someone entitled to receive money or property from a trust, will, or insurance policy

---

## 12 **blatant** adj.

**blatantly (adv.)**

clamorous; outright

noisy or sounding loudly in an offensive manner; openly and shamelessly obvious

---

## 13 **colossus** n.

**colossal (adj.)**

giant, titan

a huge statue, or anyone or anything of great size, influence, or power

## 14 **commingle** v.

blend, put together
to mix or combine

## 15 **deity** n.

divinity, immortal
(the state or position of being) a god, goddess, or any divine being

## 16 **dejected** adj.

**dejection (n.)**
depressed, disheartened
sad or low in spirits

## 17 **desultory** adj.

casual; wandering; discouraging
having no definite purpose, plan, or enthusiasm; not connected with the main idea or
subject; disappointing in performance or quality

## 18 **deviate** v.

**deviant (n./adj.), deviation (n.)**
divert, stray
to move away from a set course, standard, norm, doctrine, etc.

## 19 **dragnet** n.

search, manhunt; fishnet, trap
a systemized network to capture suspects or criminals; a net drawn along the bottom
of water or across ground to catch fish or small animals

## 20 **embroider** v.

**embroidery (n.)**
knit, ornament; dramatize, overstate
to decorate with needle and thread of assorted colors; to exaggerate a story or event

vocabulary

## 21 genealogy n.

genealogical (adj.), genealogist (n.)

 lineage, line

an account or recorded history of the descent, origin, or development of a person, animal, plant, etc., traced from an ancestor

---

## 22 guise n.

 pretense; costume; image

a false or misleading appearance; a style or form of dress; an outward or external appearance

---

## 23 hunker v.

hunkering (adj.)

 squat; fortify; apply oneself

to crouch down low; to settle or dig in, mainly to take a defensive position; to work diligently on a certain task

---

## 24 impregnable adj.

impregnability (n.)

 unconquerable, impenetrable; firm, unwavering

too strong to be taken forcefully or broken into; incapable of being shaken or refuted

---

## 25 incarcerate v.

incarceration (n.)

 imprison, lock up; restrain, restrict

to put in jail; to enclose or confine

---

## 26 innate adj.

 inborn, natural

existing since birth, or coming from or driven by instinct

---

## 27 insular adj.

insularity (n.)

 narrow-minded; isolated

ignorant or inward-looking; having little or no contact with other people; of, relating to, or like an island

## 28 **joust** v.

clash; tilt

to combat or compete for superiority or supremacy; to fight with lances while riding on a horseback

## 29 **justification** n.

justify (v.), justifiable (adj.)

defense, rationale; text alignment

a reason or excuse showing or explaining something to be correct, righteous, or reasonable; the arrangement of lines of text by proper spacing

## 30 **louse** n.

lice (pl.)

parasite; scoundrel

a tiny (parasitic) insect that lives mostly on other organisms; a bad, deceitful, or contemptible person

## 31 **lynch** v.

lynching (n.)

put to death, execute illegally

to murder (especially by hanging) by mob action without a proper or legal trial

## 32 **magnate** n.

tycoon, mogul

a wealthy and powerful person in a particular area, especially in business

## 33 **matriarch** n.

matriarchal (adj.), matriarchy (n.)

queen, grande dame

a woman who rules a family, tribe, or state, or a revered elderly woman

## 34 **maverick** n.

free spirit, individualist

an independent person who does not abide by the rules of a group or party; an unbranded animal, especially a strayed or motherless calf

### 35 **motley** adj./n.

assorted; rainbow; harlequin; jokester

made up of many incongruously varied elements; having a variety of colors; a multi-colored clothes; a jester or fool

---

### 36 **Occident** n.

**Occidental (adj.), Occidentalism (n.)**

the West

the Western world

---

### 37 **ogre** n.

**ogress (fem.), ogreish (adj.)**

monster, giant; brute, villain

a huge and terrifying creature that feeds on humans (from folklore or fairy tales); a cruel, dreaded, or hideous person or thing

---

### 38 **ordeal** n.

suffering, trouble; trial by fire

a difficult or painful experience; a primitive trial method of determining guilt or innocence by subjecting the accused to painful tests

---

### 39 **ostracize** v.

**ostracism (n.)**

exile, ignore

to banish or exclude from a group, community, or society

---

### 40 **papal** adj.

**papacy (n.)**

pontifical, apostolic

having to do with the pope or the Roman Catholic Church

---

### 41 **pessimism** n.

**pessimistic (adj.), pessimist (n.)**

negativity, cynicism

a tendency to see or expect the worst aspect of things or possible outcome

## 42 **plenary** adj.

unrestricted, whole

complete, full, or absolute; for or in full attendance by all the members of an organization or group

## 43 **potentate** n.

sovereign, autocrat

a monarch, ruler, or a person who holds great power

## 44 **preferment** n.

promotion, rise

advancement to a higher office, station, or position

## 45 **presentiment** n.

foreboding, intuition

a feeling that something, especially one that is undesirable, is going to take place

## 46 **presumptuous** adj.

**presumption (n.)**

arrogant, overconfident

not observing the limits of what is considered proper or appropriate

## 47 **prognosis** n.

**prognostic (adj.)**

foretelling, prophecy

a forecast of the likely course of, or the chance of recovery from, a disease; a prediction of the probable outcome

## 48 **prognosticate** v.

**prognosticative (adj.), prognosticator (n.), prognostication (n.)**

predict, foreshadow

to foretell or warn a future event

vocabulary

### 49 **turgid** adj.

**turgidity (n.)**

bloated, distended; pretentious, flowery

swollen or congested; tediously or overly pompous or difficult in language or style

---

### 50 **vivacious** adj.

**vivacity (n.)**

high-spirited, lively

animated and full of energy

---

# List 5

= Synonyms, related words

---

## 01 **abhorrent** adj.

**abhorrence (n.), abhor (v.)**

 awful, detestable

causing hatred or disgust

---

## 02 **abomination** n.

**abominate (v.), abominable (adj.)**

 evil, revulsion

something that causes (or a feeling of) great disgust and hatred

---

## 03 **acclimate** v.

**acclimatize (v.), acclimation (n.)**

 adapt, get used to

to adjust to a new environment

---

## 04 **acoustic** adj.

**acoustics (n.)**

 audio, auditory

related to the sense or organs of hearing or the science of sounds

---

## 05 **adage** n.

 proverb, maxim

a short, old saying that conveys a general truth

---

## 06 **aficionado** n.

 devotee, enthusiast

a person who knows about and has great interest in a particular subject

---

## 07 **allay** v.

 ease, relieve

to put fear or worry to rest, or to lessen pain or suffering

---

## 08 **amorphous** adj.

amorphism (n.)

☞ vague, irregular

not having a definite form or shape

---

## 09 **antagonistic** adj.

antagonism (n.), antagonist (n.), antagonize (v.)

☞ hostile, unfriendly

showing or feeling hatred, or in strong or violent disagreement

---

## 10 **berate** v.

☞ rebuke, lecture

to scold sternly

---

## 11 **biped** n.

bipedal (adj.)

an animal that utilizes two feet to move around

---

## 12 **bludgeon** n./v.

☞ club; strike; harass

a short stick with a thick, heavy end; to hit with a heavy weapon or anything physically hard; to coerce aggressively

---

## 13 **broker** n.

brokerage (n.)

☞ mediator, intermediary

a person who acts as an agent

---

## 14 **browbeat** v.

browbeater (n.)

☞ bully, scare

to intimidate with abusive words or in a stern manner

---

## 15 **carnage** n.

☞ massacre, slaughter; corpses, gore

death and destruction; the flesh or bodies of slain humans or animals

---

## 16 chronometer n.

**chronometry (n.), chronometric (adj.)**

⌐ clock, timepiece

a device or instrument that measures time with great accuracy

## 17 cliché n.

**clichéd (adj.)**

⌐ commonplace, banality

something that is overused to the point that it becomes very uninteresting or is considered too common

## 18 convivial adj.

**conviviality (n.)**

⌐ sociable, companionable

relating to or fond of festive activities, such as feasting and drinking

## 19 corpuscle n.

**corpuscular (adj.)**

⌐ speck, fleck

any tiny particle; a cell (in biology); electron, atom, etc. (in physics)

## 20 corrosive adj.

**corrosion (n.), corrode (v.)**

⌐ erosive; sharp-tongued

having the power to wear away or cause deterioration; bitterly or stingingly sarcastic

## 21 curt adj.

**curtness (n.), curtly (adv.)**

⌐ terse; blunt; minimized

not using too many words to convey information; too brief, to the point of being rude; concise or shortened

## 22 diatribe n.

⌐ condemnation, tirade

an abusive, bitter criticism, particularly in speech or writing

## 23 discern v.

**discernible (adj.), discernibly (adv.)**

notice, perceive

to see clearly or understand, or to be able to recognize the difference

---

## 24 distrain v.

**distrainer, distrainor (n.)**

confiscate, take possession of

to force a person to do something by seizing property, or to seize a property as security until a debt is paid

---

## 25 duress n.

coercion, pressure; custody, confinement

threats forcing someone to do something; imprisonment

---

## 26 encryption n.

**encrypt (v.), encrypted (adj.)**

hide, conceal

the process of coding information or data so as to make it unreadable for outsiders

---

## 27 expiate v.

**expiation (n.)**

mend, compensate

to atone or pay for an offense, guilt, or wrongdoing

---

## 28 extenuate v.

**extenuating (adj.), extenuation (n.)**

defend, justify; weaken, impair

to make (a fault, offense, etc.) appear less serious by providing reasons or making excuses; to lessen or lower the effect or strength of

---

## 29 fitful adj.

sporadic, disrupted

active or occurring irregularly

---

## 30 **genuflect** v.

**genuflection (n.)**

 kneel, bow down

to bend the knee as a sign of worship or respect, or to act or behave in a submissive manner

## 31 **grapple** v.

**grappling (adj.)**

 grip; sort out; wrestle

to seize and hold securely; to try to cope or deal with something; to fight hand-to-hand without using weapons

## 32 **havoc** n.

 ruin, catastrophe; disorder, disarray

widespread destruction or devastation; great confusion or disorganization

## 33 **inebriate** v.

**inebriation (n.)**

 intoxicate

to make, become, or cause to be drunk

## 34 **jurisdiction** n.

 control; judicature; district

the authority or the extent of the power to make legal decisions; a court, or a system of law courts; the territorial limits of authority

## 35 **logos** n.

 logical appeal

a means of persuasion through logic or reason

## 36 **lucid** adj.

**lucidity (n.)**

 comprehensible; sane; luminous

understandable, or clearly expressed; mentally sensible or sound; bright or transparent

## 37 **martyr** n.

**martyrdom (n.)**

saint; victim

a person who chooses to suffer or be tortured or killed rather than giving up a belief, faith, or principle; a constant sufferer of pain or misery

---

## 38 **necrosis** n.

**necrotic (adj.)**

the death of cells or tissues in a certain part of the body

---

## 39 **orthopedic** adj.

**orthopedics (n.)**

of or relating to the branch of medicine dealing with bones, joints, muscles, etc.

---

## 40 **pension** n.

benefit, allowance; rental, room and board

a regular payment made to a person; a boardinghouse

---

## 41 **placid** adj.

**placidity (n.)**

serene, even-tempered

peaceful, undisturbed, or not easily excited

---

## 42 **prerequisite** n.

precondition, requirement

a thing required or necessary as a condition for something that follows

---

## 43 **proffer** v.

submit, propose

to present or offer for acceptance

---

## 44 **prudery** n.

**prude (n.), prudish (adj.)**

primness, moralism

the quality or state of being excessively proper or modest in behavior and morals

## 45 **sentient** adj.

**sentience** (n.)

aware, conscious

able to feel or perceive

## 46 **surly** adj.

ill-natured; threatening

bad-tempered, rude, or unfriendly; menacing or gloomy (as in weather)

## 47 **temerity** n.

**temerarious** (adj.)

rashness, nerve

reckless or foolish boldness or confidence

## 48 **tumultuous** adj.

**tumult** (n.)

uproarious, deafening; intense, violent

characterized by loud, excited noise; confused or disorderly

## 49 **vignette** n.

scenario, portrayal

a brief literary sketch or a scene in a film or play; a picture that shades off gradually at the edge; a design of vine branches in a book

## 50 **whimsical** adj.

**whim** (n.), **whimsy** (n.), **whimsicality** (n.)

playful, quaint; impulsive, capricious

oddly or amusingly fanciful, attractive, or appealing; subject to unpredictable behavior or change

vocabulary

### 01 **abyss** n.

**abyssal (adj.)**

✐ chasm, pit

a deep opening; a difficult or destructive situation most likely to happen

### 02 **accession** n.

✐ elevation; addition; consent

the obtaining of rank or power; an increase by something added; the act of agreeing or accepting

### 03 **adjure** v.

**adjuration (n.)**

✐ implore, entreat; order, obligate

to urge or request earnestly; to issue a formal command

### 04 **amplitude** n.

✐ extent, range

the measure of the size of something; the distance between the highest and the lowest point of a wave

### 05 **appendage** n.

**append (v.)**

✐ addition, accessory; arm, leg

a part that is added to something more important; any external part of an organism, such as a limb, tail, branch, etc.

### 06 **arbiter** n.

✐ judge, referee; expert, authority

a person with the authority to settle a dispute; a person whose opinions have huge influence over social trends

## 07 **battery** n.

**batter (v.), battered (adj.)**

✎ cannonry; assault; array

a fortress to place heavy guns; the act of striking someone or something repeatedly and violently; a series or arrangement of similar things

---

## 08 **bray** v.

**braying (adj.)**

✎ neigh, shriek; pound, mill

to utter, laugh, or make a loud cry, almost like that of a donkey; to crush or grind into a powder

---

## 09 **burgeoning** adj.

**burgeon (v.)**

✎ flourishing, prospering

beginning to grow, develop, or expand rapidly

---

## 10 **bursar** n.

**bursary (n.), bursarial (adj.)**

✎ treasurer

an official in charge of funds and finances, as at a school or college

---

## 11 **cerebral** adj.

✎ brainy, analytical

relating to the cerebrum (a part of the brain) or the intellect (as opposed to emotions)

---

## 12 **circumspect** adj.

**circumspection (n.)**

✎ prudent; guarded

careful and tending to think before acting; not willing to take risks

---

## 13 **concoct** v.

**concoction (n.), concoctive (adj.)**

✎ put together, create; fabricate, devise

to prepare by mixing various ingredients; to make up or come up with something

## 14 **condescending** adj.
condescend (v.), condescension (n.)

snobbish, patronizing

showing a tone of superiority

## 15 **convergent** adj.
converge (v.), convergence (n.)

merging, connecting

moving toward one point to come closer together (as in lines, forces, characteristics, ideas, etc.)

## 16 **crucible** n.

melting pot, vessel; ordeal, challenge

a container in which substances can be heated up or even melted; a very difficult test, trial, or experience

## 17 **culmination** n.
culminate (v.), culminant (adj.)

climax, prime

the reaching of the highest altitude or decisive point

## 18 **culvert** n.

channel, conduit

a drain or tunnel that passes under a road, railroad, path, etc.

## 19 **deprecate** v.
deprecation (n.), deprecating (adj.)

frown upon; withdraw; put down

to express disapproval of; to discourage the use of something in favor of a better option; to speak negatively of someone or something

## 20 **desolate** adj.
desolation (n.)

lifeless, deserted; gloomy, miserable

having no visitors or inhabitants, or showing signs of neglect or abandonment; lonely, or having no warmth or hope

## 21 **elated** adj.

elate (v.), elation (n.)

⌐ ecstatic, overjoyed

extremely happy or in high spirits

## 22 **gamut** n.

⌐ spectrum, extent

a complete or entire range or series; a complete musical scale

## 23 **grandiose** adj.

grandiosity (n.)

⌐ grand, majestic; showy, pompous

imposing and impressive in size, scope, or extent; trying to appear important

## 24 **gratuity** n.

⌐ tip, reward

money or gift given willingly, usually for some service rendered

## 25 **humanities** n.

⌐ arts, classics

academic disciplines concerned with human culture, such as literature, history, language, music, philosophy, etc.

## 26 **idiosyncrasy** n.

idiosyncratic (adj.)

⌐ habit, mannerism; susceptibility

a characteristic, quality, or trait peculiar to an individual, group, place, or thing; an individual's peculiar physical reaction to a drug or food

## 27 **incipient** adj.

incipience, incipiency (n.)

⌐ emerging, developing

in the first or initial stage, or beginning to be noticeable

## 28 **incursion** n.

**incursive (adj.)**

raid; inroad

a sudden attack or invasion; the act of entering into an activity, venture, etc.

## 29 **indigenous** adj.

native, regional; inborn, innate

originating in a particular place or environment; present or existing from birth

## 30 **indisposition** n.

**indisposed (adj.), indispose (v.)**

unwillingness, distaste; ailment, sickness

reluctance, dislike, or lack of enthusiasm; a mild or minor illness

## 31 **infantile** adj.

**infant (n.), infancy (n.)**

newborn; initial; immature

relating to babies; in an early or the earliest stage of development; childish or juvenile

## 32 **infectious** adj.

**infection (n.)**

contagious, catching

likely or able to be transmitted from one organism to another (as in disease), or spreading rapidly from one person to another (as in news, fads, etc.)

## 33 **inkling** n.

hint, suspicion

a slight suggestion or knowledge

## 34 **lampoon** v.

mock, make fun of

to ridicule or satirize, especially in the form of public criticism

## 35 **lodge** v.

*appeal; stay; deposit; embed; flatten; confer upon*

to accuse or complain; to rent (or to settle or live in) a place; to place for safekeeping; to fix firmly; to beat down; to bestow powers upon

---

## 36 **misogynist** n.

**misogyny (n.), misogynous (adj.)**

*sexist, male chauvinist*

one who hates or is extremely prejudiced against women

---

## 37 **monarch** n.

**monarchy (n.)**

*sovereign; standout; monarch butterfly*

the ruler or constitutional head of a state; one surpassing in power or position; a large butterfly with orange-brown wings native to North America

---

## 38 **nuance** n.

*subtlety, hint*

a slight distinction or variation

---

## 39 **palatable** adj.

**palatability (n.)**

*delicious, tasty; satisfactory, desirable*

pleasing to the sense of taste; acceptable, or to one's liking

---

## 40 **paramount** adj./n.

*foremost, ultimate; sovereign*

of utmost importance, or above all others; a supreme ruler

---

## 41 **picayune** adj./n.

*insignificant; narrow-minded; half dime*

of little value or consequence; petty or small-minded; a coin of little value

---

## 42 **pneumatic** adj.

**pneuma (n.)**

 spiritual; curvy

of, relating to, or containing gas, wind, or air; having cavities filled with air; of or relating to the soul; having a full, shapely feminine figure

---

## 43 **potable** adj.

 drinkable

fit or safe to drink

---

## 44 **protocol** n.

 agreement; etiquette; guideline

an official record of a transaction or negotiation; an acceptable behavior or code of conduct; the set of rules or instructions

---

## 45 **suffrage** n.

**suffragist (n.)**

 franchise; ballot; petitions

the right to vote; a vote in deciding on a specific candidate or issue; a short prayer done on behalf of another

---

## 46 **torpor** n.

 sluggishness, idleness

a state of being physically or mentally inactive

---

## 47 **trove** n.

 treasure, storehouse

a collection of valuables

---

## 48 **vertigo** n.

**vertiginous (adj.)**

 dizziness

a condition in which one feels the sensation of whirling or one's surroundings seem to whirl about

---

## 49 **winsome** adj.

⬦ attractive, loveable

pleasant or appealing in a charming or engaging way

---

## 50 **wizen** v.

⬦ shrink, shrivel

to wither, dry up, or become wrinkled

---

# List 7

## 01 **acquit** v.
**acquittal (n.)**
 clear, release
to declare or find not guilty

## 02 **acute** adj.
 clever, keen; dire, serious
having a remarkably quick and perceptive understanding; severe or terrible

## 03 **addle** v.
 daze, muddle
to confuse or make difficult to think properly

## 04 **annex** v./n.
**annexation (n.)**
 take over; appendix
to take by force, especially a territory of a state; an addition to a building, document, etc.

## 05 **apostate** n.
**apostasy (n.)**
 defector, deserter
a person who gives up a religion, faith, or political belief

## 06 **apprehension** n.
**apprehend (v.), apprehensive (adj.)**
 dread; comprehension; seizure
fear that something unpleasant might happen; quickness in understanding; the act of arresting a person

## 07 **attribute** n./v.

**attributable (adj.)**

✎ trait, quality; ascribe; connect

a characteristic of someone or something; to explain the reason by specifying a cause; to associate ownership or authorship to someone

---

## 08 **beset** v.

**besetting (adj.)**

✎ assault; encircle; stud

to attack or cause trouble; to surround; to decorate or cover thickly with ornaments, jewels, etc.

---

## 09 **caustic** adj.

**causticity (n.), caustically (adv.)**

✎ acid, burning; critical, scornful

able to corrode or destroy (especially organic tissue) by chemical action; harshly or bitterly sarcastic

---

## 10 **chronicle** n.

**chronicler (n.)**

✎ annals, archive; portrayal, account

a factual, historical record of events in the order in which they occurred; a fictitious or actual story of connected events

---

## 11 **constable** n.

✎ marshal; warden; patrolman

a high official of a royal or noble household; a caretaker or guard of a castle; an officer maintaining order (mostly in a small town)

---

## 12 **dinghy** n.

✎ raft, bark

an inflatable rubber boat, or a small boat used for recreation or sports or as a lifeboat

---

## 13 **diversion** n.

**diversionary (adj.)**

✎ detour; distraction; recreation

the act of veering away from a course; the act of turning someone's attention away from something; a pastime

## 14 **dowry** n.

marriage settlement; skill, competence

the gift or money (especially property) that a bride offers to her husband at marriage; a natural ability or talent

---

## 15 **embalm** v.

**embalmment (n.)**

mummify; preserve; perfume

to treat a corpse in order to prevent decaying; to cherish or protect the memory of; to add or fill with something fragrant

---

## 16 **entrails** n.

intestines, guts; inner workings

the internal parts of a person or animal; the innermost parts of something

---

## 17 **entrench** v.

**entrenchment (n.)**

institute; fortify; wear down; trespass

to establish (an attitude, belief, etc.) firmly; to dig or surround with a trench for defense; to cut into or erode; to enter upon illegally

---

## 18 **epigram** n.

**epigrammatic (adj.)**

play on words, proverb

a short saying or poem that is usually clever, wise, or satirical

---

## 19 **exigent** adj.

**exigency, exigence (n.)**

urgent, critical; demanding, challenging

calling for or requiring immediate help or attention; requiring more than is necessary or reasonable

---

## 20 **expunge** v.

**expunction (n.)**

eliminate, wipe out

to delete, erase, or destroy

## 21 **facetious** adj.

*humorous, witty*

joking or trying to be funny, often done deliberately and considered inappropriate

## 22 **gala** n.

*fair, carnival*

a festival, celebration, or public entertainment

## 23 **incumbent** adj.

**incumbency (n.)**

*present; required; lying*

currently in or holding office or power; imposed as an obligation or duty; resting or reclining on something

## 24 **indelible** adj.

**indelibility (n.)**

*permanent; unforgettable*

not able to be erased or removed; memorable or lasting

## 25 **lament** v./n.

**lamentation (n.)**

*wail; repent; complain; elegy*

to weep loudly; to regret strongly; to express disappointment; a song or literary composition expressing grief

## 26 **loquacious** adj.

**loquacity (n.)**

*wordy, garrulous*

tending to be very talkative

## 27 **magisterial** adj.

*accomplished; official; domineering*

suitable for or showing the skill of a master or expert; relating to authority; dictatorial or pompous

vocabulary

## 28 **manifesto** n.

announcement, proclamation

a public declaration or statement of policy, intent, aims, etc.

---

## 29 **masquerade** n./v.

masque; outfit; pose as, impersonate

a ball where attendees wear masks or costumes; attire worn at a masked ball; to pretend or disguise oneself

---

## 30 **mitigate** v.

**mitigation (n.)**

appease, alleviate, downplay

to make less hostile (as in aggression), painful (as in suffering), or serious (as in offense)

---

## 31 **nocturnal** adj.

**nocturnality (n.)**

nightly, nighttime

of or relating to, or occurring or active at, night

---

## 32 **nostalgia** n.

**nostalgic (adj.)**

longing, homesickness

a sentimental yearning for something past or far away (especially one's home or home-land)

---

## 33 **obstinate** adj.

**obstinacy (n.)**

headstrong; persistent

unreasonably stubborn or uncooperative; not easy to fix, remove, or conquer

---

## 34 **odyssey** n.

journey, quest

a voyage that is long and adventurous, or an intellectual or spiritual exploration

## 35 **omnipotent** adj.

omnipotence (n.)

✔ almighty, all-powerful

having unlimited power, influence, or authority

## 36 **pacifist** n.

pacifism (n.)

✔ conscientious objector, dove

a person who opposes war or violence or who supports a policy of nonresistance

## 37 **paucity** n.

✔ fewness, bit; shortage, lack

smallness of number or quantity; insufficiency in size or amount

## 38 **philologist** n.

philology (n.), philological (adj.)

a person who studies literature and its related disciplines

## 39 **predilection** n.

✔ liking, taste

an established preference or fondness for something

## 40 **propriety** n.

✔ appropriateness, suitability

the condition or (rules of) behavior that is considered correct, fitting, or socially acceptable

## 41 **pulmonary** adj.

relating to or affecting the lungs

## 42 **remonstrate** v.

remonstration (n.), remonstrative (adj.)

✔ object, protest

to oppose or express disapproval

## 43 **subpoena** n.

summons, writ

a written legal command requiring a person to appear in court

## 44 **tirade** n.

condemnation, harangue

a long, emotionally charged speech of accusation or denunciation

## 45 **translucent** adj.

**translucence (n.)**

semitransparent; clear; genuine

letting light to pass through but diffusing it so as not to be fully transparent; clear or transparent; real, or not disguised

## 46 **trenchant** adj.

**trenchancy (n.)**

incisive; acute; clear-cut

powerfully or aggressively effective and articulate; keenly perceptive; certain or distinct

## 47 **umbrage** n.

**umbrageous (adj.)**

offense; foliage; suspicion; sign

a feeling of annoyance or resentment; shady leaves or branches; doubtful feeling; a vague suggestion or hint

## 48 **upbraid** v.

**upbraiding (n.)**

reproach, lecture

to criticize or scold sharply or severely

## 49 **waif** n.

**waiflike, waifish (adj.)**

stray; drop

a homeless or neglected person or animal, especially a homeless child; something found but unclaimed

## 50 **wanton** adj.

✎ inhumane; luxuriant; sensual; undisciplined

merciless or malicious; lavish or extravagant; lewd or lustful; mischievous or pampered

# List 8

## 01 **adjunct** n.
**adjunctive** (adj.)
✐ supplement, accessory
something attached to something else as an addition rather than an essential part

## 02 **aghast** adj.
✐ horrified, appalled
shocked or filled with horror

## 03 **alcove** n.
✐ recess, arbor
a small room set off from a larger one, or a secluded leafy shade in a garden

## 04 **allocate** v.
**allocation** (n.), **allocable** (adj.)
✐ allot, assign
to set aside for a specific purpose or distribute according to a plan

## 05 **anemometer** n.
✐ wind gauge, windsock
an instrument that measures and records wind speed or gas current

## 06 **arboreal** adj.
**arborist** (n.), **arboretum** (n.)
resembling, relating to, or adapted for living in a tree

## 07 **babble** v.
✐ ramble, prattle
to talk rapidly without pause or make muddled sounds in a senseless, excited, or incomprehensible way

## 08 **bibulous** adj.

spongy; intemperate

extremely absorbent; relating to or having a strong love for alcohol

## 09 **blasé** adj.

unimpressed, indifferent

lacking interest in something because of having or experiencing it too frequently

## 10 **buttress** n.

reinforcement, prop

a structure built against a wall or building as a support, or anything that supports or provides strength

## 11 **carnal** adj.

**carnality (n.)**

material, terrestrial; lustful, pleasing

relating to the body or flesh, or worldly or earthly; marked by bodily needs or pleasures

## 12 **cohesion** n.

**cohesive (adv.)**

solidarity, unity; attachment; bond

the state or tendency to unite or act together as a single unit; the merger of similar plant parts; the molecular force that holds particles together

## 13 **constellate** v.

**constellation (n.)**

assemble, gather

to unite or cluster

## 14 **contemporary** adj./n.

current, modern; simultaneous; peer

relating to the present period; occurring or living at the same time; a person or thing of the same (or nearly the same) age as another

vocabulary

## 15  counterintuitive adj.

⌁ unreasonable, contradictory

contrary to what one would logically expect

---

## 16  delirium n.

**delirious (adj.)**

⌁ madness, temporary insanity; frenzy, ecstasy

a mental disturbance caused by fever, intoxication, etc.; an uncontrolled excitement

---

## 17  devious adj.

⌁ deceptive, sneaky; curved, twisted

not honest or straightforward; moving away from the proper or straight path

---

## 18  disparage v.

**disparaging (adj.), disparagement (n.)**

⌁ belittle, degrade

to criticize or discredit someone or something in a disrespectful manner

---

## 19  duplicitous adj.

**duplicity (n.)**

⌁ dishonest, crooked

deceptive or deceitful

---

## 20  eclectic adj.

⌁ assorted, diverse

taking things from or composed of various sources, methods, doctrines, etc.

---

## 21  embezzle v.

**embezzlement (n.), embezzler (n.)**

⌁ run off with, take for oneself

to steal something (such as money or property) entrusted to one's care

---

## 22  encyclical adj./n.

⌁ common; papal document

addressed to all or for general circulation; the Pope's letter addressed to the bishops

---

### 23 **eponymous** adj.

**eponym (n.)**

*identifying*

relating to or being the person or thing after which it is named

---

### 24 **facet** n.

**faceted, facetted (adj.)**

*face, part; factor, characteristic*

a surface or one side of something; a specific aspect of something

---

### 25 **felicity** n.

**felicitous (adj.)**

*bliss, joy; properness, suitability*

extreme happiness; the ability to find appropriate or pleasing expression

---

### 26 **folio** n.

an individual leaf of paper, or a page or page number of a book; a sheet of paper folded in half (or a book with such sheets of paper)

---

### 27 **fortuitous** adj.

**fortuity (n.)**

*unforeseen; fortunate*

happening by coincidence or chance; happening by luck

---

### 28 **furrow** n.

*depression, trench; crinkle, crease*

a groove made in the earth by a plow, or anything that resembles such a groove; a deep wrinkle on the face

---

### 29 **harbinger** n.

*sign, foreshadowing; forerunner, pioneer*

someone or something that comes before to indicate what is to follow; someone or something that starts or causes a major change

vocabulary

## 30 **inclination** n.

incline (v.)

 habit, bias; bow, nod; slope, angling

one's natural tendency to act or feel in a particular way or like something; a bending of the head or body; a slant or tilt

---

## 31 **levity** n.

 frivolity; irregularity

lightness or lack of sincerity in handling serious matters; lack of constancy or stability

---

## 32 **malady** n.

 infection, ailment; problem, difficulty

a disease or illness; a harmful or desperate condition

---

## 33 **meme** n.

 trend, fad

a unit of culture (such as behavior, belief, style, etc.) that passes from person to person, or a humorous or interesting item spread extensively online

---

## 34 **ornate** adj.

 elaborate; flowery

intricately or extravagantly decorated; complex or fancy in construction or style (as in literary or musical composition, performance, etc.)

---

## 35 **pantheon** n.

 shrine; hall of fame

(a temple dedicated to) all the gods of a people or religion; a classification for famous people, or a place where they are buried or honored

---

## 36 **pensive** adj.

 meditative, reflective

engaged in or suggestive of sad or serious thought

---

## 37 **piety** n.

**pious (adj.)**

devoutness, reverence; attachment, commitment

devotion to or strong belief in a religion or religious faith, duties, or practices; loyalty or fidelity to parents or other natural obligations

---

## 38 **plebiscite** n.

**plebiscitary (adj.)**

referendum, popular vote

a vote by the people (of a district, region, country, etc.) on an important public issue

---

## 39 **posterity** n.

offspring, progeny

the descendants of a specific individual, or all the succeeding or future generations

---

## 40 **progeny** n.

offspring; disciples; product

children or descendants of a person, animal, or plant; followers or successors; an outcome or result

---

## 41 **ravenous** adj.

starving, voracious

extremely hungry, or very eager for satisfaction

---

## 42 **recondite** adj.

deep; secret; concealed

difficult for the ordinary mind to comprehend; relating to something little known; hidden or obscure

---

## 43 **remiss** adj.

careless, irresponsible

neglecting or failing to perform one's duty or obligations

## 44 **requital** n.

**requite (v.)**

compensation, retaliation

an act of giving (or something given) in return, good (as in payment) or bad (as in revenge)

---

## 45 **revocation** n.

**revoke (v.)**

abandonment, calling off

the act or instance of canceling or calling back

---

## 46 **ruminate** v.

**rumination (n.), ruminative (adj.)**

consider, think over

to contemplate or ponder over; to chew over and over (as in cow chewing the cud)

---

## 47 **transverse** adj.

crosswise, side to side

lying, placed, or extending across

---

## 48 **treatise** n.

exposition, discourse

a book or article that explains, describes, or discusses a subject in a formal and systematic way

---

## 49 **tribulation** n.

hardship, trouble

a cause or state of great dress, pain, or suffering

---

## 50 **verdant** adj.

grassy, flourishing; immature, naive

green in color or with plants or lush vegetation; inexperienced or unsophisticated

# List 9

## 01 **aberration** n.
**aberrant (adj.)**
deviation, freak
a departure from what is considered normal, proper, or correct

## 02 **acerbic** adj.
**acerbity (n.)**
acidic, sharp; critical, cruel
sour or bitter tasting; harsh or direct in the way one speaks

## 03 **aeronautics** n.
**aeronautical (adj.), aeronaut (n.)**
aviation, flight
the theory and practice of aircraft and other flying objects

## 04 **affront** n.
offense, provocation
a word or action to insult someone intentionally

## 05 **altercation** n.
**altercate (v.)**
quarrel, wrangle
a noisy dispute carried on with anger

## 06 **anomaly** n.
**anomalous (adj.)**
exception, abnormality
something that departs from a common rule or different from what is considered normal

## 07 **apex** n.

✎ summit, peak

the greatest or highest point of something; the most successful period

---

## 08 **bauble** n.

✎ trinket, novelty

a cheap, showy piece of ornament or jewelry

---

## 09 **blunt** adj.

✎ dull; direct

having an edge that is not sharp; abrupt or honest in speech, often to the point of being insensitive

---

## 10 **calamity** n.

**calamitous (adj.)**

✎ disaster, tragedy

an event (or a state brought about by an event) so devastating as to cause great misery, distress, or confusion

---

## 11 **commencement** n.

**commence (v.)**

✎ initiation; graduation

the beginning or the earliest existence of something; a ceremony or the day to award diplomas or academic degrees

---

## 12 **consummate** v./adj.

**consummation (n.)**

✎ succeed, conclude; expert

to achieve, complete, or perfect; to make a relationship (especially marriage) complete through physical intimacy; highly skilled or accomplished

---

## 13 **crag** n.

**craggy (adj.)**

✎ ridge, rock face

a rough, steep cliff or rock

---

## 14 **crystalline** adj.

✐ clear-cut, see-through

very clear or transparent (like a crystal or in literary terms), or relating to or composed of crystals

---

## 15 **cusp** n.

**cusped (adj.), cuspate (adj.)**

✐ tip, apex; turning point, verge

a pointed end, or a sharp point; a moment of transition between two situations or historical periods

---

## 16 **cynosure** n.

✐ notable, cornerstone, compass; North Star, Polaris

someone or something that is the center of attention or admiration, or that acts as a guide or direction; a star in the constellation Ursa Minor

---

## 17 **directive** n./adj.

✐ command, decree; directional, managing

a decision or order issued by a high-level official or official body; serving or tending to guide or influence

---

## 18 **dismember** v.

**dismemberment (n.)**

✐ disjoint, amputate; divide, partition

to tear or cut off the limbs of a person or animal; to cut or separate into pieces or parts

---

## 19 **encroach** v.

**encroachment (n.)**

✐ trespass, invade; overpass, overreach

to intrude on (a property, territory, the rights of a person, etc.); to advance or go over the normal or proper limits

---

## 20 **enigma** n.

**enigmatic (adj.)**

✐ mystery, puzzle

a person or thing that is mysterious or hard to understand

### 21 **extol** v.

**extolment (n.)**

glorify, celebrate

to praise highly or enthusiastically

---

### 22 **fastidious** adj.

demanding; dainty

extremely critical and too concerned about details; overly picky about cleanliness and order

---

### 23 **forerun** v.

**forerunner (n.)**

precede; imply; forestall

to run or go before; to be a sign of something to follow; to prevent something from happening by taking early action

---

### 24 **grandiloquent** adj.

**grandiloquence (n.)**

flowery, pretentious

using language or expressions in a showy, extravagantly colorful way in order to impress

---

### 25 **harangue** n.

rant, tirade

a long, noisy, and aggressive speech, writing, or lecture

---

### 26 **hawkish** adj.

**hawk (n.)**

militarist, warmonger

supporting an aggressive policy, especially having a warlike attitude and advocating swift action

---

### 27 **hoodwink** v.

fool, mislead

to trick or deceive

---

## 28 **intermediary** n./adj.

**intermediation (n.)**

negotiator, mediator; mid, halfway

a person acting as a go-between; being or happening between or in the middle

## 29 **intrepid** adj.

**intrepidity (n.)**

bold, adventurous

fearless, daring, or brave

## 30 **irrepressible** adj.

**irrepressibility (n.)**

uncontainable, undying

not able to be controlled or repressed

## 31 **irrevocable** adj.

**irrevocability (n.)**

unalterable, permanent

unable to be changed or reversed

## 32 **locomotion** n.

**locomotive (adj.)**

movement, mobility

the act of moving or the ability to move from place to place

## 33 **malicious** adj.

**malice (n.)**

cruel, vicious

having or showing a desire or intention to do evil or cause harm to someone

## 34 **malleable** adj.

**malleability (n.)**

pliable; susceptible; adjustable

capable of being beaten or pounded to bend or shape without breaking; easily controlled or influenced; adaptive to change

## 35 **opulence** n.

**opulent (adj.)**

wealth, luxury; abundance, profusion

immense fortune or affluence; an ample supply or large quantity

## 36 **overwrought** adj.

agitated, overwhelmed; overdone, ornate

extremely tense or excited; too complicated or elaborate

## 37 **penance** n.

atonement, self-abasement

a self-imposed punishment to serve as reparation for a wrongdoing or sinful act

## 38 **perchance** adv.

maybe, possibly

perhaps, or by chance

## 39 **peripatetic** adj.

**Peripateticism (n.)**

nomadic, wandering; Aristotelian

moving from place to place, or not remaining in one place; having to do with Aristotle or his philosophy

## 40 **perseverance** n.

**persevere (v.), perseverant (adj.)**

determination, persistence

the act or power of continuing in a course of action despite difficulties or opposition

## 41 **plutocracy** n.

**plutocrat (n.), plutocratic (adj.)**

government by the wealthy; a controlling class whose power and influence comes from its wealth

## 42 **precocious** adj.

**precocity (n.)**

gifted; untimely

having developed advanced abilities at an abnormally early age; exceptionally mature or ahead in development

## 43 **prospectus** n.

brochure, pamphlet

a printed statement that advertises or describes a book, business enterprise, institution, etc.

## 44 **providential** adj.

lucky; miraculous

occurring at an opportune time; involving divine intervention

## 45 **prowess** n.

skill, mastery; valor, heroism

extraordinary ability or expertise in a particular field; courage or bravery, especially in battle

## 46 **punctilious** adj.

thorough, precise; proper, formal

very attentive to details; careful about correct behavior

## 47 **rampart** n.

fortification, bulwark

a stone or dirt wall built around a castle or fort for defense, or any protective wall or barrier

## 48 **termagant** n.

shrew

a scolding, quarrelsome, or overbearing woman

## 49 **tryst** n.

engagement, date

an arrangement or the place to meet secretly, especially between lovers

## 50 **vociferous** adj.
**vociferate (v.), vociferation (n.)**

🖊 vocal, outspoken

characterized by a loud, vehement outcry in expressing one's feelings

---

◔ = Synonyms, related words

---

## 01 **acme** n.

◔ peak, apex

the highest point of achievement or full maturity

---

## 02 **ad hoc** adj.

◔ provisional, spontaneous

created for a particular purpose or on the spur of the moment

---

## 03 **aesthetic** adj.

**esthetic (adj., alt.), aesthetics, esthetics (n.)**

◔ pleasing, elegant

concerned with beauty, artistic impression, or appearance

---

## 04 **anhydrous** adj.

◔ arid, dehydrated

containing little or no water

---

## 05 **autocracy** n.

**autocrat (n.), autocratic (adj.)**

◔ dictatorship, tyranny

a system of government or a state ruled by one person who has absolute power

---

## 06 **bombastic** adj.

**bombast (n.)**

◔ high-sounding, inflated

trying to sound impressive but having no real meaning in speech or writing

---

## 07 **bovine** adj.

◔ sluggish, dense

affecting, belonging to, or having the qualities of cattle; slow and dull like cattle

---

Part 1

vocabulary

## 08 **bullish** adj.

 bright, confident

hopeful or optimistic about success, especially regarding rising prices (as in stock market)

---

## 09 **chivalrous** adj.

**chivalry (n.)**

 heroic; gentlemanly; noble, knightly

behaving honorably and bravely; courteous and kind (especially to women); relating to the medieval knighthood system or spirit

---

## 10 **communicable** adj.

**communicability (n.)**

 exchangeable; infectious; conversable

capable of conveying information, ideas, feelings, etc.; capable of being transmitted, especially disease; talkative or sociable

---

## 11 **crux** n.

**cruces (pl.)**

 mystery; core; the Southern Cross

a difficult problem or a question that is puzzling or unsolved; the central or essential point; a constellation in the Southern Hemisphere

---

## 12 **dendrology** n.

**dendrologist (n.)**

the study of trees

---

## 13 **efficacy** n.

**efficacious (adj.)**

 effectiveness, efficiency

the ability to produce an effect or desired result

---

## 14 **egregious** adj.

 outrageous, blatant

exceptionally bad, shocking, or obvious

---

## 15 **embolism** n.

**embolic (adj.)**

lump, clump; insert, fit in

the blockage in a blood vessel, mostly caused by blood clot or air bubble; the adding
of days into the calendar for adjustments (as in leap year)

---

## 16 **epiphany** n.

**epiphanic (adj.)**

revelation, discovery; manifestation

a sudden or revealing moment of realization; an appearance of a divine or supernatural being

---

## 17 **exhort** v.

**exhortation (n.)**

encourage, press

to urge, advise, or warn strongly or earnestly

---

## 18 **faculty** n.

capability; control; staff

an ability to do something specific; a power given by a higher authority; the teachers
and administrators (or department) in a school or college

---

## 19 **fracas** n.

brawl, fight

a noisy or loud disturbance or quarrel

---

## 20 **fray** n./v.

**frayed (adj.)**

quarrel; wear away

a fight, dispute, or competition; to become weakened, shredded, or worn

---

## 21 **gait** n.

bearing, pace

a manner of walking, movement, or progress

## 22  inadvertently adv.
inadvertent (adj.)

accidentally, unwittingly
by mistake or without intention

## 23  inflection n.
inflect (v.)

angle, twist; modulation, variation
the act or result of curving, turning, or bending; a change in loudness or pitch (voice), in curvature (mathematics), or word form (grammar)

## 24  insurrection n.
insurrectionist (n.)

rebellion, revolution
a revolt or uprising against an establishment authority or government

## 25  interpolation n.
interpolate (v.)

insertion, introduction
the act of adding a new or artificial thing to something else

## 26  laureate n.
laureateship (n.)

honoree, receiver
the recipient of award or honor for outstanding achievement

## 27  littoral adj./n.

seaside, coastline
(of, relating to, or situated or growing on) coastal region or seashore

## 28  maelstrom n.

vortex, swirl; chaos, turmoil
a huge, powerful whirlpool; any confusing and violent situation

## 29 **mellifluous** adj.

**mellifluent (alt.)**

soothing, harmonious

sounding sweet, smooth, or musical

---

## 30 **module** n.

**modular (adj.)**

piece, capsule; diameter, width

a compartment, section, or unit having a specific function; a standardized unit of measurement

---

## 31 **mooring** n.

**moor (v.)**

dock, anchor; reassurance

the act of securing (or a place or device used to secure) a vessel or aircraft; beliefs or practices that one abides by to feel secure

---

## 32 **omniscient** adj.

**omniscience (n.)**

all-wise, all-knowing

having infinite knowledge, awareness, or understanding

---

## 33 **patronize** v.

**patronizing (adj.)**

condescend, talk down; endorse; habituate

to treat or act kindly but also show a tone of superiority; to sponsor, support, aid, or protect; to frequent a business

---

## 34 **penchant** n.

inclination, fondness

a strong liking or taste for something

---

## 35 **pilfer** v.

**pilferage (n.)**

filch, lift

to steal, especially things that have little value and done in small quantities

### 36 **preemptive** adj.

**preempt (v.)**

preventive, deterrent

intended as an initiative against an anticipated situation that could be dangerous or troublesome

---

### 37 **privation** n.

loss, absence; poverty, neediness

the state of being deprived, or the act of depriving; the state of not having the basic necessities of life

---

### 38 **procrastinate** v.

**procrastination (n.)**

put off doing, wait

to postpone or delay taking action

---

### 39 **provisional** adj.

**provision (n.)**

temporary, interim

existing or serving for the time being

---

### 40 **pugnacious** adj.

**pugnacity (n.)**

aggressive, combative

quick to argue or fight

---

### 41 **ramification** n.

**ramify (v.)**

outcome, effect; offshoot

the possible consequence or result of an action; a branch, or an arrangement of branches

---

### 42 **recompense** v.

reward, indemnify

to repay or compensate for a service rendered or for harm, injury, or damage incurred

### 43 **retrogression** n.

**retrogress (v.), retrogressive (adj.)**

*reversion, regression*

the process of declining or deteriorating to an earlier state, or a return to an earlier, less complex level or state

---

### 44 **sacrosanct** adj.

*hallowed, untouchable*

too important, sacred, or holy to be challenged or tampered with

---

### 45 **scion** n.

*graft; heir*

a bud or shoot of a plant; a descendant, especially one from a wealthy or influential family

---

### 46 **sequester** v.

**sequestration (n.)**

*separate, isolate; confiscate, impound*

to segregate, seclude, or withdraw; to take over or seize by authority

---

### 47 **spinster** n.

**spinsterhood (n.), spinsterish (adj.)**

an unmarried, older woman; a woman whose occupation involves spinning thread

---

### 48 **surety** n.

*sponsor; assurance; doubtlessness*

one who takes legal responsibility for another's failure in duty; something that acts as a security or guarantee; the state of being certain

---

### 49 **unconscionable** adj.

*unethical; outrageous; extreme*

not done in good conscience; unfair or unjust; unreasonably or unduly excessive

---

Part 1

vocabulary

## 50 **vivisection** n.

**vivisect (v.)**

animal experimentation; evaluation

the practice of performing surgical operations or other experiments on a living animal; a keenly detailed examination, analysis, or criticism

# List 11

⌐ = Synonyms, related words

## 01 **abstruse** adj.

⌐ complicated, obscure

difficult to comprehend or hard to understand

## 02 **accountable** adj.

⌐ answerable, liable

expected to be held responsible

## 03 **adumbrate** v.

**adumbration (n.), adumbrative (adj.)**

⌐ sketch; indicate; foretell; conceal

to present an outline; to show faintly; to foreshadow or symbolize; to obscure

## 04 **aerate** v.

**aeration (n.)**

⌐ aerify, circulate

to supply with air, or to add air into something

## 05 **aggrieve** v.

**aggrieved (adj.)**

⌐ oppress, abuse

to cause pain or sorrow unjustly, especially by infringing upon one's rights

## 06 **ambidextrous** adj.

**ambidexterity (n.)**

⌐ two-handed; versatile

having the ability to use both hands equally well; exceptionally skillful in many areas

## 07 **anthology** n.

**anthological (adj.)**

compilation, collection

a literary work collection, such as poems or short stories created by different writers

---

## 08 **artifice** n.

ingenuity; scam

a clever skill; a crafty trick

---

## 09 **balmy** adj.

gentle, temperate; absurd, idiotic

having soothing qualities, or mild and pleasant (as in weather); foolish or crazy

---

## 10 **blazon** v.

announce; bedeck; show

to proclaim or make widely known; to adorn or decorate; to display prominently or publicly; to describe or portray a coat of arms

---

## 11 **calibrate** v.

**calibration (n.), calibrator (n.)**

assess; systemize, fine-tune, calculate

to determine the ability, quality, or competence of; to standardize, adjust, or measure accurately

---

## 12 **capillary** adj./n.

threadlike; vein

pertaining to hair or a tube, especially one being slender and narrow; a tiny blood vessel

---

## 13 **chaff** n.

**chaffy (adj.)**

banter; outer coverings; waste

a lighthearted teasing; the husks separated from the grain; anything unwanted or worthless

## 14 **chicanery** n.

chicane (v.)

dishonesty, stunt

words or actions cleverly used or taken to trick or deceive people

---

## 15 **concord** n.

concordance (n.), concordant (adj.)

friendship, peace; accord, alliance

a state of agreement or harmony; a pact or treaty establishing peaceful relations between nations

---

## 16 **consecrate** v.

consecration (n.), consecratory (adj.)

bless; anoint; pledge

to make or declare holy or sacred; to make someone a (religious) leader or ruler by a ceremony; to devote or dedicate fully

---

## 17 **conundrum** n.

dilemma, difficulty; riddle, brain-teaser

a complex and difficult problem; a question asked for fun, typically involving a play on words

---

## 18 **covenant** n.

covenantal (adj.)

contract, pledge

an agreement that is binding and often obligatory

---

## 19 **cryptic** adj.

mysterious, confusing; veiled, concealed

difficult to understand or having hidden meaning; serving as or having good camouflage

---

## 20 **defunct** adj.

extinct, discontinued, obsolete

no longer living, existing, or in use

### 21  **din** n./v.

 racket, commotion; instill, drill

an unpleasantly loud and continued noise; to make someone understand or learn by relentless repetition

---

### 22  **discerning** adj.

 wise, perceptive

having or showing good taste, insight, or judgment

---

### 23  **disingenuous** adj.

 deceitful, underhanded

not honest, straightforward, or sincere, especially by pretending ignorance

---

### 24  **disposition** n.

**dispositional (adj.)**

 inclination; placement; authority; settlement; delegation

a person's inherent qualities or tendency; the arrangement of specific things; the power to control; the final decision; a transfer to the care of another

---

### 25  **elocution** n.

**elocutionary (adj.), elocutionist (n.)**

 articulation, oratory

the art, skill, or style of speaking effectively, especially in public

---

### 26  **emanate** v.

**emanation (n.)**

 discharge, emit

to come or spread out from a source

---

### 27  **evanescent** adj.

**evanescence (n.)**

 fading, momentary

tending to vanish (from memory, sight, existence, etc.)

---

## 28 **extrajudicial** adj.

✎ out-of-court, off-the-record

beyond or not within the authority of a court, or (a punishment or sentence) carried out without legal authorization

## 29 **fecund** adj.

**fecundity (n.)**

✎ fertile, prolific

highly fruitful or productive

## 30 **fetter** n.

✎ shackle, cuffs; limitation, impediment

a chain or object that binds, mainly for the feet; anything that restricts action or progress

## 31 **fiasco** n.

✎ flop, blunder; flask

a sudden, unexpected, or complete failure; a straw-covered bottle, especially one for wine

## 32 **finesse** n.

✎ artistry; prudence; slyness

intricate delicacy or refinement (as in workmanship, texture, skill, etc.); the skill in taking care of difficult situations; cunning or craftiness

## 33 **foolhardy** adj.

✎ rash, overconfident

bold or reckless to the point of being foolish

## 34 **fretful** adj.

**fret (v.)**

✎ uneasy, agitated

tending to worry or be distressed

## 35 **gargantuan** adj.

✎ enormous, massive

huge or tremendous

## 36 **gradient** n.

 hill, ramp; angle, slant

a slope of a road or railway; the degree of a given slope

---

## 37 **insipid** adj.

**insipidity (n.)**

 tasteless, unsavory; dull, boring

having little or no flavor; not stimulating or interesting

---

## 38 **inure** v.

**inurement (n.)**

 accustom, toughen; take effect

to get used to something undesirable or unpleasant; to come into use or operation

---

## 39 **Lilliputian** adj.

 miniature, minute; insignificant, minor

very small or tiny; petty or trivial

---

## 40 **maudlin** adj.

 overemotional, weepy

tearfully sentimental, especially when drunk

---

## 41 **moratorium** n.

**moratoria (pl.)**

 ban, postponement

a temporary suspension or prohibition of activity, usually a legal authorization to delay debt payment

---

## 42 **mordant** adj./n.

**mordancy (n.)**

 sarcastic; dye fixative; acid

(especially of humor) harshly critical; a chemical used when dying a fabric material; any corrosive substance used in etching to cut into a metal surface

---

## 43 neologism n.
coinage, new term

a new word or expression, or a new meaning of a traditional word or expression

## 44 perennial adj.
long-lasting, eternal; recurrent, repeated

present or lasting throughout the entire year, for a long time, or infinitely; continually recurring

## 45 preordained adj.
preordain (v.), preordination (n.)

fated, predestined

determined or decided in advance

## 46 profusion n.
profuse (adj.)

abundance; extravagance

a great quantity or something; lavish or wasteful expenditure

## 47 sedulous adj.
sedulity (n.)

persevering, constant

diligent or persistent

## 48 tenuous adj.
weak, flimsy; thin, fine

insignificant, or having little strength; not thick or dense

## 49 torpid adj.
torpidity (n.)

inert; lethargic; asleep

inactive or unmoving; lazy or apathetic; dormant, as in hibernating

## 50 **vehement** adj.

**vehemence (n.)**

✎ powerful; fervent; antagonistic

having great force or energy; strongly passionate or emotional; bitterly hostile

---

= Synonyms, related words

## 01 **airborne** adj.

aerial, flying

in, through, or carried by the air

## 02 **anagram** n.

**anagrammatic (adj.)**

rearrangement, reposition

a word or phrase that is created by moving around the letters of another word or phrase

## 03 **anemia** n.

**anemic (adj.)**

weakness, lifelessness

a medical condition marked by a lack of red blood cells; lack of vigor or strength

## 04 **appellate** adj.

having the power to review appeals and reverse any decision made by a lower court

## 05 **approbation** n.

**approbate (v.), approbative (adj.)**

praise, acceptance

an act of approving or agreeing

## 06 **astute** adj.

keen, insightful; calculating, scheming

having or showing an ability to understand accurately; cunning or shrewd

## 07 **avian** adj.

feathered, winged

relating to or resembling a bird

## 08 **baleful** adj.

*hostile, menacing*

very harmful or threatening, or suggesting potential danger

---

## 09 **boisterous** adj.

*wild, lively; blustery, gusty*

noisy or loud in a rowdy, unruly, or cheerful and energetic manner; stormy or turbulent (as in wind, water, etc.)

---

## 10 **calumny** n.

**calumniate (v.), calumnious (adj.)**

*slander, attack*

a falsified and spiteful statement meant to damage someone's reputation

---

## 11 **conscription** n.

**conscript (v./adj./n.)**

*draft, obligation*

a mandatory service (mostly the military) officially required by the government

---

## 12 **consolation** n.

**console (v.), consolable (adj.), consolatory (adj.)**

*reassurance, condolence*

the act (or a person or thing) that comforts, especially in time of suffering or grief

---

## 13 **curtail** v.

**curtailment (n.)**

*shorten, abridge; regulate, keep in check*

to reduce the duration of something; to limit or impose restrictions

---

## 14 **debacle** n.

*setback, blow; washout, flooding*

a total failure or defeat; the breaking up of a river's ice and the ensuing surge of water

## 15 **den** n.

*cavern, lair; hideout, refuge; study, studio*

a home for wild (especially predatory) animals; a place used for hiding or for secret or shady activities; a cozy, comfortable room

---

## 16 **destitute** adj.

**destitution (n.)**

*lacking, penniless*

not having something that is desirable or needed, or not having the basic necessities of life

---

## 17 **disheveled** adj.

**dishevel (v.), dishevelment (n.)**

*unkempt, messy*

marked by disorder or untidiness, especially of one's hair, clothes, appearance, etc.

---

## 18 **dispensation** n.

**dispense (v.)**

*allocation; arrangement; immunity*

an act of distributing or something distributed; a system of order or organization; an exemption from a rule, law, oath, vow, etc.

---

## 19 **exacting** adj.

*rigorous, firm; delicate, exhausting*

very demanding or strict; needing great care, effort, or patience

---

## 20 **excrement** n.

**excremental (adj.)**

*dropping, dung*

solid waste discharged from the body

---

## 21 **exorbitant** adj.

**exorbitance (n.)**

*extravagant, excessive*

going over or beyond what is considered reasonable or appropriate, especially regarding prices or charged amounts

---

Part 1

vocabulary

## 22 **extemporaneous** adj.

**extemporize (v.)**

✏ improvised; makeshift

spoken or performed on the spur of the moment; made or put to use temporarily

---

## 23 **fatuous** adj.

✏ dense, foolish

stupid or silly

---

## 24 **gnash** v.

✏ grate, crunch

to grind (the teeth) together, usually as a sign of anger or pain

---

## 25 **heterogeneous** adj.

**heterogeneity (n.)**

✏ diverse, mixed

composed of unrelated, differing, or opposite elements

---

## 26 **homage** n.

✏ reverence; tribute

a show of respect or honor; something done (such as artistic work) following as a model of another in a praising way; a formal oath to a feudal lord

---

## 27 **impalpable** adj.

**impalpability (n.)**

✏ intangible; indistinct

not capable of being felt by the sense of touch; not easily understood or comprehended

---

## 28 **improvident** adj.

**improvidence (n.)**

✏ shortsighted, wasteful

reckless or not caring or providing for the future

### 29 **inalienable** adj.

**inalienability (n.)**

inherent, absolute

not capable of being surrendered or transferred

---

### 30 **inexorable** adj.

**inexorability (n.)**

adamant; unstoppable

unable to be influenced or persuaded; impossible to alter or prevent

---

### 31 **innocuous** adj.

safe, innocent; unoffending, peaceful

producing no harm or injury; not offensive or controversial

---

### 32 **inquisitive** adj.

curious, interested; nosy, prying

tending to ask many questions or having the desire to seek information or knowledge; overly or unduly curious

---

### 33 **isolationism** n.

**isolationist (n.)**

noninvolvement, nonengagement

a policy or attitude supporting or favoring non-interaction with the political affairs of other nations

---

### 34 **jarring** adj.

**jar (v.)**

bizarre, discordant; jolting, shaking

shockingly inharmonious or clashing; producing vibration or physical shock

---

### 35 **mete** v./n.

allot, distribute; borderline, bound

to deliver or give out in portions, especially in dispensing justice, punishment, etc.; a limit or boundary

### 36 **minutia** n.

**minutiae (pl.)**

trifle, triviality

a small or relatively minor detail

---

### 37 **misappropriate** v.

**misappropriation (n.)**

embezzle, pocket

to steal or make use of something (especially money) for own use or illegal purposes

---

### 38 **monogamy** n.

**monogamous (adj.)**

loyalty, faithfulness

the practice of having only one marriage partner or mate (in zoology) at a time

---

### 39 **nefarious** adj.

evil, villainous

blatantly wicked or vile

---

### 40 **officious** adj.

meddlesome, prying; casual, off-the-record

intrusively offering unnecessary and unwanted advice or help; informal or unofficial

---

### 41 **onslaught** n.

assault, rush

a violent or fierce attack

---

### 42 **paleontology** n.

**paleontological (adj.), paleontologist (n.)**

the branch of science dealing with life forms from the past through studying fossils

---

### 43 **pendulum** n.

**pendular (adj.)**

a weight suspended from a fixed point and swings from side to side; a state or situation that alternates between two extremes

---

## 44 **physiology** n.

**physiological (adj.), physiologist (n.)**

the branch of biology concerned with the functions of living organisms; the processes of living organisms or the way their bodily parts function

---

## 45 **pivotal** adj.

**pivot (n.)**

 critical, vital; medial

of vital importance; of or relating to a central point on which something turns

---

## 46 **plumage** n.

**plume (n.)**

the feathers of a bird, collectively

---

## 47 **sedition** n.

**seditious (adj.)**

 uprising, revolt

incitement of resistance or rebellion against the authority or government in power

---

## 48 **soliloquy** n.

**soliloquize (v.), soliloquist (n.)**

 aside, monologue

the act of speaking to oneself, especially in theater in which the performer reveals his or her thoughts to the audience

---

## 49 **status quo** n.

 state of affairs, normality

the existing situation or condition, or the way things are at the present

---

## 50 **usury** n.

**usurer (n.), usurious (adj.)**

the lending of money at an excessively high rate of interest

# List 13

### 01 **abdicate** v.

**abdication (n.)**

renounce, step down

to surrender one's power or position as a ruler

### 02 **abysmal** adj.

awful, hopeless

extremely bad or severe

### 03 **accumulate** v.

**accumulation (n.), accumulative (adj.)**

store, amass

to build up, grow, or increase in quantity or number

### 04 **advent** n.

appearance, emergence

the arrival of someone or something worthy of attention

### 05 **assay** v.

**assayer (n.)**

assess, measure

to analyze or determine the composition, value, or worth of a metal, ore, drug, etc.

### 06 **attest** v.

**attestation (n.), attestable (adj.)**

confirm, certify

to verify officially, provide proof, or put under oath

### 07 **bastion** n.

stronghold; defender

a projecting segment of a fortress, or a fortified position; a person or system that strongly upholds a principle or attitude

## 08 **benefactor** n.

**benefaction (n.)**

⬦ patron, sponsor

someone who supports a person, charity, or cause, especially through financial means

---

## 09 **brusque** adj.

⬦ curt, tactless

short and sudden, blunt, or harsh in manner or speech

---

## 10 **chronic** adj.

**chronicity (n.), chronically (adv.)**

⬦ persistent; incurable; rooted, habitual

continuing for a long time or indefinitely; recurring (problem, illness, etc.); marked by custom or habit

---

## 11 **commensurate** adj.

**commensuration (n.)**

⬦ comparable, proportionate

equal in measurable standard (such as size, amount, degree, etc.)

---

## 12 **construe** v.

⬦ deduce, take to mean

to analyze the construction of words of a clause, sentence, etc., or to interpret, explain, or translate (with respect to a specific situation)

---

## 13 **de facto** adj./adv.

⬦ true, in reality

actual in practice or in fact (whether or not someone or something is legally or officially recognized)

---

## 14 **emaciate** v.

**emaciation (n.), emaciated (adj.)**

⬦ weaken, waste away

to make or cause to be extremely or abnormally thin

vocabulary

## 15 **emblazon** v.

**emblazonry (n.), emblazoned (adj.)**

decorate, depict; commend, celebrate

to display or inscribe (names, symbols, coat of arms, etc.) on something; to praise highly or glorify

---

## 16 **esquire** n.

a member of the English social position who ranks below a knight; a knighthood candidate; a title of respect, mostly used to address lawyers

---

## 17 **fallow** n./v./adj.

unsown land; plow; motionless; light yellowish-brown

a piece of land allowed to remain idle without seeding; to break up soil; resting or inactive; pale or brownish-yellow

---

## 18 **faux pas** n.

mistake, impropriety

an embarrassment or blunder, especially in etiquette or social situations

---

## 19 **feces** n.

**fecal (adj.)**

dung, excrement

waste material expelled from the bowels

---

## 20 **fief** n.

**fiefdom (n.)**

estate; domain

land given by a feudal lord in return for service; something which a person or organization has control over

---

## 21 **flagrant** adj.

**flagrance, flagrancy (n.)**

blatant, conspicuous

offensive in an obvious way

---

## 22 **flamboyant** adj./n.

**flamboyance (n.)**

eye-catching; royal poinciana

showy or flashy in behavior or appearance; a tropical tree native to Madagascar

---

## 23 **galvanize** v.

**galvanization (n.)**

motivate; electrify; cover

to shock or stir someone into taking action; to stimulate by an electric current; to coat metal with zinc

---

## 24 **garrulous** adj.

**garrulity (n.)**

chatty, verbose

excessively or needlessly talkative, especially on matters that are unimportant

---

## 25 **incandescence** n.

**incandescent (adj.)**

glow, radiance; fervor, rage

the emission of light caused by heat; strong emotion or extreme anger

---

## 26 **inimical** adj.

adverse, unfavorable; antagonistic, unkind

tending to harm; hostile or unfriendly

---

## 27 **isothermal** adj.

**isotherm (n.)**

of, relating to, or indicating equality of temperature or any changes of volume or pressure at constant temperature

---

## 28 **jockey** v./n.

contend; cheat; horseman; controller

to plan out or manipulate for position or advantage; to swindle or trick; a racehorse rider; one who operates a specified vehicle, machine, device, etc.

## 29 laconic adj.
*brief, concise*
using few words

## 30 latitude n.
**latitudinal (adj.)**
*parallel; leeway*
the angular distance (in degrees) north or south from the equator; the relative freedom
of action, conduct, choice, opinion, etc.

## 31 linguist n.
**linguistic (adj.), linguistics (n.)**
*polyglot, philologist*
one skilled in or who studies languages

## 32 lurid adj.
*startling; overbright; pasty*
causing shock or revulsion; excessively colorful or unpleasantly bright; appearing
ghastly pale; glowing red, as fire covered by smoke

## 33 malaise n.
*uneasiness, unhappiness*
a vague feeling of anxiety or discomfort without knowing its exact cause

## 34 naysayer n.
**naysay (v.)**
*doubter, pessimist*
a person who consistently denies, opposes, or criticizes

## 35 opine v.
*observe, comment*
to hold, express, or state an opinion openly

## 36 **ossify** v.

**ossification (n.)**
 petrify; stagnate
to transform or turn into bone; to become conventional or inflexible, as in attitude, habit, practice, etc.

## 37 **pejorative** adj.

**derogatory, disrespectful**
expressing disdain or disapproval

## 38 **polyhedron** n.

**polyhedral (adj.), polyhedra (pl.)**
a solid figure with several plane faces

## 39 **precipice** n.

**precipitous (adj.)**
 cliff, bluff; verge, threshold
a very steep or overhanging rock face; the brink of an extremely risky or dangerous situation

## 40 **preternatural** adj.

 abnormal, supernatural
beyond or differing from what is normal or natural

## 41 **ratification** n.

**ratify (v.)**
 sanction, authorization
the act or process of giving formal or official confirmation to a treaty, amendment, contract, etc.

## 42 **recreant** adj.

 cowardly; disloyal
lacking in courage; unfaithful to duty, belief, or allegiance

### 43 **rectitude** n.

integrity, virtue; straightness

righteousness or uprightness of character, or correctness of judgment, procedure, or opinion; the state or quality of not being bent

---

### 44 **regicide** n.

**regicidal (adj.)**

the killing of (or one who kills) a king

---

### 45 **requisition** n.

claim, order

a formal demand, application, or request for the use or surrender of equipment, supply, service, a fugitive criminal, etc.

---

### 46 **reticent** adj.

**reticence (n.)**

silent; controlled

habitually disinclined to speak; having a restrained, unpretentious quality

---

### 47 **scrupulous** adj.

**scruple (n.)**

honest, upright; diligent, attentive

very careful about not doing anything morally wrong; extremely precise or thorough

---

### 48 **sophistry** n.

**sophist (n.), sophism (n.)**

fallacy, trickery

a seemingly plausible argument using misleading or deceptive reasoning

---

### 49 **staunch** adj./v.

devoted; sturdy; fit; block

loyal or reliable; firmly or strongly constructed; watertight or seaworthy; to stop or lessen the flow of

---

## 50 **stupor** n.

daze, oblivion
a state of dulled consciousness or sensibility

## 01 **agrarian** adj./n.

**agrarianism (n.)**

rural, agricultural

relating to the ownership or cultivation of land; person who fights for farmers or land redistribution

## 02 **antedate** v.

predate, backdate

to occur before (or assign a date to a document or occurrence earlier than) a specific event or time

## 03 **aperture** n.

gap, crack

a hole or an opening, such as through which light travels (as in a photographic lens of a camera)

## 04 **auxiliary** adj.

supplementary, backup

providing additional or extra support

## 05 **bane** n.

**baneful (adj.)**

hardship, curse

a cause or source of misery, harm, or death

## 06 **bequeath** v.

**bequest (n.)**

bestow, hand down

to leave something (as in personal fortune or estate by will) or pass something on to the generations to follow

## 07 **centurion** n.

*commander, captain*

a commanding officer of a Roman military unit made up of 100 soldiers

---

## 08 **circulation** n.

**circulate (v.), circulator (n.)**

*flow, motion; distribution, readership*

the act of moving around in a circle or system; freely passing from a place or person to another, or its extent (as of currency, publication, etc.)

---

## 09 **compensate** v.

**compensation (n.), compensative (adj.)**

*counterbalance; fix; settle; adapt*

to offset; to make up for something, such as a loss, error, weakness, etc.; to pay or reward someone for a favor or work done; to adjust to a change

---

## 10 **conducive** adj.

*helpful, beneficial*

making something possible

---

## 11 **confluent** adj./n.

**confluence, conflux (n.)**

*joining, connecting; tributary*

converging or flowing together; a stream coming together to flow as one

---

## 12 **connive** v.

**conniving (adj.)**

*overlook, conspire, plot*

to ignore, scheme, or cooperate with others in secret to engage in a wrongdoing

---

## 13 **consolidate** v.

**consolidation (n.)**

*centralize; fuse; strengthen*

to join or unite into a single unit; to combine into a single mass; to make stronger

Part 1

vocabulary

## 14 **countermeasure** n.

🖋 solution, canceller

something created to act as a device of retaliation or neutralization of another

---

## 15 **delineate** v.

**delineation (n.)**

🖋 draw, mark; portray, describe

to sketch out or trace an outline; to provide a representation or depict in words

---

## 16 **deputize** v.

🖋 appoint, commission; stand in for, replace

to officially empower someone; to act (or name someone) as a substitute

---

## 17 **doleful** adj.

🖋 mournful, cheerless

causing or filled with sadness or grief

---

## 18 **ecclesiastic** adj./n.

**ecclesiastical (adj., alt.)**

🖋 clerical, religious; clergyman

relating or pertaining to a church; a minister or priest

---

## 19 **exonerate** v.

**exoneration (n.), exonerative (adj.)**

🖋 acquit, pardon; relieve, liberate

to clear from blame, accusation, or charges; to release from hardship, duty, or obligation

---

## 20 **gentry** n.

🖋 aristocracy, elite; type, circle

people of the upper or ruling class; people belonging to a particular kind, class, or group

---

## 21 **gesticulate** v.

**gesticulation (n.)**

motion, signal

to make gestures when speaking, or to express through gestures

## 22 **illuminate** v.

**illumination (n.), illuminant (adj.)**

elucidate; brighten; adorn

to explain or help clarify; to shine or make brighter with light; to decorate or make spectacular

## 23 **incisor** n.

narrow-edged tooth

a tooth at the front of the mouth used mainly for cutting

## 24 **indemnify** v.

**indemnity (n.)**

insure; compensate

to secure or protect against harm, loss, damage, or legal responsibility; to repay or make up for incurred loss or damage

## 25 **inertia** n.

**inertial (adj.)**

inactivity, inaction

the tendency of a matter to remain at rest or keep moving in uniform direction unless affected by an external force; a tendency to remain passive

## 26 **infringe** v.

**infringement (n.)**

breach, disobey; intrude, trespass

to violate or break a law, agreement, treaty, rights, etc.; to encroach or go beyond the proper or set limits

## 27 **interdependence** n.

**interdependent (adj.)**

interconnection, linkage

the state of being dependent on each other, or the mutual relationship stemming from such a condition

## 28 **intrinsic** adj.

⌐ inherent; essential

belonging naturally, or being the basic trait of someone or something; vital or necessary; originating or situated within a tissue, organ, muscle, etc.

## 29 **ire** n.

⌐ wrath, fury

intense anger

## 30 **lithography** n.

**lithograph (n.), lithographic (adj.)**

⌐ engraving, impression

the printing process from a flat surface, such as stone or metal plate

## 31 **litter** n.

⌐ sedan chair, stretcher; junk; young

a structure for carrying a passenger or injured person; trash or waste; the animal offspring born in one birth; material for animal waste or bedding

## 32 **maroon** v./n.

⌐ strand; reddish purple

to place or leave abandoned in an isolated place, especially a deserted island; dark red or dark brownish red

## 33 **mortar** n.

⌐ cannon; dish; adhesive

a short-barreled device for firing shells (bombs), firework, lifelines, etc.; a bowl used for grinding; a mixture for bonding bricks or stones

## 34 **nondescript** adj.

⌐ indefinable, indescribable; ordinary, dull

not belonging to any specific class or kind; lacking distinctive or interesting characteristics or features

## 35 **ordinance** n.

*decree; observance*

an authoritative or government order or law; a set or accepted practice (such as religious ritual); something commanded by fate or a god

---

## 36 **paragon** n.

*exemplar, paragon*

an ideal model or example of perfection or excellence; a flawless diamond of 100 carats or more, or a large pearl that is flawlessly round

---

## 37 **paranoia** n.

**paranoid (adj.)**

*delusions; doubt*

mental illness characterized by a false belief of conspiracy or persecution against the person; extreme and irrational suspicion or mistrust of people

---

## 38 **parlance** n.

*language, idiom*

a certain style or manner of speaking or using words

---

## 39 **parochial** adj.

**parochialism (n.)**

*narrow, small-minded*

having a limited range, scope, or outlook; pertaining to a church parish

---

## 40 **pauper** n.

**pauperize (v.), pauperization (n.), pauperism (n.)**

*beggar, dependent*

an extremely poor person, or one living on or eligible for government aid or public charity

---

## 41 **pernicious** adj.

*dangerous, deadly*

causing great harm, destruction, or death

## 42 **perspicacious** adj.

**perspicacity (n.)**

perceptive, observant

having keen insight or awareness

---

## 43 **preconception** n.

**preconceived (adj.)**

assumption, prejudice

an idea or opinion formed prior to obtaining actual knowledge or experience

---

## 44 **prenatal** adj.

antenatal, fetal

occurring or existing before birth, or relating to pregnancy

---

## 45 **pupilage** n.

the condition, state, or period of being a student

---

## 46 **repercussion** n.

**repercussive (adj.)**

effect, outcome

a consequence of some action or event, especially one that is unforeseen and undesirable

---

## 47 **revile** v.

**revilement (n.)**

criticize, condemn

to attack through the use of abusive language

---

## 48 **servile** adj.

**servility (n.)**

obedient, subservient

of or like that of a slave, or excessively humble or submissive

---

## 49 **sophomoric** adj.

 pretentious, inexperienced

self-assured or overconfident despite lacking knowledge, or lacking in taste or maturity

---

## 50 **voluble** adj.

**volubility (n.)**

 talkative; rotating; twining

talking fluently, quickly, or incessantly; easily turning or rolling; twisting like a vine

---

# List 15

## 01 **ammunition** n.
cartridge, ammo
objects used in charging firearms such as bullets and shells

## 02 **archetype** n.
**archetypal (adj.)**
prototype, standard
an original model or an ideal example

## 03 **auricular** adj.
auditory, acoustic
relating to the ear or the sense of hearing

## 04 **bight** n.
inlet; loop
a bend or curve in a coastline, river, etc.; a curve or loose part in a rope

## 05 **boon** n./adj.
blessing; festive
something to be thankful for or that is beneficial; relating to being merry (as in drinking, feasting, having good company, etc.)

## 06 **boorish** adj.
**boor (n.)**
impolite; uncultured
having rough or rude manners; behaving in an uneducated manner

## 07 **brethren** n.
brothers; comrade
a plural form of brother; members of an organization, especially of a religion or sect

## 08 **cadaverous** adj.

**cadaver (n.)**

corpselike, bony

relating to or resembling a dead body, or deathly thin or pale

---

## 09 **campaign** n.

warfare; promotion

a series of focused military operations; planned actions to achieve a specific goal (for an election, advertisement, etc.)

---

## 10 **chiffon** n./adj.

softness ornament; frothy

a sheer, light fabric (silk, nylon, etc.); decorative accessories on a dress (laces, ribbons, etc.); made light by adding whipped food ingredients

---

## 11 **circuitous** adj.

**circuitously (adv.)**

roundabout; devious; twisting

not being direct in words or actions; being deceptive or dishonest; having a lengthy and winding route or course

---

## 12 **copious** adj.

ample, profuse, extensive

plentiful in quantity, full of thought or information, or abundant with words, expressions, or ideas

---

## 13 **coronation** n.

**coronate (v.)**

enthronement

the act or ceremony of crowning a king or queen

---

## 14 **crass** adj.

mindless; coarse, insensitive; money-oriented

lacking intelligence; crude or unrefined; downright materialistic

---

## 15 **demagogue** n.

**demagogy, demagoguery (n.)**

*agitator, rabble-rouser*

a politician or leader who tries to seek support or gain power by emotionally stirring up the people

---

## 16 **dilapidate** v.

**dilapidation (n.)**

*decay, deteriorate*

to cause to become ruined or fall into a state of disrepair, mostly due to misuse or neglect

---

## 17 **downtrodden** adj.

*persecuted, abused*

oppressed or trampled on

---

## 18 **edict** n.

**edictal (adj.)**

*decree, announcement; instruction*

an official, authoritative proclamation or order; a command or demand

---

## 19 **effigy** n.

*image, model*

a crude representation or figure, especially of a person disliked or ridiculed

---

## 20 **equity** n.

**equitable (adj.)**

*neutrality, impartiality; worth, valuation*

justice or fairness; the value of a company's shares or property

---

## 21 **extrude** v.

**extrusion (n.)**

*eject, expel; cast, mold*

to thrust or push out; to shape or form metal, plastic, etc., by squeezing it through a shaped opening

---

## 22 **incendiary** adj.

incendiarism (n.)

flammable; rebellious

capable of causing destruction by fire; tending to excite or stir up conflict

---

## 23 **ineffable** adj.

ineffability (n.)

unspeakable, inexpressible

too great, extreme, or sacred to utter or describe in words

---

## 24 **infidel** n.

nonbeliever, doubter

one who opposes or does not accept a particular religion, principle, theory, etc.

---

## 25 **insubstantial** adj.

insubstantiality (n.)

weak, unstable; untouchable, imaginary

having little or no strength; not solid, tangible, or real

---

## 26 **levy** v.

gather, charge

to impose, collect, require, or enlist by authority (such as tax, fine, military service, etc.)

---

## 27 **livid** adj.

black-and-blue; pallid; furious

changed in color by a bruise; lacking color or deathly pale; extremely angry

---

## 28 **maladroit** adj.

incompetent, clumsy

ineffective or awkward

---

## 29 **mar** v.

disfigure, tarnish

to ruin or spoil the appearance or quality of someone or something

## 30 **menagerie** n.

assortment, jumble

a collection of wild or exotic animals kept for exhibition, or any diverse collection or mixture

---

## 31 **mercurial** adj.

fickle, volatile; sly, cunning

characterized by sudden, unpredictable mood changes; shrewd, clever, or thievish; pertaining to the element mercury or planet Mercury

---

## 32 **metronome** n.

**metronomic (adj.)**

timer

a device that marks precise time by means of regular, repeated ticks

---

## 33 **ministry** n.

**ministerial (adj.)**

priesthood; bureau

the profession or functions of a clergyman; a government department in certain countries

---

## 34 **obtuse** adj.

stupid; unclear; blunt

insensitive, or lacking intellect; not precise, or hard to comprehend; not pointed or sharp; more than 90 degrees but less than 180 degrees (angle)

---

## 35 **paradox** n.

**paradoxical (adj.)**

inconsistency, dichotomy

something or someone with qualities that are contradictory

---

## 36 **patrician** n.

aristocrat, noble

a person of high birth or social rank

---

## 37 **patron** n.

**patronize (v.)**

benefactor; client; guardian

a wealthy or powerful person who sponsors or supports an organization, cause, artist, writer, etc.; a regular customer; one who defends or protects

---

## 38 **penitent** adj.

**penitence (n.)**

repentant, remorseful

feeling sorrow and regret for one's sins or offenses

---

## 39 **ponderous** adj.

clumsy, heavy; tedious, unnatural

(hard to carry or move because) of very great weight; dull or labored

---

## 40 **portent** n.

**portend (v.), portentous (adj.)**

omen, foreshadowing; marvel, prodigy

a sign or warning that an event, especially something big or unfortunate, is likely or about to occur; something extraordinary

---

## 41 **prostrate** adj.

**prostration (n.)**

prone; weakened; overcome

lying flat with face downward in submission; having no vitality or physically exhausted; completely helpless

---

## 42 **pusillanimous** adj.

**pusillanimity (n.)**

timid, cowardly

showing a lack of courage, resolution, or determination

---

## 43 **rancid** adj.

**rancidity (n.)**

stale, rank; appalling, dreadful

smelling or tasting unpleasant; offensive or distasteful

---

vocabulary

## 44 **rapport** n.

bond, affinity

a close, harmonious relationship

---

## 45 **squalid** adj.

dirty, shabby; dishonest, improper

unpleasant and filthy from neglect, poverty, or unsanitary conditions; deserving contempt, or having a lack of moral standards

---

## 46 **swarthy** adj.

dusky, dark-skinned

of a dark color or complexion

---

## 47 **tenure** n.

tenancy; term

the conditions of occupying a building or land; the period, status, or right to permanent employment of a position or office

---

## 48 **timorous** adj.

timid, fearful

having or showing little confidence, or easily frightened

---

## 49 **unbridled** adj.

**unbridle (v.)**

uncontrolled, unrestricted

unrestrained or uncontainable

---

## 50 **wont** n.

routine, practice

a habitual or customary behavior

---

# List 16

= Synonyms, related words

## 01 **accelerate** v.
**acceleration** (n.), **accelerant** (n.)
⌐ quicken, hasten
to cause to move faster or begin to move more quickly

## 02 **administer** v.
**administration** (n.), **administrator** (n.), **administrative** (adj.)
⌐ regulate; dispense; execute; help
to manage, operate, or govern; to give a drug to patients; to deliver punishment; to provide aid or service

## 03 **adversary** n.
**adversarial** (adj.)
⌐ competitor, enemy
an opponent or rival

## 04 **beguile** v.
**beguiling** (adj.)
⌐ captivate, fascinate; mislead, con
to charm or interest someone; to trick or deceive

## 05 **beleaguer** v.
**beleaguered** (adj.)
⌐ besiege; harass
to be surrounded (as by army or enemy); to cause or create constant problems or difficulties

## 06 **bourgeois** adj.
**bourgeoise** (fem.), **bourgeoisie** (n.)
⌐ conservative, capitalistic
relating to the social middle class, often with the idea of being conventional or materialistic in belief and attitude

## 07 **chastity** n.

**chaste (adj.)**

➤ purity; honor; uncomplicated

the state of avoiding physical intimacy or anything considered immoral; a person's integrity; simplicity in design, expression, or style

---

## 08 **chide** v.

**chidingly (adv.)**

➤ reproach, admonish

to scold or rebuke mildly

---

## 09 **consequential** adj.

**consequent (adj., alt./n.), consequence (n.)**

➤ ensuing, resulting; major, substantial

relating to a result that follows as a secondary or indirect effect; very important or significant

---

## 10 **craft** n.

**crafty (adj.)**

➤ competence; cunning; occupation; vessel

skill in creating and executing a plan; skill in trickery; a trade requiring specific skills; a boat, ship, aircraft, etc.

---

## 11 **dabble** v.

**dabbler (n.)**

➤ dally, fiddle with; dip, moisten; splash

to have an interest in something superficially or in a casual manner; to wet by spattering or dipping slightly in liquid; to play or paddle in water

---

## 12 **decapitate** v.

**decapitation (n.)**

➤ behead; oust, overthrow

to cut off the head of a person or animal; to weaken or destroy a group, organization, or state by removing its leader or ruling body

## 13 **derail** v.

**derailment (n.)**

deviate; obstruct; frustrate; come off

to move away from the intended course or purpose; to block a progress; to weaken someone's composure; to cause to run off the tracks

---

## 14 **détente** n.

peace, agreement

a relaxing or lessening of tension or hostility, especially between countries

---

## 15 **disparate** adj.

**disparity (n.)**

uneven, disproportionate; distinct, dissimilar

unequal (as in age, social class, income, etc.); essentially unlike in quality or character

---

## 16 **draconian** adj.

severe, harsh

very strict or cruel

---

## 17 **effervescent** adj.

**effervescence (n.), effervesce (v.)**

fizzy, sparkling; lively, animated

giving off or forming bubbles; high-spirited or enthusiastic

---

## 18 **efflorescence** n.

**efflorescent (adj.), effloresce (v.)**

sprouting; climax; rash

the period when flowers start blooming or appearing; the peak stage of development; a skin redness or eruption

---

## 19 **fiducial** adj.

trustworthy; guiding

based or founded on strong faith or trust; taken or used as a standard of reference for measuring something

## 20 **flippant** adj.
**flippancy (n.)**
 cocky, rude
not showing or having little or no seriousness or respect

---

## 21 **forte** n.
 talent, strength
something that one is particularly good at; the stronger part (between the handle and the middle) of a sword blade; a loud part in music

---

## 22 **gossamer** n.
a fine film or strand of cobwebs drifting in the air, or anything extremely light, thin, or delicate

---

## 23 **huckster** n./v.
 peddler; advertising copywriter; deal
one who sells (especially aggressively or dishonestly) small items; one who writes ads for radio or TV; to bargain or haggle

---

## 24 **humdrum** n.
 boring, monotonous
dull or lacking variety

---

## 25 **immaculate** adj.
**immaculacy (n.)**
 spotless; perfect; pure
flawlessly clean or tidy; having no flaws or free from mistakes or error; without sin or free from moral corruption

---

## 26 **immiscible** adj.
**immiscibility (n.)**
 incompatible, discordant
incapable of combining to attain a uniform mixture

---

## 27 **immolate** v.

immolation (n.), immolator (n.)

blaze, offer up

to kill (yourself or someone else), destroy, or offer as sacrifice, especially by burning

## 28 **incognito** adv./adj.

concealed, under cover

under disguised name or appearance

## 29 **ingenuity** n.

ingenious (adj.)

creativity, imagination

the quality of being (or a device that is) clever or original

## 30 **injunction** n.

injunctive (adj.)

order, directive; writ, decree

an act of commanding or prohibiting; a court order requiring a party to do or not do a certain act

## 31 **inquisition** n.

interrogation, inquiry

an intensive questioning or investigation, or a judicial examination or a jury's finding

## 32 **insinuate** v.

insinuation (n.)

slip, insert; imply, infer

to introduce or enter gradually or unnoticeably; to suggest or hint in an indirect and often unpleasant way

## 33 **irate** adj.

furious, outraged

extremely angry

vocabulary

## 34 **magnanimous** adj.

magnanimity (n.)

considerate, merciful

extremely generous or forgiving

## 35 **millennium** n.

millennia (pl.), millennial (adj.)

golden age, utopia

a period or anniversary of a thousand years; a period of great or universal happiness, prosperity, or peace

## 36 **minuscule** adj./n.

minute, microscopic; small letter

extremely small or tiny; a lowercase letter; a small and simplified cursive writing style used in medieval manuscripts

## 37 **misadventure** n.

misfortune, mishap

an unfortunate accident or incident

## 38 **modish** adj.

modiste (n.)

trendy, latest

conforming to current style or fashion

## 39 **muse** v./n.

contemplate; motivation; bard

to think deeply for a long time or speak thoughtfully; an inspirational source; a poet; any of the nine goddesses of the arts and sciences

## 40 **narrative** n.

narrate (v.), narration (n.)

record, chronicle

a spoken or written account or story

## 41 **nestle** v.

snuggle; situate

to settle down, or to press closely, cozily, or affectionately; to lie partly concealed or in shelter

## 42 **ostentatious** adj.

**ostentation (n.)**

pretentious, showy

intended to impress or attract notice, admiration, or attention

## 43 **preoccupation** n.

**preoccupy (v.)**

concentration; obsession

the state of being absorbed in something; something that engrosses a person

## 44 **proletariat** n.

**proletarian (n., alt./adj.)**

wage earners, the masses

the working class, or the lowest social or economic class

## 45 **promenade** n.

**promenader (n.)**

boardwalk, stroll; dance movement; prom

(a place for) a walk for leisure or display; a dance motion done in a walk; a formal dance or ball

## 46 **propagate** v.

**propagation (n.)**

breed, multiply; make known, disseminate

to cause to continue or reproduce; to promote or spread a theory, belief, idea, etc.; to transmit (sound, motion, etc.) through a medium

## 47 **purveyor** n.

**purvey (v.), purveyance (n.)**

vendor, supplier; propagator, disseminator

a person who provides or sells food, particular goods, or even information; a person who spreads stories, views, ideas, etc.

Part 1

vocabulary

## 48 **subterfuge** n.

*trickery, artifice*

any deception used to hide or achieve one's objective

## 49 **taciturn** adj.

**taciturnity (n.)**

*quiet, unresponsive*

habitually silent or disinclined to speak

## 50 **zealot** n.

**zealous (adj.), zealotry (n.)**

*fanatic, extremist*

one who is too passionate about or uncompromising in achieving or upholding a specific objective or belief

= Synonyms, related words

vocabulary

## 01 **ameliorate** v.
**amelioration (n.)**
⌐ ease, alleviate
to improve or make something more bearable

## 02 **antediluvian** adj.
⌐ ancient, antique
belonging to the time period before Noah's Flood; extremely primitive or old-fashioned

## 03 **arbitrary** adj.
⌐ personal, random; tyrannical, dictatorial
based on individual whim or judgment rather than any objective reason or system;
unlimited in exercising absolute power

## 04 **bellicose** adj.
⌐ hostile, combative
showing an aggressive tendency

## 05 **blasphemy** n.
**blasphemous (adj.)**
⌐ desecration, sacrilege
the act of insulting or disrespecting a god or anything considered holy

## 06 **calligraphy** n.
**calligrapher (n.), calligraphic (adj.)**
⌐ penmanship, chirography
(the art of producing) elegant and stylized handwriting

## 07 **cantankerous** adj.
⌐ disagreeable, cranky
ill-tempered or hard to deal with

## 08 **cataclysm** n.

**cataclysmic (adj.)**

deluge; calamity; crisis, turmoil

a great, disastrous flood; a large-scale natural disaster; an unexpected, violent political or social disruption or upheaval

## 09 **claimant** n.

petitioner, applicant

a person making a claim (to a right, property, or title) or receiving a benefit of some sort; a person who starts a lawsuit

## 10 **clout** n.

authority, weight; beat; slam; rag

power, influence, or advantage; a blow, especially with the hand; a hard hit (in baseball); cloth for patching or cleaning

## 11 **collate** v.

**collator (n.), collation (n.)**

match, verify

to collect, compare, or combine in the right order, or to make sure such an order is correct or accurate

## 12 **conspicuous** adj.

**conspicuity (n.), conspicuously (adv.)**

obvious; eye-catching

easy to see or notice; attracting or drawing attention

## 13 **covert** adj./n.

secret, undercover; shelter; plume; twill-weave fabric

not openly admitted or shown; a cover or hiding place; feathers covering a specific part of a bird; a type of durable cloth

## 14 **decadence** n.

**decadent (adj.)**

degeneration, deterioration

a process or period of moral or artistic decline

## 15 **demographic** adj.

**demography (n.)**

relating to various statistics (such as density, distribution, etc.) of human populations

---

## 16 **didactic** adj.

**didacticism (n.)**

instructive; patronizing

intended to teach, especially moral observations or with the inclusion of entertaining elements; overly preachy or inclined to teach

---

## 17 **effluvium** n.

**effluvia (pl.)**

exhaust, odor; rubbish, refuse

an invisible outflow of vapor or steam mainly characterized by foul smell; an unpleasant by-product or waste

---

## 18 **enrapture** v.

**enrapt (adj.)**

thrill; captivate

to fill with delight or great joy; to fascinate

---

## 19 **exultant** adj.

**exult (v.)**

thrilled, proud

extremely or triumphantly happy

---

## 20 **farce** n./v.

**farcical (adj.)**

humor; foolishness; cram

a dramatic composition or work characterized by satire and comedy; an absurd act, situation, or event; to fill or stuff

---

## 21 **forbearance** n.

**forbear (v.)**

patience; leniency

self-control or tolerance; a refraining from enforcing a right, obligation, debt that is due, etc.

## 22 **fulcrum** n.

**fulcra (pl.)**

prop, axis; heart, basis

the point or support on which a lever turns; something that acts as a central role

---

## 23 **gregarious** adj.

sociable; collective

fond of being with other people; (animals) living or traveling in herds or packs, or (plants) growing in clusters

---

## 24 **holistic** adj.

**holism (n.)**

comprehensive, integrated

relating to the whole instead of analyzing or breaking up into parts

---

## 25 **impervious** adj.

immune; impermeable

unable to be damaged, harmed, or disturbed; not allowing passage or penetration

---

## 26 **impromptu** adj./adv.

improvised, spontaneous

done on the spur of the moment or without preparation

---

## 27 **incongruous** adj.

**incongruity (n.)**

unsuitable, inappropriate

not agreeing, proper, or compatible

---

## 28 **industrious** adj.

**industry (n.)**

busy, diligent

constantly active or hard-working

---

## 29 **malevolence** n.

**malevolent (adj.)**

❝ hatred, ill will

hostile feeling, attitude, or behavior

## 30 **metaphor** n.

**metaphorical, metaphoric (adj.)**

❝ analogy, symbol

a figure of speech carrying an implied comparison and not to be taken literally

## 31 **missive** n.

❝ message, memorandum

a letter or written communication

## 32 **monotonous** adj.

**monotony (n.)**

❝ flat, droning; tedious, boring

marked by unvarying tone, pitch, or intensity; dull or having little or no variety

## 33 **notorious** adj.

**notoriety (n.)**

❝ infamous, disreputable

widely known and discussed, typically in an unfavorable way

## 34 **novice** n.

❝ apprentice; novitiate

a new or inexperienced person in a particular job or activity; a probationary member of a religious order prior to taking vows

## 35 **ostensibly** adv.

**ostensible (adj.)**

❝ superficially, supposedly

on the surface, or so as to appear to be true or give the impression

## 36 **palisade** n.

barricade, paling; bluff

a fence of strong wooden or iron stakes or poles for defense or enclosure; a line of steep, high cliffs

---

## 37 **panorama** n.

**panoramic (adj.)**

scenery; overview; cyclorama

an unobstructed view of an entire area; a comprehensive survey or presentation of a subject; a circular picture exhibition surrounding the spectators

---

## 38 **penury** n.

**penurious (adj.)**

poorness, destitution

extreme poverty

---

## 39 **pinnacle** n.

peak, crag; prime

a tall, pointed piece of rock or mountain; the highest point (of achievement, development, etc.)

---

## 40 **predisposition** n.

**predispose (v.), predisposed (adj.)**

vulnerability, weakness; preference, inclination

the state of being susceptible to a particular condition, especially a health problem; the tendency to behave in a certain way

---

## 41 **privy** adj./n.

informed of, in on; outhouse, latrine

allowed to share in a secret or private knowledge; an outside toilet

---

## 42 **profess** v.

**professed (adj.), profession (n.)**

pretend; affirm

to claim in words only; to declare, confess, or admit one's belief in, faith in, or allegiance to

---

## 43 **rapine** n.

seizure, plunder

the taking of someone's property by force

## 44 **recourse** n.

resort, hope

the act of seeking (or the source of) help, strength, or advice; the right to demand compensation

## 45 **risible** adj.

**risibility (n.)**

comical, amusing

causing, associated with, or prone to laughter

## 46 **savvy** adj.

shrewd, well-informed

perceptive or knowledgeable

## 47 **serendipity** n.

**serendipitous (adj.)**

luck, chance

the gift for or occurrence of finding unexpected but beneficial things or events

## 48 **siphon** v./n.

steal; pipe

to transfer, especially illegally; a bent tube used to transfer liquid; a tubular organ used for moving water in and out of an animal's body

## 49 **travail** n.

toil, exertion; distress, misery

painful or excessive work or labor; intense agony or suffering; labor pains, especially that of childbirth

## 50 **vindictive** adj.

⟐ vengeful, unforgiving

involving, intended for, or showing a tendency to seek revenge

# List 18

### 01 **adeptness** n.
*deftness, adroitness*
skillful ability in doing something

### 02 **advocate** v.
**advocacy (n.)**
*recommend, urge*
to plead in favor of or defend by argument

### 03 **affinity** n.
**affinitive (adj.)**
*affection, fondness; similarity, resemblance*
a natural attraction to someone or something; the way in which something is related to another

### 04 **anarchy** n.
**anarchist (n.), anarchism (n.), anarchic (adj.)**
*disorder, chaos*
a state of disorder due to a lack of an authoritative governing body

### 05 **arrears** n.
*dues, obligation*
debts that are not yet paid, or duties that are not yet completed

### 06 **atone** v.
**atonement (n.)**
*compensate, redeem*
to make up for an offense, crime, or sin one has committed

### 07 **awry** adj./adv.
*amiss, wrong*
veering away or off from the appropriate or planned course

Part 1

vocabulary

## 08 **banal** adj.

**banality (n.)**

common, unoriginal

boring, having no originality, or obvious because of overuse

---

## 09 **bard** n.

storyteller; barding

a poet, traditionally one who composes, recites, or sings poetry about epics or heroes; a piece of armor put on a horse

---

## 10 **blare** v./n.

**blaring (adj.)**

boom, blast; flamboyance, gaudiness

to make a loud, harsh sound or noise; brilliance, often to the point of being too much

---

## 11 **brood** v./n.

ponder; guard; incubate; overshadow; young

to contemplate moodily or feel depressed; to protect (offspring); to sit on (eggs); to hover or loom; offspring of a family

---

## 12 **chasm** n.

**chasmal (adj.)**

gorge, fissure; disagreement, gap

a deep rift or gap in the earth's surface; a profound separation or difference of feelings, views, interests, etc.

---

## 13 **conservative** adj.

**conservatism (n.)**

conventional; inflexible; guarded

relating to traditional taste, attitudes, or values; resisting change; moderate or cautious

---

## 14 **contagion** n.

**contagious (adj.)**

transmission, infection

the spreading of or something that spreads emotion, custom, or especially something undesirable (bad influence, disease, etc.)

---

### 15 **continent** adj./n.

**continence (n.)**

*◌* disciplined, temperate; mainland, landmass

being able to control oneself or relating to self-restraint; one of the world's major divisions of land

---

### 16 **culpable** adj.

**culpability (n.)**

*◌* blameworthy, guilty

deserving or meriting blame

---

### 17 **cumbersome** adj.

*◌* awkward, inconvenient; complicated, inefficient

not easily managed because of size or weight; difficult to deal with because of complexity, extent, slowness, etc.

---

### 18 **defraud** v.

**defraudation (n.)**

*◌* cheat, swindle

to obtain (money, property, etc.) illegally by the use of deception

---

### 19 **discomfit** v.

**discomfiture (n.)**

*◌* discomfort, confound; prevent, disappoint

to embarrass or confuse; to spoil the plans, hopes, or expectations of

---

### 20 **dispatch** v./n.

*◌* expedite; put an end to, do away with; report

to finish or send off or out (shipment, message, etc.) quickly; to kill, destroy, or get rid off; a news item sent by a journalist

---

### 21 **emporium** n.

**emporia (pl.)**

*◌* outlet, marketplace

a large store or a trading center selling many different kinds of goods

## 22 **entreaty** n.

**entreat (v.)**

appeal, petition

a humble request or earnest plea

## 23 **epigraph** n.

**epigraphic (adj.)**

heading, excerpt; engraving, etching

a quotation written at the beginning of a chapter or book to suggest its theme; an inscription on a statue, monument, building, etc.

## 24 **exacerbate** v.

**exacerbation (n.)**

aggravate, complicate

to make something worse or more intense

## 25 **expenditure** n.

**expend (v.)**

costs, expense; labor, effort

the amount of funds that can be or are spent; the use of energy, time, etc., to produce a result

## 26 **expository** adj.

**exposition (n.)**

explanatory, descriptive

intended to give an explanation of something

## 27 **gnarl** n./v.

**gnarled, gnarly (adj.)**

lump; tangle; grunt

a knot or twisted grain on a tree; to twist or knot something into a state of deformity; to growl or snarl

## 28 **hindsight** n.

looking back, retrospect

realization of the importance of an event after it has taken place

## 29 impasse n.

deadlock, dilemma; blind alley, cul-de-sac

a situation in which no escape, solution, or progress is offered or can be made; a road or passage with no exit or one that is closed at one end

## 30 kaleidoscopic adj.

**kaleidoscope (n.)**

multicolored; varied

having bright, complex, and continuously changing patterns of colors; composed of a diverse mix of elements

## 31 lachrymose adj.

tearful, weepy; sad, moving

likely to shed tears frequently or easily; tending to induce tears

## 32 mallet n.

a hammer with a large head and small handle; a long-handled stick used in polo or croquet; a beater used for playing certain musical instruments

## 33 mead n.

honey wine; meadow

an alcoholic drink fermented from water and honey, malt, yeast, etc.; a field of grassland or pasture

## 34 millet n.

any of several small-seeded grasses grown as cereal crops or grains for animal feed and human food

## 35 monochrome adj.

solid, uniform

relating to visual images in black, white, or varying tones of one color

## 36 moribund adj.

dying; obsolete; frail

nearing death; nearing the end, or in decline; lacking vitality or vigor

### 37 **municipal** adj.

**municipality** (n.)

local, civic

relating to any of a nation's administrative division (town, district, etc.) or its self-government

---

### 38 **overture** n.

proposal, advance; prelude, opening

an approach or offer made to show willingness to negotiate or establish a relationship; a musical piece introduction, or anything introductory

---

### 39 **petulant** adj.

**petulance** (n.)

bad-tempered, peevish

rude, impatient, or childishly sulky or irritable

---

### 40 **philanthropy** n.

**philanthropist** (n.), **philanthropic** (adj.)

humanism, benevolence

the desire, effort, or act to promote the welfare of humankind

---

### 41 **plebeian** adj.

lowly; unrefined; unremarkable

characteristic of or relating to the lower class or the common people; vulgar or uncultured in manner or style; common or ordinary

---

### 42 **punitive** adj.

disciplinary, penal

involving or inflicting punishment

---

### 43 **repartee** n.

banter, retort

a (skill in making) quick and witty comment or reply

---

## 44 **salubrious** adj.

⌐ health-giving, beneficial

promoting health or well-being

## 45 **somniferous** adj.

⌐ drowsy, hypnotic

causing or tending to induce sleep

## 46 **stalwart** adj./n.

⌐ robust; valiant; resolute; supporter

strong and sturdy; brave or courageous; firm or unyielding; a dependable person loyal to a cause

## 47 **stipulate** v.

**stipulation (n.)**

⌐ specify, set down

to add or make a specific demand as a requirement or condition in an agreement or contract

## 48 **tantamount** adj.

⌐ equal to, much the same as

equivalent in value, force, effect, etc.

## 49 **theocracy** n.

**theocrat (n.), theocratic (adj.)**

⌐ hierocracy, church-state

a system of government controlled by a state-sponsored religion

## 50 **vernal** adj.

⌐ young

of, appropriate to, or occurring in spring; youthful, or new or fresh

= Synonyms, related words

## 01 **abscond** v.

escape, hide

to flee secretly, particularly to avoid arrest

## 02 **adulation** n.

**adulate (v.), adulatory (adj.)**

adoration, respect

unrestrained admiration or praise

## 03 **affliction** n.

**afflict (v.), afflictive (adj.)**

illness, distress

a state of or something that causes pain or suffering

## 04 **afoot** adv./adv.

happening, going on

in progress, motion, or action; on foot

## 05 **agnostic** n.

**agnosticism (n.)**

nonbeliever, skeptic

a person who doubts the existence of any god

## 06 **amalgamate** v.

**amalgamation (n.)**

combine, integrate

to merge to create a single system or organization

## 07 **annals** n.

journal, chronicle

a written report or description of events year by year; historical records

## 08 **antechamber** n.

✐ anteroom, foyer

a small room or reception area leading to a larger, main room

---

## 09 **belie** v.

✐ conceal, mislead

to disguise, misrepresent, or contradict

---

## 10 **belligerent** adj.

**belligerence (n.)**

✐ militant; ill-tempered

engaged in war; characterized by eagerness to fight

---

## 11 **bode** v.

✐ foreshadow, indicate

to be a sign of what is to come

---

## 12 **brooding** adj.

**brood (v.)**

✐ grave; grim, dark

thoughtful or serious in a moody and gloomy manner; causing an anxious or uneasy feeling or atmosphere

---

## 13 **cacophony** n.

**cacophonous (adj.)**

✐ racket, noise; clutter, mess

a harsh or inharmonious sound; a jumbled, unnatural, or bizarre mixture or combination

---

## 14 **canny** adj.

✐ acute, cautious, frugal

clever or shrewd in action, careful or prudent in behavior, or thrifty with money

---

## 15 **carp** v./n.

✐ whine, grumble

to complain or nag about a minor fault; a fish belonging to the family Cyprinoidea

## 16 **catapult** v./n.

*hasten; fling; ballista*

to quickly move up or ahead to a better position or status; to hurl or launch something; an ancient war engine used to fire weapons

## 17 **celibate** adj.

**celibacy (n.)**

*unwed, pure*

unmarried or not engaging in physical intimacy, mainly because of a religious vow

## 18 **chronology** n.

**chronological (adj.), chronologist (n.)**

*record, register; timetable, chart*

the science of measuring time or dating events in which they occurred; a list or table arranged in sequential order of time

## 19 **clement** adj.

**clemency (n.)**

*temperate, balmy; forgiving, tolerant*

mild (as in weather); merciful or lenient (as toward a person or action)

## 20 **corollary** n.

*conclusion, complement*

something that naturally follows or inferred from another that is already proven

## 21 **critique** n.

*evaluation, assessment*

an analysis reviewing or criticizing a piece of work

## 22 **debauchery** n.

**debauch (v.), debaucher (n.)**

*immorality, degeneracy*

unrestrained indulgence or fulfillment in sensual pleasures

## 23 **desecrate** v.

**desecration (n.)**

 taint, defile; spoil, ruin

to damage or violate something pure, holy, or respected; to treat or change in a disrespectful or destructive way

---

## 24 **diaphanous** adj.

 lightweight, transparent; uncertain, indefinite

so fine or light in texture as to be very delicate or capable of being seen through; vague or not very distinct

---

## 25 **dogma** n.

**dogmata (pl.), dogmatic (adj.)**

 doctrine, canon

a belief or opinion held as established principle, code, or truth, whether or not there is evidence to support it

---

## 26 **doldrums** n.

 listlessness, dejection

the state of being bored or in low spirits; ocean regions around the equator characterized by calmness and light shifting breezes

---

## 27 **endemic** adj.

**endemism (n.)**

 local, native

belonging to a particular region or nation (organisms, people, culture, etc., and especially diseases)

---

## 28 **extortion** n.

**extort (v.), extortionist (n.)**

 coercion, blackmail

the act of obtaining something (especially money) by using force, threats, official position, etc.

---

## 29 **fruition** n.

 realization, achievement; pleasure, delight

the state of bearing fruit or results; the enjoyment gained from using or having something

## 30 **furtive** adj.

sneaky; sly

done in secret or gained dishonestly; displaying a look of guilt or secrecy

---

## 31 **gratuitous** adj.

needless, unjustified; costless, for nothing

lacking good reason or not necessary; given or received free of charge

---

## 32 **indispensable** adj.

**indispensability (n.)**

essential, needed

totally necessary or not subject to being ignored or neglected

---

## 33 **infiltrate** v.

**infiltration (n.), infiltrative (adj.)**

permeate, seep into; invade, sneak into

to pass into something by filtering through small openings or pores; to enter, gain access, or take over secretly or stealthily

---

## 34 **jocular** adj.

**jocularity (n.)**

joking, playful

characterized by humor, or meant to be funny

---

## 35 **juxtaposition** n.

**juxtapose (v.)**

adjacency, proximity

the placing of two things side by side so as to create an effect or to emphasize or notice the differences between them

---

## 36 **lapse** n.

slip; expiration; gap

a temporary failure (as in concentration, memory, status, etc.); a decline or termination; an interval of time

---

## 37 **lascivious** adj.

 indecent, lewd
feeling or expressing lust or desire

## 38 **lingo** n.

 dialect, terminology
a language peculiar to a specific individual, group, region, nation, field of study or
interest, etc.

## 39 **machination** n.

**machinate (v.)**
 ploy, conspiracy
an artful plot or scheme, usually formulated for evil purposes

## 40 **mandate** n.

**mandatory (adj.)**
 decree; authorization
an official order or command; the power to act as a representative of the people

## 41 **mayhem** n.

 chaos, uproar
a state of great disorder and destruction

## 42 **monocracy** n.

 autocracy, dictatorship
a system of government by a single individual

## 43 **obdurate** adj.

**obduracy (n.)**
 inflexible, unyielding; heartless, cold
stubbornly resistant in changing one's opinion or behavior; having little or no sympathy

## 44 **ominous** adj.

 threatening, sinister
giving the impression of a coming ill, or being a bad or evil omen

## 45 **permeate** v.

**permeation (n.)**

⌐ pervade, suffuse

to affect throughout (such as an idea or opinion spreading throughout society), or to pass, diffuse, or spread through

---

## 46 **perpetrator** n.

**perpetration (n.), perpetrate (v.)**

⌐ offender, violator

one who makes, carries out, or commits a mistake, offense, crime, etc.

---

## 47 **piecemeal** adv./adj.

⌐ gradually; apart; step-by-step

one bit at a time; into parts or fragments; made or done one piece or stage at a time

---

## 48 **principality** n.

⌐ sovereignty, realm

the rank or jurisdiction of, or the territory ruled by, a prince

---

## 49 **probity** n.

⌐ uprightness, integrity

the quality of having correct or strong moral principles

---

## 50 **propensity** n.

⌐ inclination, proneness

a natural tendency or preference

---

# List 20

## 01 **adhere** v.

**adherence** (n.), **adherent** (adj.)

 bond, attach; obey, comply with

to stick fast to something; to hold on to or follow an idea or belief

## 02 **ambience** n.

**ambiance** (alt.)

 air, aura

the mood or atmosphere of a particular place

## 03 **antithesis** n.

**antithetical** (adj.)

 inverse, reverse

the clear opposite of someone or something

## 04 **azure** n.

 bright blue, sky blue

a color like that of a cloudless sky

## 05 **baffle** v.

**baffling** (adj.), **bafflement** (n.)

 perplex, bewilder; hinder, prevent

to frustrate or confuse completely; to interfere or stop the flow of something

## 06 **belle** n.

 beauty, sensation

an attractive and popular girl or woman, usually in a specific group or at an event

## 07 **blight** n.

 disease, withering

anything that destroys or prevents growth of plants or any aspect of life (such as situations, conditions, ideas, hopes, ambitions, etc.)

Part 1

vocabulary

## 08 **bulwark** n.

stronghold; support

a wall or structure built for defense; anything or anyone serving as protection

## 09 **buoyancy** n.

**buoy (v./n.), buoyant (adj.)**

lightness; resilience

the ability to float or remain afloat in water or air; the ability to maintain or recover immediately from present or negative situation

## 10 **butte** n.

a steep, isolated hill characterized by having a flat top

## 11 **cessation** n.

termination

a pause, discontinuance, or stopping of something

## 12 **consternation** n.

**consternate (v.)**

anxiety, dismay

an amazement or shock (usually because of something unexpected) that causes confusion

## 13 **debilitation** n.

**debilitate (v.), debilitating (adj.)**

weakening, deterioration

the act or process of losing strength or energy

## 14 **demulcent** adj.

**calming, easing**

soothing or alleviating

## 15 **dissimulate** v.

**dissimulation (n.)**

pretend, conceal

to put on false appearance

## 16 **effete** adj.

sterile; weakened; feminine

no longer able to produce; having lost character, vigor, or strength; unmanly or womanlike

---

## 17 **enamored** adj.

**enamor (v.)**

captivated, fascinated

filled with love or admiration for someone or something

---

## 18 **endowment** n.

**endow (v.)**

fund, grant; ability, quality

a gift or donation that provides an income or support for a nonprofit institution or person; a natural gift or talent

---

## 19 **exuberant** adj.

**exuberance (n.)**

cheerful; plentiful

full of energy or excitement; growing lavishly and abundantly

---

## 20 **forthright** adv.

honest, no-nonsense

direct and straight to the point

---

## 21 **fractious** adj.

rebellious, troublesome; quarrelsome, bad-tempered

unruly or difficult to manage; easily irritated or excited

---

## 22 **gastronomy** n.

**gastronomic (adj.), gastronome (n.)**

cookery; cuisine

the practice, science, or art of eating good food; the cooking style or customs of a particular area or region

### 23 **gouge** v.

dig; overcharge

to make a hole or cut or scoop out; to push out an eye with the thumb; to charge too much money without a justified reason

---

### 24 **governess** n.

nanny

a woman hired to care for and educate children in their own home

---

### 25 **granary** n.

storehouse, barn; breadbasket

a facility for storing threshed grain; a fertile region producing a large amount of grain

---

### 26 **gyrate** v.

gyration (n.)

revolve, spin

to rotate in a circle or spiral

---

### 27 **homologous** adj.

homologize (v.)

comparable, correlative

showing or having a degree of similarity (in relation, position, structure, etc.)

---

### 28 **intelligible** adj.

intelligibility (n.)

understandable, unambiguous

able to be comprehended, or clear to the intellect (not to the senses)

---

### 29 **interminable** adj.

interminability (n.)

nonstop, ceaseless

occurring without interruption, or seemingly endless

---

### 30 **irreconcilable** adj.

conflicting, at odds

impossible to be brought into agreement

---

## 31 **layman** n.

*amateur, nonprofessional; parishioner*

a person without knowledge or skill in a particular subject or given field; someone who is not a member of the clergy

## 32 **liquidate** v.

**liquidation (n.)**

*close down; convert; settle; murder*

to dissolve a company by distributing assets and debts; to sell off assets for cash; to clear a debt; to eliminate, especially by killing

## 33 **masonry** n.

**mason (n.)**

*stonework*

something constructed of bricks, stones, concrete, etc.

## 34 **mollify** v.

**mollification (n.)**

*soften, pacify*

to reduce the intensity, rigidity, anger, or violence

## 35 **monogram** n.

**monogrammatic (adj.)**

*symbol, mark*

a design or figure of letters (especially initials of a name) used as a logo or sign of identity

## 36 **morbid** adj.

**morbidity (n.)**

*pathologic; twisted; gory*

relating to, characterized by, or affected with disease; having or showing interest in grisly or horrific subjects; disgusting or gruesome

## 37 **novelty** n.

**novel (adj.)**

*originality; ornament*

something (or the quality or state of being) new, fresh, or unusual; a small, often inexpensive, manufactured trinket or toy

Part 1

## 38 **ocular** adj.

optic, visual

connected with or relating to the eye or eyesight

## 39 **onomatopoeia** n.

**onomatopoeic (adj.)**

echoism

a word formed from a sound associated with what it represents (e.g., boom, bang)

## 40 **pecuniary** adj.

financial, fiscal

of, relating to, measured in, or consisting of money

## 41 **penultimate** adj.

next-to-last, last but one

second to the last

## 42 **placate** v.

**placation (n.)**

appease, mollify

to calm or pacify anger, hostility, etc.

## 43 **polytheism** n.

**polytheistic, polytheistical (adj.)**

belief in or worship of multiple gods

## 44 **pretext** n.

pretense, excuse

a false reason given to conceal the actual one

## 45 **reconnaissance** n.

exploration, inspection

a preliminary survey, research, or observation (especially by the military) to gain information

## 46 **redoubtable** adj.

formidable, dreadful; eminent, distinguished
causing fear; commanding or worthy of respect

## 47 **thearchy** n.

a government ruled by a god or gods; a system of hierarchy of gods

## 48 **titular** adj.

ceremonial; identifying
in name or title only; mentioned or referred to in the title

## 49 **verity** n.

truth, actuality; righteousness, integrity
a principle, statement, belief, etc., regarded as true; the quality or state of being true,
real, or honest

## 50 **visage** n.

countenance; aspect
one's face or facial expression; the surface, image, or appearance of something

## 01 **acculturate** v.

**acculturation (n.)**

⌐ assimilate, merge

to change because of the influence of a different culture

## 02 **allotment** n.

**allot (v.)**

⌐ ration, share

the specific amount that one is allowed to get

## 03 **altruistic** adj.

**altruism (n.), altruist (n.)**

⌐ humanitarian, self-sacrificing

showing genuine concern for the well-being of others

## 04 **anathema** n.

**anathematize (v.)**

⌐ taboo; hate

a formal ban or curse by a religious organization; something that is strongly disliked by somebody

## 05 **annul** v.

**annulment (n.)**

⌐ nullify, cancel

to make something no longer valid

## 06 **anticlimax** n.

**anticlimactic (adj.)**

⌐ letdown, disappointment

an unsatisfying conclusion to a story or an event

## 07 **arbitration** n.

**arbitrator (n.), arbitrate (v.)**

↗ mediation, judgment

the settling of a dispute between two parties by an uninvolved third party

## 08 **aviary** n.

↗ birdhouse

a large cage or building for housing birds

## 09 **bona fide** adj.

↗ honest; real

made with sincerity; genuine

## 10 **buffoonery** n.

**buffoon (n.), buffoonish (adj.)**

↗ foolishness, nonsense

a silly but amusing behavior

## 11 **cavalier** adj./n.

↗ casual; jolly; cocky; dandy; knight

unconcerned about important things; energetic and high-spirited; arrogant or acting superior; a mannerly gentleman; a soldier skilled in horsemanship

## 12 **centrifugal** adj.

**centrifuge (n.)**

↗ outward, deviating

tending, proceeding, or causing to move away from the central point

## 13 **chaperone** n.

**chaperon (alt.)**

↗ escort, supervisor

a person who accompanies a young woman or young people to ensure proper appearance or behavior in public or at a social gathering

## 14 **cogitate** v.

**cogitation** (n.), **cogitative** (adj.)

contemplate, meditate

to ponder or think deeply about something

---

## 15 **conjecture** n.

**conjectural** (adj.)

guesswork, supposition

an unproven opinion, statement, idea, or conclusion based on incomplete evidence

---

## 16 **countenance** n.

visage; control; approval; agree

one's face, facial features, or facial expression; calmness or composure; encouragement or support

---

## 17 **cower** v.

flinch, cringe

to shrink away in fear from threats or possible physical blows

---

## 18 **detract** v.

**detraction** (n.), **detractive** (adj.)

lower, discredit

to reduce, divert from, or take away the worth or effectiveness of something or someone

---

## 19 **dilettante** n.

**dilettantism** (n.)

dabbler, amateur

a person who has a casual interest in a subject or area without having much understanding of it

---

## 20 **dolorous** adj.

anguished, bitter

marked by great sorrow or misery

---

### 21 **euphemism** n.

**euphemistic (adj.), euphemize (v.)**

✐ softening, indirectness

(the use of) a pleasant word or phrase used in place for one that is too blunt, offensive, or harsh

---

### 22 **expropriate** v.

**expropriation (n.)**

✐ confiscate, seize

to take away a private possession or property, mainly for public benefit

---

### 23 **foreshadow** v.

**foreshadowing (n.)**

✐ indicate, foretell

to suggest or warn what is to come

---

### 24 **gourmand** n.

**gourmandize (v.)**

✐ big eater, glutton; gourmet, foodie

a person who enjoys good food to the point of being greedy or excessive; a person who knows and appreciates good food

---

### 25 **homogeneous** adj.

**homogeneity (n.)**

✐ alike, identical

having similar or uniform parts or elements

---

### 26 **immutable** adj.

**immutability (n.)**

✐ unalterable, ageless

unchanging or not susceptible to change

---

### 27 **introgression** n.

✐ entry, infiltration

the introduction or transfer of a gene from one species to another

## 28  **liaison** n.

**liaise (v.)**

connection; mediator; love affair; mixture

cooperation between two parties; an intermediary or go-between; an illicit romantic relationship; a binding or thickening substance (in cooking)

---

## 29  **logistic** adj.

**logistical (alt.), logistics (n.)**

organizational, administrative

relating to planning, organizing, or managing

---

## 30  **lugubrious** adj.

mournful, gloomy

appearing or sounding exaggeratedly sad or depressed

---

## 31  **modulation** n.

**modulate (v.)**

inflection; alteration; regulation

a variation of stress, tone, or pitch of the voice or musical key; the process of shifting from one form or state into another; the act of adjusting

---

## 32  **nadir** n.

bottom, base

the lowest point; (in astronomy) the point on the celestial sphere opposite of the zenith (and directly below the observer)

---

## 33  **pander** v.

gratify, indulge

to cater to or tempt with immoral or improper desires

---

## 34  **pendulous** adj.

dangling; drooping; indecisive

suspended so as to swing or hang loosely; bending downward; hesitant or irresolute

---

## 35 **personification** n.

**personify (v.)**

✎ embodiment, representation

a person or thing exemplifying a certain quality or idea, or a figure of speech in which a thing or idea is portrayed as a human

---

## 36 **phonetics** n.

**phonetic (adj.)**

the science dealing with the study of speech sounds or processes

---

## 37 **plaintiff** n.

✎ complainant

a person bringing a legal action in a court of law

---

## 38 **polarization** n.

**polarize (v.), polarity (n.)**

✎ separation, disunion

division into two opposites or contrasting groups

---

## 39 **premeditated** adj.

**premeditate (v.), premeditation (n.)**

✎ intentional, calculated

planned or thought out in advance

---

## 40 **presage** n.

✎ hunch, omen

an intuition, or something that warns or serves as a sign of a future event

---

## 41 **prevalent** adj.

**prevalence (n.)**

✎ widespread, popular; predominant

widely preferred or practiced; governing or prevailing over others

vocabulary

## 42 **prohibition** n.

**prohibit (v.), prohibitive (adj.)**

banning, barring

an order, law, or regulation that forbids or disallows; the forbidding by law of the manufacture or sale of alcohol

---

## 43 **prosaic** adj.

commonplace, ordinary; factual, heavy

unimaginative or dull; characteristic of prose rather than poetry

---

## 44 **protract** v.

**protraction (n.), protracted (adj.)**

prolong protrude

to draw out or extend in duration; to thrust out

---

## 45 **renege** v.

back out, go back on

to break a promise or contract

---

## 46 **soporific** adj.

hypnotic; monotonous

causing sleep or tending to lessen alertness; tediously dull or boring

---

## 47 **statutory** adj.

**statute (n.)**

legitimate, legal

established, declared, or authorized by a rule, regulation, or law

---

## 48 **surreptitious** adj.

concealed, stealthy

done, made, kept, or acting secretly

---

## 49 **transient** adj.

**transience (n.)**

impermanent, passing

lasting only briefly; staying or working temporarily in a particular place

---

## 50 **wispy** adj.

**wisp (n.)**

faint, delicate

fine, thin, or feathery (as in hair, thread, cloud, smoke, etc.)

## 01 **accoutre** v.

**accouter (v., alt.), accoutrement, accouterment (n.)**

✎ gear, fit

to equip, dress, or furnish

## 02 **admissible** adj.

✎ permissible, justifiable

allowable as evidence in a court of law

## 03 **akin** adj.

✎ resembling; connected

similar or alike; related, especially by blood

## 04 **annotation** n.

**annotate (v.), annotative (adj.)**

✎ note, commentary

an added comment or explanation to a text or diagram

## 05 **apogee** n.

✎ crest, peak

the point in an orbit about Earth (or any planet) that is the farthest distance from it; the farthest or highest point

## 06 **apostle** n.

✎ messenger, champion

any of Christ's twelve disciples; a pioneer or early advocate of a specific cause or belief

## 07 **ascertain** v.

**ascertainment (n.), ascertainable (adj.)**

✎ confirm, verify

to find out absolutely or with certainty

## 08 **atheist** n.

**atheism (n.), atheistic (adj.)**

⬚ agnostic

a person who denies the existence of a god or gods

## 09 **colloquial** adj.

**colloquialism (n.)**

⬚ conversational, casual

relating to the use of language in an ordinary, familiar, or informal way

## 10 **cornucopia** n.

**cornucopian (adj.)**

⬚ plenty; cone

abundance or overflowing supply; a container in the form of a horn

## 11 **countervail** v.

**countervailing (adj.)**

⬚ compensate; counteract

to make up for something (mostly by offsetting it with another of equal force); to go against (usually something considered harmful or evil)

## 12 **criterion** n.

**criteria (pl.)**

⬚ standard, scale

a point of reference by which someone or something may be judged or compared

## 13 **custody** n.

**custodial (adj.), custodian (n.)**

⬚ guardianship, maintenance; confinement, arrest

the legal right to take care of (or temporary possession or care of) a child or someone's property; the state of being detained by the authorities

## 14 **deportation** n.

**deport (v.)**

⬚ expulsion, expelling

the act of removing a foreigner from a country

## 15 **diaspora** n.

 exodus, relocation

the dispersion, movement, or settlement of a people away from their ancestral land; the Jews who live outside Israel

## 16 **disavow** v.

**disavowal (n.)**

 disclaim; reject

to deny any knowledge of or responsibility for something; to refuse to recognize

## 17 **distend** v.

**distension (n.), distensible (adj.)**

 bulge, puff up; extend, unfold

to expand or swell from internal pressure; to stretch or spread out

## 18 **enunciate** v.

**enunciation (n.), enunciable (adj.)**

 articulate; declare

to speak or pronounce clearly or effectively; to announce or proclaim

## 19 **equivocal** adj.

**equivocate (v.)**

 ambiguous; undecided; suspicious

having more than one meaning as to be misleading; having uncertain feeling toward someone or something; having questionable behavior

## 20 **esoteric** adj.

**esoterica (n.)**

 mysterious, obscure; confidential, restricted

hard to understand, or made to be understood only by a few; private or limited to a small circle or group

## 21 **estimable** adj.

 praiseworthy, commendable; measurable, calculable

worthy of respect; able to be estimated

## 22 **fugacious** adj.

 short-lived, brief

lasting only momentarily or tending to pass quickly away

---

## 23 **hallow** v.

**hallowed (adj.)**

 sanctify, consecrate; venerate, revere

to honor or regard as holy or sacred; to regard with great respect and admiration

---

## 24 **indomitable** adj.

**indomitability (n.)**

 unbeatable, unshakeable

not easily conquered or discouraged

---

## 25 **insidious** adj.

 subtle; seductive; crafty

producing harm in a slow and gradual manner so as to be unnoticeable; attractive or alluring but harmful; treacherous or sly

---

## 26 **interpose** v.

**interposition (n.)**

 insert; step in; intrude

to place or come between someone or something; to intervene or involve oneself; to interrupt a debate, discussion, conversation, etc.

---

## 27 **laden** adj.

 loaded, filled

weighed down or burdened

---

## 28 **liberal** n./adj.

**liberalism (n.)**

 reformist; impartial; various; giving; plentiful

one favoring political and social progress or reform; tolerant or open-minded; not restricted; generous or unselfish; large or abundant

vocabulary

### 29 **marginal** adj.

**margin (n.)**

borderline; minor; irregular; basic; disputable

placed at the edge; secondary or less important; outside the mainstream; limited or minimal; very close (such as decision, distinction, etc.)

### 30 **modicum** n.

bit, speck

a small or limited amount or portion

### 31 **myriad** n./adj.

abundance; innumerable

a countless or vastly great number; various and numerous

### 32 **parse** v.

examine, dissect

to break a sentence into its parts and analyze their grammatical arrangements and roles; to scrutinize or analyze critically

### 33 **pedantic** adj.

**pedant (n.), pedantry (n.)**

perfectionist; pretentious; dull

overly concerned with conventional rules and trivial details of learning; showy of one's knowledge; unimaginative or ordinary

### 34 **pedigree** n.

**pedigreed (adj.)**

family tree; history

a record of one's ancestral line or history; the origin and background of something; a prominent ancestry; the record proving a breed to be purebred

### 35 **perambulate** v.

**perambulation (n.), Perambulatory (adj.)**

cross, cover

to walk or travel over or through (especially for pleasure), or to walk around in order to officially inspect the boundary of an area (estate, forest, etc.)

### 36 **percipience** n.

percipient (n./adj.)

comprehension, sharpness

a capacity for understanding, or the quality of being highly insightful or perceptive

### 37 **perdition** n.

damnation; netherworld

eternal condemnation or punishment; hell

### 38 **pillage** v.

pillaging (n.)

loot, plunder

to rob (town, village, etc.) using force or violence, especially in war

### 39 **precursor** n.

precursory (adj.)

predecessor, herald

one that comes before another or indicates an approaching phenomenon; a substance or component from which another is formed

### 40 **preeminent** adj.

preeminence (n.)

leading, outstanding

above or exceeding others in rank, importance, quality, etc.

### 41 **prescription** n.

prescribe (v.), prescriptive (adj.)

decree; instruction

the action of setting down a rule or guide; the authorization or direction for the use of a drug, medicine, or treatment

### 42 **probate** n.

the action or process of officially proving a will, or the court that has jurisdiction over such matters

### 43 **protagonist** n.

star, principal; champion, supporter

the leading character in a drama, movie, novel, etc., or a prominent figure in a real event or situation; an advocate of a particular cause

### 44 **rote** n.

pattern, drill

(learning through) habitual routine or repetition; the noise of surf pounding on the shore; a medieval harp-like stringed instrument

### 45 **sanctimonious** adj.

**sanctimony (n.)**

self-righteous, hypocritical

pretending to be holy or morally superior to other people

### 46 **savant** n.

intellectual, sage

a learned person, especially an eminent scholar

### 47 **tremulous** adj.

unsteady, quivering; fearful, shy

shaking or trembling; timid, or not confident

### 48 **tundra** n.

a treeless, frozen area of flat land in arctic or subarctic regions

### 49 **tyro** n.

newcomer, learner

a beginner or novice in learning or doing something

### 50 **ursine** adj.

of, relating to, or characteristic of a bear

# List 23

☞ = Synonyms, related words

Part 1

---

## 01 **abolition** n.

**abolish (v.), abolitionary (adj.)**

☞ ending, elimination

the act of officially ending something, usually a system or practice

---

## 02 **achromatic** adj.

☞ colorless, achromous

having no color; referring to white, grey, or black color

---

## 03 **adroit** adj.

☞ deft, nimble

quick or skillful in thoughts or actions

---

## 04 **ancillary** adj.

☞ secondary, subordinate

providing support

---

## 05 **apocryphal** adj.

☞ made-up, fictitious

doubtful or not genuine (in describing a statement or story)

---

## 06 **axiom** n.

**axiomatic (adj.)**

☞ saying, adage

a statement widely recognized as true

---

## 07 **begrudgingly** adv.

**begrudge (v.)**

☞ hesitantly, unwillingly

in an envious or reluctant manner

---

## 08 **benchmark** n.

*standard, example*

a reference point by which something may be measured

---

## 09 **brazen** adj.

*brash, unabashed; metallic, clanging*

shamelessly brave or offensive; made of, the color of, or sounding harsh like striking brass

---

## 10 **cadence** n.

**cadent (adj.)**

*beat, accent*

the rhythm or rhythmic flow of a dance, music, voice, motion, etc.

---

## 11 **capitulate** v.

**capitulation (n.)**

*give in, yield*

to surrender (especially after agreeing to terms or conditions) or end all resistance

---

## 12 **catharsis** n.

**cathartic (adj.)**

*relief; purgation*

a release of emotional tension; the cleaning out of the bowels

---

## 13 **cede** v.

**cession (n.)**

*hand over; renounce*

to yield or give up (as in power, territory, one's rights, etc.); to transfer or give away one's title, position, or possession

---

## 14 **churn** v.

*swirl, whip*

to agitate or stir fiercely, or to produce or make (butter, foam, etc.) by doing so; to encourage active purchases and sales to make money

### 15 **compelling** adj.

compel (v.)

fascinating, powerful, persuasive

captivating, demanding, or convincing

---

### 16 **consensus** n.

understanding; unity

an judgment or opinion held by all or almost all; a general agreement among a given group

---

### 17 **consonance** n.

consonant (adj.)

agreement, balance

harmony or compatibility between actions or opinions; a harmonic combination of musical notes; recurrence of sounds

---

### 18 **constituent** n./adj.

constituency (n.)

voter; component; representative

a resident in an electoral district; a necessary part of a whole; having the authority to create or revise a government or its basic principles and laws

---

### 19 **contemporaneous** adj.

contemporaneously (adv.)

simultaneous, coexisting

existing, happening, or created in the same period of time

---

### 20 **conventional** adj.

convention (n.), conventionalize (v.)

customary; normal, unoriginal; congregational; nonnuclear

following accepted behaviors or agreement; commonplace, standard, or even boring; relating to assembly or meeting; not nuclear (as in weapons)

---

### 21 **creed** n.

creedal (adj.)

faith, credo

a formal statement or system of religious belief, or a set of guiding principles or rules of conduct

## 22 **cursory** adj.

**cursorily (adv.)**

careless, half-hearted

hastily and oftentimes superficially done or made

---

## 23 **decree** n.

command, mandate

an official order or proclamation issued by a legal or religious authority

---

## 24 **ductile** adj.

**ductility (n.)**

pliant, flexible; responsive, yielding

capable of being drawn out into a thin wire (mostly metal) or of being made into a new form; easily influenced

---

## 25 **egress** n.

doorway, departure

a way out, or the act or process of exiting; (in law) the right or freedom to leave

---

## 26 **espouse** v.

**espousal (n.)**

wed; embrace

to marry or give in marriage; to accept or support an idea, cause, etc.

---

## 27 **expurgate** v.

**expurgation (n.)**

censor, edit

to cleanse or remove something considered harmful or offensive (as from a publication, presentation, etc.)

---

## 28 **germane** adj.

appropriate, fitting

related or relevant to the topic or subject being considered or discussed

---

## 29 **ghastly** adj.

**ghastliness (n.)**

pasty; frightful; offensive

pale or ghostlike in appearance; horrifying or shocking; extremely bad or unpleasant

---

## 30 **inroad** n.

headway, strides; raid, attack

an advance or progress made toward realizing an objective; a sudden incursion or invasion

---

## 31 **insolent** adj.

**insolence (n.)**

rude, offensive; overconfident, arrogant

disrespectful or insulting in speech or manner; shamelessly bold

---

## 32 **interdisciplinary** adj.

comprehensive, integrative

relating to or a linkage between more than one fields of study or artistry

---

## 33 **licentious** adj.

promiscuous; unrestrained

having strong lustful desires; having little or no regard for accepted rules or conventions

---

## 34 **macrocosm** n.

**macrocosmic (adj.)**

entirety; cosmos

a portrayal of something on a bigger scale or as a whole; the great world, or the universe

---

## 35 **matinee** n.

afternoon show

a showing of a movie or performance held in the daytime

---

### 36 **metabolism** n.

metabolize (v.), metabolic (adj.)

the chemical and physical reactions or processes occurring in cells and organisms

### 37 **mortality** n.

**mortal (n./adj.)**

impermanence; fatality; death rate; mankind

the state or condition of being exposed to death; the loss of life in large numbers; the number of deaths or rate of loss; the human race

### 38 **nomenclature** n.

**nomenclatural (adj.)**

designation, terminology

a system or set of terms, names, or symbols used in a particular field of study or activity

### 39 **nonchalant** adj.

**nonchalance (n.)**

calm, indifferent

not showing interest, enthusiasm, or concern

### 40 **pediatric** adj.

**pediatrics (n.), pediatrician (n.)**

of or relating to the branch of medicine that deals with children and their care, development, treatment, etc.

### 41 **percolate** v.

**percolation (n.), percolator (n.)**

filter; permeate

to drain, pass, or seep through a porous substance; to spread gradually or throughout; to prepare (coffee) in a brewing machine; to become lively

### 42 **prolific** adj.

**prolificacy (n.)**

fertile; creative; bountiful

producing (young, fruit, foliage, etc.) in abundance; producing works or results (books, music, paintings, etc.) in abundance; plentiful

### 43 **rotund** adj.

**rotundity (n.)**

circular; portly; full-toned

round in shape; having a plump body; characterized by fullness of sound

---

### 44 **salvo** n.

barrage, bombardment; outburst, eruption

a discharging or releasing of a number of guns, bombs, etc., simultaneously or in quick succession; a sudden or spirited burst or attack

---

### 45 **sanguine** adj.

hopeful; blood-red; murderous

optimistic or confident; of blood color or relating to blood; bloody or bloodthirsty

---

### 46 **spurious** adj.

fake, counterfeit; deceitful, fallacious

false, or not genuine; misleading in nature or quality

---

### 47 **strident** adj.

**stridency, stridence (n.)**

grating; hostile

loud and harsh-sounding; expressing feelings or opinions in an excessively forceful or uncomfortable way

---

### 48 **treble** adj.

soprano; shrill; threefold

of the highest voice, instrument, or part in harmonic musical composition; high-pitched; triple in number, or having three parts

---

### 49 **truism** n.

commonplace, platitude

a self-evident truth, one so obvious as to be boring or uninteresting

---

### 50 **waylay** v.

ambush; intercept

to lie in wait for and attack; to wait for and approach suddenly and unexpectedly

---

*= Synonyms, related words*

---

## 01 **abjure** v.

**abjuration (n.)**

*disavow, reject*

to strongly renounce or abandon a cause or a belief

---

## 02 **abusive** adj.

**abuse (v.)**

*offensive, cruel*

tending to treat someone badly

---

## 03 **acquisition** n.

*acquirement, addition*

the purchasing or obtaining of an asset, object, knowledge, or skill

---

## 04 **affable** adj.

**affability (n.)**

*friendly, courteous*

receiving others or talking to them kindly

---

## 05 **affiliation** n.

**affiliate (n./v.)**

*partnership, alliance*

a close or official connection with an another person or specific organization

---

## 06 **badger** v.

**badgering (n.)**

*pester, harass*

to bother someone (usually to make one do something) annoyingly and persistently

---

## 07 **bide** v.

endure, reside; await, anticipate

to remain in a certain state, condition or place; to wait or be in expectation

---

## 08 **bohemian** adj.

**bohemia (n.)**

free spirit, nonconformist

a person (usually a writer, poet, artist, etc.) who leads a lifestyle that is not typical or traditional

---

## 09 **bole** n.

stem; mud

a tree trunk; soft, reddish-brown types of clay usually used as natural coloring substance

---

## 10 **brandish** v.

wield, wave; flaunt, boast

to swing (a weapon or tool) threateningly or excitedly; to display in a way that attracts attention

---

## 11 **cascade** n.

**cascading (adj.)**

rapids; sequence; surge

a series (or one) of small waterfalls; something happening in stages; something rushing forth in great numbers

---

## 12 **circumscribe** v.

**circumscription (n.)**

encircle; mark off; restrain

to draw a line around; to surround to mark a boundary of something; to restrict an activity in a limited way

---

## 13 **clinical** adj.

cold; methodical; treatable

emotionless and cool; analytical and efficient; relating to clinic or direct and practical treatment of patients

## 14 **congeal** v.

congealment (n.)

harden; clot; establish

to solidify from a liquid state; to thicken or form into a jelly-like state; to form into a complete or satisfying whole (such as ideas)

---

## 15 **console** n./v.

consolation (n.) consolable (adj.), consolatory (adj.)

cupboard; control panel; soothe

a cabinet (for housing TV, games, etc.); a unit containing controls for electronic systems; to comfort someone who is suffering

---

## 16 **counterpart** n.

equal; complement; duplicate

one that resembles another in form, position, or function; something that completes the other; a copy of something (such as legal document)

---

## 17 **daunting** adj.

daunt (v.)

disheartening, intimidating

discouraging or overwhelming

---

## 18 **derivative** adj.

derive (v.), derivation (n.)

by-product, secondary; unimaginative, dull

received, taken from, or based on another source or substance; having no originality

---

## 19 **dissemble** v.

dissemblance (n.), dissembler (n.)

conceal, disguise; simulate, imitate

to hide one's true motives, feelings, or beliefs; to fake an act

---

## 20 **domicile** n.

home, residency

the place where one lives

## 21 **durance** n.

confinement, detention

a state of being restrained physically or imprisoned

## 22 **emancipation** n.

emancipate (v.)

liberation, freedom

the act or state of freeing or being freed from control or power

## 23 **engender** v.

engenderment (n.)

cause, produce

to give rise to or come into existence

## 24 **eugenics** n.

eugenic (adj.)

the science of improving the human species through controlled breeding

## 25 **explicate** v.

explication (n.)

clarify, expand

to make clear or explain in detail

## 26 **facility** n.

simplicity; skill; institution

the quality of being easy; a talent or ability to do or learn something; a place for a specific purpose

## 27 **fervid** adj.

fervidity (n.)

blazing, fiery; emotional, zealous

intensely hot or burning; extremely passionate or fervent

## 28 **foreclosure** n.

**foreclose (v.), foreclosable (adj.)**

seizure, takeover

the act of taking possession of a mortgaged property as a result of payment failure

---

## 29 **fraternal** adj.

**fraternity (n.)**

friendly, intimate

of or relating to brother or a group of people connected by a common interest or purpose; of twins developed from separate ova

---

## 30 **fulminate** v./n.

**fulmination (n.)**

speak out; blow up

to denounce or make strong protest; to explode or develop suddenly and violently; a type of salt used as an explosive ingredient

---

## 31 **hierarchy** n.

**hierarchical (adj.)**

ordering, ladder; officials, authority

people or groups ranked according to grade, class, status, authority, etc.; a group of people in power in a organization

---

## 32 **hyperbole** n.

**hyperbolic (adj.)**

overstatement, amplification

exaggerated statement or comment meant to stress a point

---

## 33 **incessant** adj.

**incessancy (n.)**

nonstop, unending

continuing without stopping, especially to the point of being unpleasant

---

## 34 **incontrovertible** adj.

indisputable, undeniable

not debatable or open to question

## 35  ingraft v.

**engraft (alt.)**

embed; transplant

to insert or fix firmly or permanently into place; to insert a shoot or twig of a tree or plant into another

## 36  jostle v.

push and shove, brush against; compete, contend

to bump into, push aside, or come into contact with; to vie or struggle in order to acquire or achieve something

## 37  lackadaisical adj.

uncaring, lazy

showing no interest or enthusiasm, or lacking vigor or life

## 38  lyre n.

a small U-shaped harp, used especially by the ancient Greeks

## 39  malignant adj.

**malignancy (n.)**

spiteful; virulent; cancerous

having a evil nature or influence; very harmful or infectious; tending to invade or infiltrate and cause death

## 40  matrimony n.

**matrimonial (adj.)**

wedlock, marriage

the state of being married, or the ceremony of becoming husband and wife

## 41  melodramatic adj.

**melodrama (n.)**

overdone, theatrical

exaggeratedly emotional or sensational

### 42 **necromancer** n.

**necromancy (n.)**

*wizard, witch*

one who practices magic or sorcery

---

### 43 **oblong** adj.

*elliptical*

elongated in shape, such as a rectangle or oval

---

### 44 **onerous** adj.

*demanding, challenging*

burdensome or troublesome; having to do with a legal obligation that outweighs the benefit

---

### 45 **parapet** n.

*rampart, breastwork*

a low wall or railing along the edge of a roof, platform, bridge, etc., or a wall or elevation (of stone, sandbags, etc.) to protect soldiers

---

### 46 **pervade** v.

**pervasive (adj.), pervasion (n.)**

*diffuse, permeate*

to spread through, be present, or apparent throughout

---

### 47 **procreate** v.

**procreation (n.), procreative (adj.)**

*propagate, reproduce*

to produce offspring

---

### 48 **rapprochement** n.

*agreement, reconciliation*

an establishment or restoration of friendly relations, especially between two nations

## 49 **repose** n.

**reposeful (adj.)**

 relaxation; composure; peace of mind

a state of sleep or rest; self-possession or calmness; a mental state of tranquility

## 50 **sapid** adj.

 savory; engaging

having flavor or pleasant taste; agreeable or interesting

---

### 01 **accede** v.

comply, assent; take on, inherit

to agree or consent to a proposal or a view; to accept a position or office

---

### 02 **account** n./v.

description; consider, regard as

an explanation of an event or experience; to take into consideration

---

### 03 **accrue** v.

accruement (n.)

amass, build up

to increase in number or amount over time

---

### 04 **acquaint** v.

acquaintance (n.), acquainted (adj.)

notify, introduce

to make aware of or become familiar with someone or something

---

### 05 **ambrosia** n.

ambrosial (adj.)

nectar; delicacy

food or ointments of the Greek and Roman gods; something exceptionally tasty, fragrant, or pleasing

---

### 06 **anachronistic** adj.

anachronism (n.)

misplaced; old-fashioned

belonging to a wrong time; behind the times or too conservative

---

### 07 **ape** v.

mimic, imitate

to copy the behavior of someone or something

---

## 08 **audacity** n.

**audacious (adj.)**

boldness, arrogance

a fearless and daring quality, sometimes seen as being rude or shameless

---

## 09 **bigotry** n.

**bigot (n.), bigoted (adj.)**

intolerance, narrow-mindedness

unwillingness to accept those with contrasting opinions

---

## 10 **brigade** n.

**brigadier (n.)**

troops; team, crew

a large body of soldiers; a group of people organized for specific interest or activity

---

## 11 **celestial** adj.

holy; astronomical; foremost; delightful

relating to heaven or divinity; relating to the sky, stars, planets, universe, etc.; of highest degree or quality; extremely pleasing

---

## 12 **circumvent** v.

**circumvention (n.)**

dodge, evade; hem in, trap

to get around a problem or go around an obstacle; to encircle or surround (as in to capture or stop the enemies)

---

## 13 **cogent** adj.

**cogency (n.)**

compelling, credible

convincing and appealing, or very persuasive

---

## 14 **contingent** adj./n.

**contingency (n.)**

possible; conditional; delegation

unpredictable or subject to chance; subject to certain requirements being met; a group that is a part of a larger group

## 15 **coup** n.

**coup d'état (alt.)**

overthrow, ousting; feat, stunt

a sudden and often violent removal or takeover of government; a brilliant, swift, and effective move or action

---

## 16 **cupidity** n.

greed, lust

extreme desire, especially for money or possessions

---

## 17 **dearth** n.

famine; scarcity, insufficiency

shortage of food; lacking a necessary or desirable amount or number of something

---

## 18 **defoliate** v.

**defoliation (n.), defoliant (n.)**

bare, strip

to remove leaves (from a tree, plant, etc.) mainly by using a chemical agent

---

## 19 **deluge** n.

flood; downpour; abundance

an overflowing water; a heavy rain; an overwhelming number or amount of something

---

## 20 **detrimental** adj.

**detriment (n.)**

dangerous, adverse

tending to cause harm, injury, or damage

---

## 21 **egalitarian** adj.

**egalitarianism (n.)**

democratic, fair

believing that everyone deserves social, political, and economic equality

---

## 22 **enjoin** v.

**enjoinder (n.)**

⚊ impose, enforce

to urge, instruct, or prohibit with authority or by legal means

## 23 **epicure** n.

**epicurean (adj.)**

⚊ foodie, gourmet

a person with sensitive tastes in (or one who greatly enjoys) food or wine

## 24 **genome** n.

**genomic (adj.), genomics (n.)**

the complete genetic material or information of an organism

## 25 **incentive** n.

⚊ stimulus, boost; bonus, share

something that motivates or stimulates one to take action; a reward or payment to encourage one to work harder

## 26 **indict** v.

**indictment (n.)**

⚊ charge, bring to trial

to make a formal accusation for an offense or crime

## 27 **indubitable** adj.

⚊ unquestionable, definite

too certain or clear to be doubted

## 28 **ingénue** n.

⚊ naive girl

an innocent, unsophisticated young woman

## 29 **ironclad** adj.

⚊ fixed, certain; armor-plated

not able to be changed, questioned, or disputed; covered or protected with iron or some metal (usually on naval ships)

## 30 **lofty** adj.

towering; grand; arrogant

imposingly high; noble in character, spirit, or status; haughty or self-important; firm, full, thick, and resilient (as in wool, textile fibers, etc.)

## 31 **metamorphosis** n.

**metamorphic (adj.)**

transformation, alteration

a change (natural or supernatural) of structure, substance, appearance, situation, etc.

## 32 **orthodox** adj.

strict, conservative; conventional, usual

conforming to accepted beliefs or established doctrines; standard or normal

## 33 **parry** v.

fend off, dodge

to deflect, ward off, avoid, or evade a weapon, blow, annoying question, criticism, etc.

## 34 **pathos** n.

emotional appeal

a means of persuasion through an appeal to emotion

## 35 **penal** adj.

correctional, punitive

of, relating to, or involving legal punishment of offenders

## 36 **perforate** v.

**perforation (n.)**

puncture, prick

to pierce, penetrate, or make holes

## 37 **perjury** n.

false swearing, false testimony

the deliberate telling of a lie in a court under oath

## 38  **polychromatic** adj.

✐ multicolored, colorful

having or showing various or changing colors; relating to radiation having a number of wavelengths

---

## 39  **polygamy** n.

**polygamist (n.), polygamous (adj.)**

✐ polyandry, polygyny

the custom or practice of having (or mating with) more than one spouse (or mate) at the same time

---

## 40  **pronouncement** n.

**pronounce (v.)**

✐ announcement, proclamation

a formal or official statement or declaration

---

## 41  **proxy** n.

✐ representative, substitute

the authority (or a person authorized) to act for someone else

---

## 42  **quintessential** adj.

**quintessence (n.)**

✐ model, typical

serving as the perfect example of something

---

## 43  **raconteur** n.

**raconteuse (fem.)**

✐ storyteller, narrator

someone who tells stories or anecdotes in a skillful way

---

## 44  **raucous** adj.

✐ hoarse, strident; rowdy, unruly

having an unpleasantly harsh or rough sound; loud and disorderly

---

vocabulary

## 45 **recapitulate** v.

**recapitulation (n.)**

summarize, repeat

to restate the main points briefly

## 46 **regalia** n.

insignia; finery

the emblems, symbols, decorations, etc., indicating royalty, office, or membership; magnificent clothes, dress, or costume

## 47 **transgression** n.

**transgress (v.), transgressive (adj.)**

sin, offense

an act or instance of violating a law, command, duty, etc.

## 48 **verve** n.

passion, vitality

enthusiasm, energy, or spirit, especially in the artistic sense

## 49 **visceral** adj.

**viscera (n.)**

unreasoning; splanchnic

having to do with instinct, emotion, or inward feelings rather than the intellect; of or relating to the internal organs of the body

## 50 **xenophobia** n.

**xenophobic (adj.), xenophobe (n.)**

racism, nationalism

fear or hatred of, or prejudice against, any person or thing that is strange or of foreign origin

## 01 **abject** adj.
**abjection (n.)**
◜ miserable, pathetic
existing in a state of utter hopelessness

## 02 **abstract** adj./n.
◜ conceptual, ideal; summary, outline
existing as an idea without having a physical form; a summary of a book or speech

## 03 **accursed** adj.
◜ cursed, damned; hateful, detestable
doomed to destruction or misery; strongly disliked

## 04 **alloy** n.
◜ blend, compound
a metal made by combining two or more metallic elements

## 05 **annihilate** v.
**annihilation (n.), annihilator (n.)**
◜ obliterate, wipe out
to destroy or defeat completely

## 06 **assonance** n.
**assonant (n./adj.)**
the repetition of similar or same vowel sounds

## 07 **bemuse** v.
**bemusement (n.), bemused (adj.)**
◜ puzzle; preoccupy
to find something confusing; to get lost in thought or hold someone's attention

Part 1

vocabulary

## 08 **beseech** v.

**beseeching (adj.)**

⌐ implore, plead

to ask for, request, or beg desperately

---

## 09 **brine** n.

⌐ salt water, saline solution

water that is heavily saturated with salt; the sea or ocean; the water of a salt lake or the sea

---

## 10 **bureaucracy** n.

**bureau (n.), bureaucrat (n.), bureaucratic (adj.)**

⌐ authority, red tape

an administrative system or group governed by many officials, usually marked by having complicated and unnecessary rules and procedures

---

## 11 **circumlocution** n.

**circumlocutory (adj.)**

⌐ wordiness, verboseness; indirectness, dodging

the use of many, unnecessary words; a deliberate, evasive speech

---

## 12 **coalesce** v.

**coalescence (n.), coalescent (adj.)**

⌐ connect, fuse; ally, cooperate

to grow or come together and form a whole; to band together to achieve a common goal

---

## 13 **cognitive** adj.

**cognition (n.)**

⌐ intellectual, logical

relating to mental functions, such as thinking, understanding, learning, remembering, etc.

---

## 14 **colloquy** n.

**colloquist (n.)**

⌐ dialogue, conference

a conversation, especially one that is serious, formal, or high-level

---

## 15 comestible n./adj.

provisions; eatable

food or anything that can be eaten; edible

## 16 conceive v.

conception (n.)

develop; comprehend; become fertilized

to devise or come up with something; to understand; to become pregnant

## 17 concentric adj.

concentricity (n.)

sharing a common center, with larger circles surrounding the smaller ones

## 18 delegation n.

delegate (n./v.)

authorization, appointment; commission, council

an act of giving responsibility to someone as a representative; a body of representatives

## 19 denizen n.

occupant; a regular; resident alien

an inhabitant of a particular place; a person who frequents a certain place or business establishment; a person admitted to stay or live in a foreign country

## 20 deposition n.

depose (v.), deposit (v.)

sediment; overthrow; declaration

the depositing of materials; the removal of someone from power or office; a sworn testimony made out of court

## 21 disburse v.

disbursement (n.), disbursal (n.)

expend, shell out

to pay out, mainly from a public treasury or fund

## 22 **discountenance** v.

oppose, resist; shame, put down

to disapprove or have an unfavorable opinion of; to embarrass or damage the self-confidence of

## 23 **empirical** adj.

empiricism (n.)

real, verifiable

based on or able to be shown or proven by observation or experience instead of pure logic or theory

## 24 **equestrian** adj.

equestrienne (n., fem.)

horsemanship

relating to horses, horseback riding, or knights

## 25 **executor** n.

execute (v.), executorial (adj.)

trustee; enforcer

one legally recognized to carry out a will; someone who carries out or puts something into effect

## 26 **fallacy** n.

fallacious (adj.)

flaw, error; fraud, deceit

a mistaken or incorrect idea, opinion, etc.; the quality of being deceptive

## 27 **florid** adj.

floridity (n.)

rosy, pink; showy, fancy

having a pale red color or complexion; too elaborate or ornate

## 28 **gastric** adj.

intestinal, abdominal

of or relating to the stomach

### 29 **hedonistic** adj.

**hedonism (n.), hedonist (n.)**

⌐ self-indulgent, decadent

devoted to or engaged in the pursuit of pleasure

---

### 30 **installment** n.

**instalment (alt.)**

⌐ deferred payment; episode; placing

a payment that is divided into and settled in portions; one part of a broadcast or a serial story or publication; the setting up of someone or something

---

### 31 **intemperance** n.

**intemperate (adj.)**

⌐ excessiveness; drunkenness

lack of moderation or restraint; uncontrolled or habitual drinking of alcohol

---

### 32 **monopoly** n.

**monopolize (v.)**

⌐ ownership, consortium

complete or exclusive possession, control, right, privilege, or use of something

---

### 33 **oxymoron** n.

**oxymoronic (adj.)**

⌐ contradiction, incongruity

a combination of words that have opposite meanings, usually formed intentionally for effect

---

### 34 **partiality** n.

**partial (adj.)**

⌐ favoritism; fondness, taste

unfair bias in favor of a certain person or thing; a special or particular liking or preference for something

---

### 35 **platitude** n.

**platitudinous (adj.)**

⌐ commonplace, cliché

a stale or obvious remark or statement

---

### 36 **plethora** n.

plethoric (adj.)

◝ overabundance, surplus

a large or excessive amount or number; an abnormal bodily condition characterized by an excess of blood

---

### 37 **posthumously** adv.

posthumous (adj.)

after the death of the originator or individual in question

---

### 38 **promontory** n.

◝ headland, cape

a high point of land that juts out into a body of water; a prominent part of the body

---

### 39 **proscription** n.

proscribe (v.), proscriptive (adj.)

◝ banning; censure

the act of prohibiting, especially by law; the act of condemning or criticizing

---

### 40 **protoplasm** n.

protoplasmic (adj.)

the colloidal substances that make up the living part of a cell

---

### 41 **quiescent** adj.

quiescence (n.)

◝ inactive, dormant

quiet or at rest

---

### 42 **respite** n.

◝ break, suspension

a temporary period of relief or delay

---

### 43 **restitution** n.

restitute (v.)

◝ handing back; recovery; reparation

a returning of something lost or taken away to its proper owner; a restoration to a former condition; compensation for loss or injury

## 44 **sapience** n.

**sapient (adj.)**

perceptiveness, sagacity

wisdom or insight

---

## 45 **sonorous** adj.

**sonority (n.)**

rich, ringing; high-sounding, extravagant

producing or capable of giving out a deep or resonant sound; full of impressive or imposing language

---

## 46 **syllogism** n.

**syllogistic (adj.)**

deduction, logic

a reasoning with a conclusion which must be true if the two given propositions are true; a subtle or tricky argument

---

## 47 **theism** n.

**theist (n.), theistic (adj.)**

monotheism

belief in one God; the belief that a god or gods exist

---

## 48 **utilitarian** adj.

**utilitarianism (n.)**

functional, efficient

being useful or practical; of or relating to a theory stating that a right action is one that benefits the greatest number of people

---

## 49 **vindicate** v.

**vindication (n.), vindicator (n.)**

clear; guard; justify; claim

to free from suspicion or blame; to protect or defend; to provide a just cause for; to assert or maintain a right to

---

## 50 **zenith** n.

**zenithal** (adj.)

summit, height

the highest point or peak, or the most successful or powerful state; the point in the
sky vertically above an observer

# List 27

= Synonyms, related words

## 01 **abnegate** v.

**abnegation (n.)**

abandon, abstain

to give up or deny oneself of something that is considered important

## 02 **ado** n.

commotion, ruckus

fuss over something usually considered unimportant

## 03 **aggregate** v.

assemble, combine

to form or gather into a whole

## 04 **antemeridian** adj.

ante meridiem, forenoon

relating to morning or before noon

## 05 **antigen** n.

**antigenic (adj.)**

vaccine, antiserum

a substance that helps create antibodies

## 06 **autonomy** n.

**autonomous (adj.), autonomously (adj.)**

independence, liberty

the freedom or capacity to act independently, make own decisions, or self-govern

## 07 **bask** v.

unwind; relish

to relax in a warm and pleasant setting; to feel pleased from being in a certain situation (as from getting attention)

## 08 **bedlam** n.

commotion, uproar; madhouse, asylum

a place or condition of disorder and confusion; an institution for the mentally ill

---

## 09 **benevolent** adj.

**benevolence (n.)**

humane, compassionate

doing or having the tendency to do good

---

## 10 **botanical** adj./n.

**botany (n.), botanica (n.)**

relating to plants or the science dealing with plant life and species; plant extracts used as medicine or cosmetics

---

## 11 **chateau** n.

**chateaux (pl.)**

mansion; citadel

a large country house or estate; a French feudal fortress or castle

---

## 12 **choleric** adj.

irritable, ill-tempered

having a quick temper or easily angered

---

## 13 **circumnavigate** v.

**circumnavigation (n.), circumnavigator (n.)**

circuit, compass; bypass, sidestep

to travel completely around by flying or (especially) sailing; to avoid or go past or around an obstacle

---

## 14 **contraposition** n.

polarity, inversion

a contrast or opposition, or (in logic) the relationship between propositions, such as "if not B then not A" following "if A then B"

### 15 **diagnosis** n.

diagnose (v.), diagnostic (adj.)

detection; confirmation

the identification of a disease or illness by examining its symptoms; the examination or analysis of the cause of a situation or problem

---

### 16 **discourse** n.

discussion, lecture, essay

a formal conversation, debate, or communication of ideas of a topic in speech or writing

---

### 17 **doublet** n.

pair, couple

a man's close-fitting jacket worn in Europe especially popular during the Renaissance era; something that has two similar or same parts

---

### 18 **embryonic** adj.

embryo (n.)

fetal, unborn; crude, simple

in the earlier stages of life (as in organism) or development (as in idea, plan, system, etc.)

---

### 19 **enfranchise** v.

enfranchisement (n.)

release, liberate; empower, entitle

to set free or grant freedom from slavery; to grant voting rights

---

### 20 **expostulate** v.

expostulation (n.), expostulatory (adj.)

disagree, protest

to reason with someone earnestly in order to object or to persuade not to do something

---

### 21 **extricate** v.

liberate, untangle

to release or set free from constraint, hardship, difficulty, etc.

## 22 **fallible** adj.

**fallibility (n.)**

⌐ imperfect, frail; incorrect, false

capable of making mistakes; likely or liable to be wrong or inaccurate

---

## 23 **fiscal** adj.

⌐ financial, monetary; economic, budgetary

relating to money in general; related to government spending and treasury

---

## 24 **forensic** adj.

**forensics (n.)**

⌐ legal, debatable

suitable to judicial, public, or formal discussion; relating to scientific methods or tests used in crime investigations

---

## 25 **genocide** n.

**genocidal (adj.)**

⌐ mass murder, ethnic cleansing

the deliberate and systematic killing of a particular race, nationality, or ethnic group

---

## 26 **hypodermic** adj.

relating to the area immediately beneath the skin or a shot or needle applied to this area

---

## 27 **iconoclastic** adj.

**iconoclasm (n.), iconoclast (n.)**

⌐ dissenting, heretical

characterized by rejection, destruction, or attack on established beliefs, institutions, or religious images

---

## 28 **implacable** adj.

**implacability (n.)**

⌐ inflexible, determined

unyielding or stubborn, or not able to be pacified or appeased

---

## 29  **impose** v.

**imposition (n.)**

enforce; bother; pass off; sort

to establish forcibly by authority (such as tax, fine, law, etc.); to force the attention of someone; to deceive or palm off; to arrange in proper order

## 30  **innumerable** adj.

**innumerability (n.)**

unlimited, countless

of great number, or too many to be counted or numbered

## 31  **interdict** n.

**interdiction (n.)**

ban, outlaw; intercept, cut off

to prohibit or forbid formally, officially, or with authority; to restrain or hinder the movement of enemies or supplies by using firepower

## 32  **juggernaut** n.

drive, movement

a destructive or overwhelming force or object that cannot be stopped

## 33  **knavery** n.

**knavish (adj.), knave (n.)**

prank, stunt; deceit, wickedness

a boyish trick or mischief; a dishonest or unprincipled action

## 34  **laissez-faire** n.

nonintervention, free trade

a policy, practice, or attitude allowing people to act without interference, especially in economic affairs

## 35  **larceny** n.

**larcenist (n.), larcenous (adj.)**

theft, stealing

the illegal taking of personal property

## 36 **lewd** adj.

*obscene, indecent*

vulgar or showing lustful desire in an offensive way

---

## 37 **libel** n.

**libelous, libellous (adj.)**

*slander, character assassination; pleading, declaration*

a written or published false statement that harms a person's reputation; a plaintiff's grievances in written statement

---

## 38 **magnitude** n.

**magnitudinous (adj.)**

*enormity; extent, quantity*

great size, extent, influence, or importance; spatial size or measurable number; the apparent brightness of a celestial body; an earthquake's intensity

---

## 39 **minstrel** n.

*balladeer, bard*

a medieval entertainer who traveled around singing or reciting poetry

---

## 40 **nebula** n.

**nebulae (pl.), nebular (adj.)**

a cloud consisting of gas or dust in interstellar space

---

## 41 **pliable** adj.

**pliability (n.)**

*flexible; susceptible; adaptable*

easily bent or shaped; easily persuaded or influenced; adjusting quickly and easily

---

## 42 **promulgate** v.

**promulgation (n.)**

*proclaim, make public; enact, implement*

to make known officially or widespread; to put (a law, rule, regulation, etc.) into effect

---

### 43 **protégé** n.

**protégée (fem.)**

pupil, apprentice

a person guided by another who is older and more experienced or influential

---

### 44 **ramshackle** adj.

neglected, shaky

in disrepair, or likely to collapse

---

### 45 **repatriate** v.

**repatriation (n.)**

return, restore

to send back someone or something to the country of origin or citizenship

---

### 46 **retinue** n.

entourage, staff

a body of assistants, advisers, or followers attending an important person

---

### 47 **rhapsodic** adj.

**rhapsodize (v.)**

elated, ecstatic

extravagantly emotional or enthusiastic

---

### 48 **supplicate** v.

**supplication (n.)**

beg, request

to ask or pray for humbly or earnestly

---

### 49 **surrogate** n.

**surrogacy (n.)**

proxy; probate; birth mother

a substitute; a local judicial court or its judge; a woman who becomes pregnant for another

---

## 50 **wayward** adj.

ungovernable, fickle

uncontrollable or unpredictable due to stubborn or erratic behavior

01 **abrogate** v.

**abrogation (n.)**

⌐ overturn, revoke; evade, stay away from

to put an end to something formally; to avoid something that one should do

---

02 **accolade** n.

⌐ honor, commendation

an award or an expression of praise; the act of making someone a knight

---

03 **backlash** n.

⌐ resistance, defiance

a strong, negative reaction, especially in response to a social or political development

---

04 **bristle** n./v.

⌐ filament; rage; abound

short, stiff hair of animals or plants or artificial ones like brush, broom, fiber, etc.; to show extreme anger; to be covered with or full of

---

05 **cabal** n.

⌐ faction, plot

a secret, exclusive group, usually created for political schemes, or the schemes engaged by such a group

---

06 **caucus** n.

⌐ conference, rally

an exclusive meeting (or the group attending) attended by members of the same political party or faction

---

## 07 **chauvinism** n.

**chauvinist (n.), chauvinistic (adj.)**

 bigotry, discrimination

aggressive or excessive patriotism, or belief in the superiority of or strong devotion to a group (race, sex, etc.) to which one belongs

---

## 08 **combustible** adj.

**combustibility (n.)**

 flammable, ignitable; passionate, hot-tempered

capable of catching fire or burning quickly or easily; easily excited, aroused, or annoyed

---

## 09 **comely** adj.

**comeliness (n.)**

 gorgeous, appealing

enjoyable to look at or having an attractive feature or appearance

---

## 10 **contrite** adj.

**contrition (n.)**

 ashamed, apologetic

feeling guilty or showing regret for a misdeed committed

---

## 11 **convalescence** n.

**convalesce (v.), convalescent (adj./n.)**

 healing, recuperation

a period of recovery from sickness or medical care

---

## 12 **defer** v.

**deferment (n.), deference (n.)**

 delay, postpone; yield, give in

to put off (especially the required military service) to a later date; to accept or submit to someone as a sign of respect

---

## 13 **delectable** adj.

**delectability (n.)**

 delightful, tasty

extremely pleasing or delicious

## 14 **dexterity** n.

**dexterous** (adj.)

cleverness, agility, deftness

skill or quickness in performing mental or physical tasks, especially with the hands

## 15 **dichotomy** n.

**dichotomous** (adj.)

split, contradiction

a separation or division into two parts, especially when two things are opposites of each other; a moon or planet appearing half lit and half dark

## 16 **elucidate** v.

**elucidation** (n.)

clarify, spell out

to make or give clear explanation

## 17 **errant** adj.

drifting, roaming; digressing; naughty

traveling or wandering around; straying from proper course; prone to behaving wrongly or making mistakes

## 18 **exhume** v.

**exhumation** (n.)

unearth, unbury; disclose, reveal

to take or dig out of the ground; to uncover or bring to light

## 19 **feudalism** n.

**feudal** (adj.), **feudalistic** (adj.)

a system (social, economic, political, etc.) in medieval Europe

## 20 **fresco** n.

a painting or a technique of art painted over freshly laid lime plaster

## 21 **genteel** adj.

refined, cultured

elegant, graceful, or having an aristocratic quality in manner or appearance, often to the point of being excessive or pretentious

## 22 **gibe** n.

jeer, ridicule

a taunting or insulting remark

---

## 23 **goad** v./n.

prod, spur; staff, rod

to provoke or urge into action; a pointed stick for urging on an animal

---

## 24 **heresy** n.

**heretic (n.), heretical (adj.)**

dissent, nonconformity

an opinion or practice that goes against the beliefs of a dominant religion, principle, theory, etc.

---

## 25 **ignoble** adj.

**ignobility (n.)**

lowborn, common; despicable, mean

of low birth or humble origins; dishonorable in character or quality

---

## 26 **impotent** adj.

**impotence (n.)**

incapable, weak; sterile, barren

lacking in power or strength; unproductive or incapable of bearing fruit or producing offspring

---

## 27 **inflame** v.

**inflamed (adj.)**

light, ignite; excite, stir up

to set on fire or cause to burn or glow; to arouse or increase the intensity of passion, anger, desire, etc.

---

## 28 **iniquity** n.

**iniquitous (adj.)**

sin, injustice

a wicked or unfair act or behavior

---

vocabulary

## 29 **iota** n.

*bit, shred

an extremely small quantity; the ninth letter of the Greek alphabet

---

## 30 **jettison** v.

*discharge, eject; dump, get rid of

to throw or drop something from a plane or vessel; to discard something unneeded

---

## 31 **knead** v.

*mould, shape; massage, stroke

to mix or press (clay, dough, etc.) into a pasty mass, usually with the hands; to squeeze or rub with the hands

---

## 32 **milieu** n.

**milieux (pl.)**

*background, atmosphere

social or cultural setting or environment

---

## 33 **mnemonic** n.

**mnemonics (n.)**

*prompt, cue

a device (such as a pattern, idea, association, etc.) that aids in remembering

---

## 34 **monograph** n.

**monographic (adj.)**

*treatise

a detailed study or book on a specific, specialized subject

---

## 35 **monsoon** n.

**monsoonal (adj.)**

*seasonal prevailing wind; wet season

any of a number of seasonal winds; a rainy season that typically lasts for months

## 36 **nihilist** n.

**nihilism (n.), nihilistic (adj.)**

skeptic, cynic

a person who believes that traditional or religious morals, beliefs, or principles have no value and that life or existence is meaningless

---

## 37 **nuptial** adj.

marital, nuptial

relating to marriage or a wedding; having to do with or occurring in breeding behavior or season

---

## 38 **omnipresent** adj.

**omnipresence (n.)**

everywhere, universal

present in all places simultaneously

---

## 39 **optometry** n.

**optometric (adj.), optometrist (n.)**

the practice, science, or profession of examining and treating the eyes

---

## 40 **oversight** n.

control, governance; slip, error

regulatory management, supervision, or care; an omission or mistake done without intention

---

## 41 **pedagogy** n.

**pedagogue (n.), pedagogic, pedagogical (adj.)**

schooling, guidance

the method, practice, or profession of teaching

---

## 42 **persona** n.

**personae (pl.)**

image, front; part, portrayal

one's outer appearance or personality presented to others; a role or character played by an actor

---

### 43 **preponderant** adj.

preponderance (n.)

predominant, supreme

superior in number, power, or influence

---

### 44 **provident** adj.

prudent; frugal

preparing for future needs; having great care in the use of resources so as to avoid wasting

---

### 45 **prudent** adj.

prudence (n.), prudential (adj.)

judicious; discreet; economical

wise or sagacious; careful or circumspect; frugal or not extravagant

---

### 46 **purloin** v.

purloiner (n.)

steal, thieve

to take something from another wrongfully

---

### 47 **receptacle** n.

container

an object used to hold or keep something; the part of the flower stalk on which the flower parts grow; an electrical outlet

---

### 48 **surfeit** n.

surplus; overconsumption; nausea

an excessive supply or amount; overindulgence in something, especially food or drink; discomfort or sickness due to overindulgence

---

### 49 **truant** n.

truancy (n.)

absentee

a person who neglects or stays away from work, responsibility, or school

---

## 50 **vestige** n.

**vestigial** (adj.)

remains; footprint; speck

a trace of something once in existence; a mark left on the earth by a foot; a bit, or the smallest amount or quantity

# List 29

## 01 **agglomerate** v.
**agglomeration (n.)**
cluster, pile
to collect or to gather into a mass

## 02 **aplomb** n.
coolness, composure
self-confidence or assurance, especially during a difficult situation

## 03 **autopsy** n.
necropsy; analysis
an examination determining the cause of death; a detailed evaluation of someone or something

## 04 **beget** v.
**begetter (n.)**
sire; bring about
to father a child; to cause something to happen

## 05 **benign** adj.
friendly, temperate, curable
kind or gentle, favorable (as to the environment or climate), or harmless (as to health)

## 06 **bestial** adj.
**bestialize (v.), bestiality (n.)**
animalistic, beastly; barbaric, cruel
resembling or relating to beasts; showing little intelligence or savage and brutal

## 07 **carcass** n.
remains; self; shell; bodywork
the body of a dead or slaughtered animal; a person's body; the remains of something now considered worthless; the framework of a structure

## 08 **celebrated** adj.

**celebrity (n.)**

renowned, famous

greatly admired or widely praised

---

## 09 **contravene** v.

**contravention (n.)**

violate, breach; contradict, differ

to fail to follow a rule or regulation; to deny or argue against a plan, proposal, statement, etc.

---

## 10 **credulous** adj.

**credulity (n.)**

gullible, over-trusting

too willing to believe something to the point of getting easily deceived

---

## 11 **dauntless** adj.

brave, courageous

incapable of feeling fear or cowering under intimidation

---

## 12 **delude** v.

**delusion (n.), delusional (adj.)**

deceive, fool

to mislead someone's mind or judgment

---

## 13 **embellish** v.

**embellishment (n.), embellished (adj.)**

adorn, dress up; distort, exaggerate

to improve or make more appealing by adding decorations or details; to make something sound or appear better than how it actually is

---

## 14 **forage** v.

**forager (n.)**

hunt, rummage

to seek out or make a thorough search for food or provisions

---

## 15 **foreboding** n.

**forebode** (v.)

apprehension, uneasiness

a sense of something bad or evil to come

## 16 **grate** v./n.

**grating** (adj.)

crush; scratch; bother; hearth; grill

to grind into small shreds; to make a rasping or scraping sound; to annoy or irritate; a fireplace; a frame to hold a stove

## 17 **gratis** adj./adv.

complimentary, at no cost

given for free or without charge

## 18 **hieroglyphic** n./adj.

**hieroglyphics** (n.)

graphics, drawings; unreadable, illegible

a system of writing mainly in pictures or symbols that represent words; difficult to decipher or understand in its written form

## 19 **incisive** adj.

decisive; keen; piercing

quick in judgment and direct in expression; highly intelligent, analytical, and concise; having the quality of cutting or penetrating

## 20 **incorrigible** adj.

**incorrigibility** (n.)

hopeless

not capable of being improved, corrected, or cured

## 21 **incriminate** v.

**incrimination** (n.)

accuse, charge

to provide proof of involvement in a crime or wrongdoing

### 22 **indolent** adj.

**indolence (n.)**

*lazy, idle; painless*

having or showing dislike for work, effort, or movement; hardly causing pain; slow in healing or developing

---

### 23 **invigorate** v.

**invigoration (n.)**

*revitalize, stimulate*

to give strength or vitality to

---

### 24 **jaunty** adj.

*merry, jolly; chic, trendy*

lively and cheerful; stylish or fashionable

---

### 25 **jubilant** adj.

**jubilation (n.), jubilate (v.)**

*excited, triumphant*

feeling or expressing great joy and elation

---

### 26 **languid** adj.

*sickly; casual; unenergetic*

weak from exhaustion or illness; lacking interest or enthusiasm; slow, unhurried, or relaxed

---

### 27 **languish** v.

**languishment (n.)**

*distress; deteriorate; fail*

to suffer from being in an unpleasant place, situation, or condition; to weaken or lose strength; to make little progress

---

### 28 **litigation** n.

**litigant (n.), litigate (v.)**

*lawsuit, legal dispute*

the act or process of engaging in legal action

## 29 **manifest** v./n.

**manifestation (n.)**

⌐ reveal; prove; record

to display or demonstrate; to make certain, evident, or obvious; a list of a cargo or passengers of a ship or airplane

---

## 30 **misnomer** n.

⌐ misnaming, miscalling

(a use of) a wrong, misleading, or inappropriate name or term

---

## 31 **nautical** adj.

⌐ seafaring, maritime

relating to, associated with, or involving sailors, ships, or navigation

---

## 32 **nemesis** n.

**nemeses (pl.)**

⌐ archenemy; curse; punishment

a persistent or powerful opponent or rival; a source of one's inescapable downfall; retributive justice

---

## 33 **olfactory** adj.

of or concerning the sense of smell

---

## 34 **orifice** n.

⌐ hole, aperture

a mouth, or an opening (such as pipe, tube, etc.)

---

## 35 **parable** n.

⌐ fable, allegory

a short story that illustrates a moral or religious lesson

---

## 36 **parametric** adj.

**parameter (n.)**

relating to a constant or condition that controls or is used as a referent

vocabulary

### 37 **parody** n.

satire, mockery

a literary or musical work imitating the style of an author or work in an exaggerated manner for comic effect; a poor or ridiculous imitation

---

### 38 **preclude** v.

preclusion (n.), preclusive (adj.)

forestall, rule out

to prevent something from happening, make impossible, or exclude

---

### 39 **preposterous** adj.

absurd, ridiculous

contrary to common sense

---

### 40 **pristine** adj.

primitive, original; clean, uncorrupted

in its earliest form or condition; still pure or unspoiled

---

### 41 **probation** n.

probationary (adj.)

trial period

subjection of a person to a period of evaluation; the suspension of sentence of a convicted person under the condition of supervision

---

### 42 **remuneration** n.

remunerate (v.), remunerable (adj.)

salary, compensation

a payment for a work done, service rendered, or loss incurred

---

### 43 **repertoire** n.

stock, supply; abilities, competencies

a list (of dramas, plays, operas, pieces, etc.) that a company or person is ready to show or perform; habitually-used special skills

## 44  **sardonic** adj.

mocking, scornful

critically humorous, or disdainfully sarcastic or cynical

---

## 45  **transliterate** v.

**transliteration (n.)**

convert, transcribe

to write letters or words in corresponding characters of a different language or system

---

## 46  **truculent** adj.

**truculence (n.)**

antagonistic; ferocious; insulting; devastating

quick or eager to initiate a conflict; cruel or savage; scathingly rude or harsh; causing death or destruction

---

## 47  **unfettered** adj.

**unfetter (v.)**

free, unburdened

not bound or restrained

---

## 48  **volant** adj.

aerial; nimble; in a flying position

flying or able to fly; moving quickly or lightly; having the wings extended

---

## 49  **wallow** v./n.

lie around; sway; absorb; pour; sludge

to roll about or lie relaxed; to roll or rock from side to side; to immerse oneself in; to surge or flow forth; a muddy place for animals

---

## 50  **zephyr** n.

air, breath

a gentle or refreshing breeze or wind; any of various light and soft fabrics

## 01 **acumen** n.

✎ sharpness, keenness

the skill to make quick and wise decisions

## 02 **aliment** n./v.

✎ sustenance; provide

food or nourishment; to sustain or support

## 03 **arrogate** v.

**arrogation (n.)**

✎ seize, assume

to take or claim something without right, reason, or justification

## 04 **auspice** n.

✎ backing; omen

approval, guidance, or support; a divine or favorable sign

## 05 **avarice** n.

**avaricious (adj.), avariciously (adv.)**

✎ greed, materialism

extreme desire for wealth

## 06 **billow** v.

**billowy (adj.), billowing (adj.)**

✎ surge, swell

to rise, flow outward, or move as a mass (as in smoke, flame, steam, cloud, waves, etc.)

## 07 **cajole** v.

**cajolery (n.)**

✎ coax, persuade

to talk a reluctant person into doing something through flattery or false promises

## 08 **captious** adj.

*critical, picky*

tending to find fault without a good reason or raise objections that are minor or unimportant

---

## 09 **catalyst** n.

**catalyze (v.), catalytic (adj.)**

*agent, stimulant; spur, impetus*

a substance that causes the rate of a chemical reaction to speed up; someone or something that acts as stimulus in bringing about a change

---

## 10 **chattel** n.

*belongings; servant*

any movable personal property, as opposed to real estate; a slave

---

## 11 **comport** v.

**comportment (n.)**

*conduct, carry; fit, correspond*

to behave in a manner proper to a given situation; to agree or be in agreement with

---

## 12 **connoisseur** n.

*authority, master*

an expert or specialist in a given field, especially areas related to matters of taste or the fine arts

---

## 13 **cultivate** v.

**cultivation (n.), cultivator (n.)**

*till, dig; raise, rear; pursue, acquire; woo, court*

to prepare soil for growing crops; to grow or improve plants, fish, etc.; to improve or encourage by caring or studying; to seek friendship with

---

## 14 **debunk** v.

*refute, disprove*

to prove or expose the falseness of a myth, idea, claim, belief, etc.

## 15 **deciduous** adj.

*temporary, brief*

falling off (or shed) at a particular season or in the life cycle (leaves, scales, teeth, etc.); short-lived

---

## 16 **defray** v.

**defrayable (adj.), defrayal (n.), defrayment (n.)**

*cover, settle*

to provide or pay the money for an expense or cost

---

## 17 **deranged** adj.

**derange (v.), derangement (n.)**

*insane; disorganized; abnormal*

mentally unstable or unsound; disordered or disarranged in order, function, condition, operation, etc.; extremely weird

---

## 18 **desiccant** adj.

**desiccate (v.), desiccation (n.)**

*anhydrous*

tending to dry

---

## 19 **desist** v.

**desistance (n.)**

*refrain, conclude*

to cease to continue or act

---

## 20 **despondent** adj.

**despondency (n.)**

*downcast, hopeless*

in low spirits or feeling discouraged

---

## 21 **effrontery** n.

*arrogance, nerve*

extreme or unashamed rudeness or boldness

## 22 **embroil** v.

**embroilment (n.)**

entangle, bog down; blur, complicate

to draw into or involve (someone) into a difficult or undesirable situation; to make difficult or throw into confusion

---

## 23 **equanimity** n.

**equanimous (adj.)**

composure, coolness

mental calmness, especially under stress or pressure

---

## 24 **euphoric** adj.

**euphoria (n.)**

ecstatic, elated

feeling intense happiness or excitement

---

## 25 **extraneous** adj.

foreign, outside; unessential, irrelevant

coming from or having external origin; not being important or having no connection

---

## 26 **exude** v.

**exudation (n.)**

seep, trickle; radiate, give out

to discharge or ooze out through small openings; to flow out or display abundantly (as in quality or emotion)

---

## 27 **felony** n.

**felon (n.), felonious (adj.)**

serious crime

a criminal offense of high seriousness, such as murder, rape, arson, etc.

---

## 28 **gaiety** n.

cheerfulness, merriment; finery, decoration

a festive mood or activity; elegance or flashy brightness

---

## 29 **impiety** n.

**impious (adj.)**

ungodliness, immorality

lack of respect or reverence (as toward a parent or god)

---

## 30 **innuendo** n.

hint, insinuation

an indirect comment or gesture, especially one that is derogatory or suggestive

---

## 31 **integral** adj.

**integrality (n.)**

essential; whole; component

necessary as a part of something to be complete; entire or complete; composed of parts forming a whole

---

## 32 **interim** adj./n.

provisional, short-term; meantime, interval

transitional or temporary; an intervening time or period between events

---

## 33 **itinerary** n.

**itinerate (v.)**

schedule; travel guide; travel diary

the route of a (or an outline for a planned) journey; a guidebook for travelers; a traveler's record of a journey

---

## 34 **junta** n.

faction, cabal

a military group in control of a government after seizing power

---

## 35 **leaven** n.

raising agent; influence

a substance added to create fermentation in dough or batter; anything that modifies or transforms

---

### 36 **maxim** n.

⌐ saying, proverb

a statement or observation expressing a principle, moral teaching, general truth, or rule of conduct

### 37 **minion** n.

⌐ underling, servant

a faithful follower or subordinate official of a powerful person

### 38 **notwithstanding** prep./adv./conj.

⌐ despite; nevertheless; although

in spite of; nonetheless; even though

### 39 **orchestrate** v.

**orchestration (n.), orchestrator (n.)**

⌐ organize; score

to combine, direct, or coordinate to achieve a desired effect; to compose or arrange music for an orchestra or performance

### 40 **parabola** n.

**parabolic (adj.)**

⌐ arc, bow

a bowl-shaped figure; (in geometry) a symmetrical open plane curve

### 41 **paraphernalia** n.

⌐ possessions, effects; equipment, materials

personal belongings; miscellaneous items used or required for a particular activity

### 42 **partisan** n.

**partisanship (n.)**

⌐ follower, devotee; guerrilla, freedom fighter

a firm supporter of a party, faction, cause, or person; a member of a small group of detached troops formed to fight covertly

Part 1

vocabulary

### 43 **perfunctory** adj.

* cursory, casual
done superficially or merely as a routine or duty

### 44 **permeable** adj.

**permeability (n.)**
* penetrable, porous
capable of being diffused or passed through

### 45 **prevaricate** v.

**prevarication (n.)**
* dodge, fabricate
to evade the truth

### 46 **pundit** n.

**punditry (n.)**
* expert, scholar; critic, observer
a person of great knowledge or wisdom in a particular area; a person who publicly
expresses an opinion or judgment about a subject

### 47 **quid pro quo** n.

* trade, substitute
something given in exchange for another or of equal value or compensation

### 48 **rendezvous** n.

* locale; hangout; engagement
a designated place for assembling; a popular place where people meet; an appointment to meet at a specific time and place

### 49 **trope** n.

* figure of speech; cliché
the use of a word or expression in a figurative sense; a recurring or overused theme,
style, device, etc.

## 50 **unwittingly** adv.

**unwitting (adj.)**

accidentally, inadvertently

without intention or knowing

*= Synonyms, related words*

## 01 **abstain** v.

**abstinence (n.), abstinent (adj.)**

✎ avoid, hold back from

to keep oneself away from something (especially alcohol); to refrain from casting a vote

---

## 02 **abstemious** adj.

**abstemiously (adv.)**

✎ disciplined, self-controlled

used sparingly or with moderation

---

## 03 **abundant** adj.

**abound (v.), abundance (n.)**

✎ plentiful, ample

existing in large quantity or amount

---

## 04 **adjudicate** v.

**adjudication (n.)**

✎ determine, mediate

to settle a legal case or dispute, or to act as a judge or a referee

---

## 05 **aerospace** n.

the Earth's atmosphere and the area of space around it, and their related industry and technology

---

## 06 **alacrity** n.

**alacritous (adj.)**

✎ enthusiasm, fervor; speed, swiftness

eager willingness or readiness; promptness or haste

---

## 07 **alchemy** n.

**alchemist (n.)**

pseudoscience; sorcery

the medieval form of chemistry; a magical power to change or create things

## 08 **alleviate** v.

**alleviation (n.), alleviative (adj.)**

lighten, lessen

to make difficulty or pain less severe

## 09 **alumnus** n.

**alumni (pl.), alumna (fem.), alumnae (fem., pl.)**

graduate, alum

a person, particularly male, who has attended a particular school

## 10 **ascribe** v.

**ascribable (adj.)**

associate, refer

to consider that something is caused by, comes from, or is connected to someone or something specific

## 11 **asperity** n.

meanness, bitterness; roughness, difficulty

harshness of temper or speech that expresses angry tone; harshness, as in sound, surface, weather, situation, etc.

## 12 **barometer** n.

**barometric (adj.)**

weatherglass; mark

atmospheric pressure and weather measuring instrument; something that reveals how things are changing

## 13 **befuddle** v.

**befuddlement (n.), befuddled (adj.)**

perplex; intoxicate

to confuse or baffle; to muddle one's mind, especially with alcohol

vocabulary

## 14 **belabor** v.

**belabored (adj.)**

beat, insult; dwell on, emphasize

to attack physically or with words; to spend too much time or get too much into details

## 15 **bravado** n.

boldness, bluff

a boastful show of bravery or courage, especially one done to hide one's fear

## 16 **carrion** n.

carcass, remains

flesh of a dead, rotting animal

## 17 **census** n.

tally, poll

an official count or survey taken to find out all kinds of information about a given population

## 18 **chary** adj.

**charily (adv.)**

guarded; sparing

careful or cautious; reluctant or hesitant in giving or accepting

## 19 **chromatic** adj.

**chroma (n.)**

hued, vibrant

relating to color; highly colored; capable of being stained with coloring materials; relating to musical tones (such as using semitones)

## 20 **clairvoyance** n.

**clairvoyant (n./adj.)**

foresight, sixth sense; sharpness, intuition

the power to see the future or sense things that ordinary senses cannot detect; keen awareness or perception

## 21 **clandestine** adj.

↗ undercover, underhanded

kept or done in secret, especially to hide something illegal

## 22 **culinary** adj.

**culinarian (n.)**

↗ cookery

relating to cooking or kitchens

## 23 **disseminate** v.

**dissemination (n.), disseminator (n.)**

↗ circulate, disperse

to spread widely or become widespread (such as information, ideas, principles, etc.)

## 24 **drone** n.

↗ hum, murmur; good-for-nothing

a continuous, low humming sound or speech; an idler or loafer; a male bee that mates with the queen; a flying device controlled remotely

## 25 **effusive** adj.

**effuse (v.)**

↗ enthusiastic; overflowing; extrusive

expressing unrestrained gratitude, emotion, or enthusiasm; pouring or spilling out freely; being poured out as lava and hardened afterwards

## 26 **fortitude** n.

**fortitudinous (adj.)**

↗ bravery, firmness

the courage to face pain, danger, misfortune, etc.

## 27 **hackneyed** adj.

**hackney (v.)**

↗ overused, stale

done too often or lacking originality

## 28 **harp** v.

**harping** (adj.)

dwell on, nag

to talk or write tiresomely on a particular subject

## 29 **incubation** n.

**incubate** (v.), **incubator** (n.)

nurturing, encouragement

the act of maintaining conditions that promote hatching or development; the development (period) of a disease from its cause

## 30 **infrastructure** n.

system, foundation

the basic framework and facilities necessary in operating an enterprise or society (such as roads, buildings, equipment, etc.)

## 31 **intermittent** adj.

**intermittence** (n.), **intermit** (v.)

sporadic, on-and-off

happening or existing occasionally or at irregular intervals

## 32 **jingoism** n.

**jingoist** (n.), **jingoistic** (adj.)

excessive nationalism, blind patriotism

the belief in the superiority of one's own country over others

## 33 **labyrinth** n.

**labyrinthine** (adj.)

maze, warren; complexity, intricacy; internal ear

a structure full of intricate network of passages; something that is very complicated and perplexing; a winding anatomical structure in the inner ear

## 34 **lethargic** adj.

**lethargy** (n.)

sluggish, inactive; indifferent, apathetic

slow or having little energy; lack of interest or concern

## 35 **liability** n.

**liable (adj.)**

responsibility; drawback; probability

an obligation or debt owed; something that acts as a burden or disadvantage; the likelihood of something to occur

## 36 **limpid** adj.

**limpidity (n.)**

see-through; understandable; untroubled

unclouded or transparent; clear and simple; free from emotional distress or anxiety

## 37 **natal** adj.

innate, native

associated with or relating to the time or place of one's birth

## 38 **nepotism** n.

**nepotistic (adj.)**

bias, preferential treatment

unfair practice of favoritism based on kinship

## 39 **ousting** n.

**oust (v.)**

unseating, displacement

the act of removing someone or something from a place or position, taking away a right, etc.

## 40 **perfidy** n.

**perfidious (adj.)**

betrayal, treachery

the deliberate violation of trust, faith, vow, etc.

## 41 **phlegmatic** adj.

**phlegm (n.)**

composed, collected

having or showing a calm and unemotional temperament

## 42 **precipitation** n.

**precipitate (v.)**

rain, snow; rush, rapidity

water particles that fall to the ground; sudden haste or acceleration

## 43 **prepossession** n.

**prepossess (v.)**

absorption; bias

an excessive concern with a particular idea or thing; a preconceived impression, opinion, or attitude

## 44 **rapacious** adj.

**rapacity (n.)**

covetous; ravenous; predatory

excessively greedy; having an extreme appetite; living on prey

## 45 **subliminal** adj.

subconscious, hidden

affecting one's mind in a way that one does not notice

## 46 **supercilious** adj.

haughty, pompous

behaving arrogantly as though one is better than others

## 47 **tome** n.

work, writing

a large or heavy scholarly book, or one of the volumes in a series

## 48 **usurp** v.

**usurper (n.), usurpation (n.)**

seize, assume

to take (power, office, position, rights, etc.) and maintain it by force or illegal means

## 49 verisimilitude n.

**verisimilar (adj.)**

accuracy, authenticity
resemblance to truth or reality

## 50 volition n.

will, self-determination
the capacity or power to make (or an act of making) a decision or choice on one's own

## 01 **abode** n.

✐ residence, dwelling
the place where one calls home

## 02 **amorous** adj.

✐ lustful, erotic
full of or relating to love or carnal desire

## 03 **ascetic** adj.

**asceticism (n.), ascetically (adv.)**
✐ self-denial, simple
characterized by strict self-discipline and living a simple life

## 04 **assiduous** adj.

**assiduity (n.)**
✐ diligent, attentive
hard-working or showing great care, dedication, and endurance

## 05 **behemoth** n.

✐ beast; mammoth
a huge and powerful monster; something that is great in size, power, or appearance

## 06 **bibliomania** n.

**bibliomaniac (n./adj.)**
✐ bibliophile, bookworm
strong passion for collecting and owning books

## 07 **caliber** n.

competence, stature; size, gauge

the degree of ability, quality, or importance; the diameter of a bullet, gun's bore, or any hollow cylinder

## 08 **callow** adj.

immature, naïve

lacking adult experience, knowledge, or sophistication

## 09 **cataract** n.

falls; rapids; deluge; eye condition

a huge waterfall; a rush of water in a river; a downpour or flood of water; a decrease in vision caused by a clouding in the eye

## 10 **civility** n.

**civil (adj.)**

courtesy, propriety

politeness in action or way of speaking

## 11 **cleric** n./adj.

**clerical (alt.)**

clergyperson, ecclesiastic

a member of (or relating to) a religious organization

## 12 **cognate** adj.

connected; kindred

similar in nature or alike, or having the same or common root or origin; related by blood or family

## 13 **contumacy** n.

**contumacious (adj.)**

disobedience, noncompliance

stubborn defiance or resistance to authority

## 14 **dawdle** v.

**dawdler (n.)**

lounge, waste time; stroll, dally

to spend time without haste or purpose; to move in a lazy or slow manner

## 15 **decorous** adj.

**decorum (n.)**

fitting, correct

marked by behavior that is considered to be proper, polite, and respectable

## 16 **depreciation** n.

**depreciate (v.)**

markdown, devaluation; downplaying, underrate

a reduction in the value of an asset or the buying power of money; the act of making something seem less important

## 17 **discrepancy** n.

**discrepant (adj.), discrepantly (adv.)**

inconsistency, difference

a lack of similarity or agreement between facts

## 18 **dissonance** n.

**dissonant (adj.)**

conflict, disunity; noise, cacophony

a state of disagreement, tension, or clash; a mixture of sounds striking the ear

## 19 **dregs** n.

**dreggy (adj.)**

sediment, residue; scum, refuse

matter that settles in a liquid; the least desirable or last remaining part

## 20 **dynamo** n.

**dynamic (adj.)**

generator, alternator; doer, go-getter

a machine that produces electricity; an extremely energetic person

## 21 **ebullient** adj.

**ebullience (n.)**

high-spirited, excited; blistering, bubbling

marked by overflowing enthusiasm; boiling or agitated

---

## 22 **embargo** n.

prohibition, bar

an official ban or restriction on movement of commercial ships or trade in a specific product

---

## 23 **ensconce** v.

nestle, establish; cover, hide

to settle comfortably or securely; to shelter or conceal

---

## 24 **exact** v.

**exactable (adj.)**

extort; impose; require

to obtain (payment) through threats or use of force; to insist strongly or demand (by the authorities); to call for (due to necessity or desirability)

---

## 25 **excrescence** n.

**excrescent (adj.)**

lump, growth; eyesore, disfigurement

a distinct, abnormal outgrowth (on a human, animal, or plant); a feature that is unattractive or unnecessary

---

## 26 **extradite** v.

**extradition (n.)**

deliver, surrender

to hand over an accused offender or criminal to the authorities of the nation where the alleged crime was committed

---

## 27 **feign** v.

**feigned (adj.)**

pretend, invent

to put on an act or make something up

## 28 **gratification** n.

gratify (v.)

bonus; contentment, delight

a reward or compensation; the act of pleasing, the state of being satisfied, or the source of pleasure or satisfaction

## 29 **humbug** n.

fake; impostor; nonsense; sweet

a hoax or fraud; a deceptive or insincere person; an absurd language, conduct, or idea; a hard (striped, peppermint-flavored) candy

## 30 **importunate** adj.

importune (v.), importunity (n.)

insistent, tenacious

thoughtlessly or annoyingly persistent in requesting or demanding

## 31 **impugn** v.

impugnable (adj.)

challenge, dispute

to attack, argue against, or call into question the truth or validity of

## 32 **inapt** adj.

inaptitude (n.)

unfit, irrelevant

not appropriate or suitable

## 33 **infidelity** n.

adultery, disloyalty; faithlessness

the act or state of being unfaithful to one's spouse or partner or to some moral obligation; lack of belief in a particular religion

## 34 **inflammation** n.

inflammatory (adj.)

rash, sore

a physical response of the body marked by redness, swelling, heat, etc., as a reaction to infection or injury

## 35 **lambaste** v.

condemn, censure; strike, batter
to criticize or scold harshly; to assault or beat severely

## 36 **laudatory** adj.

**laud (v.)**

glorifying, complimentary
expressing praise or appreciation, especially publicly

## 37 **milestone** n.

achievement, turning point; milepost, marker
an important event or stage in development (in history, for a person, etc.); a stone that marks the distance in miles to a specific place

## 38 **misanthrope** n.

**misanthropy (n.), misanthropic (adj.)**

cynic, pessimist
a person who dislikes or distrusts humankind

## 39 **monolith** n.

**monolithic (adj.)**

block; tower; establishment
a huge stone, usually serving as a monument; any massive structure; a huge organization acting as a single, powerful force

## 40 **munificent** adj.

**munificence (n.)**

unsparing, lavish
extremely generous or liberal in giving

## 41 **nominal** adj.

formal; unimportant; approximate; satisfactory
in name only; trivial or insignificant; theoretical or without adjustment; according to design or plan; of or relating to names; relating to nouns

vocabulary

### 42 **ode** n.

**odist (n.)**

✑ lyric poem

a poetical composition often devoted to the praise of a person or thing

---

### 43 **patriarch** n.

**patriarchal (adj.), patriarchy (n.)**

✑ father, leader

the male head or founder of a family, tribe, state, organization, etc.; a dignified elderly man; the oldest representative of a group

---

### 44 **petrify** v.

**petrification (n.), petrified (adj.)**

✑ fossilize; numb; terrify

to change (organic material) into a stony substance or form; to paralyze or make inactive; to stun with fear or amazement

---

### 45 **prerogative** n.

✑ entitlement, advantage

an exclusive right or privilege belonging to a particular individual, group, or class

---

### 46 **quixotic** adj.

✑ unrealistic, romantic

exceedingly or foolishly idealistic or impractical

---

### 47 **rationalism** n.

**rationalist (n./adj.), rationalistic (adj.)**

the belief or theory that reason should be the fundamental criteria in basing one's actions or opinions

---

### 48 **resplendent** adj.

**resplendence (n.)**

✑ dazzling, splendid

shining brilliantly or strikingly colorful

---

## 49 **suture** n.

⌐ stitch; junction

a thread used to close a wound; a fixed joint between two bones

## 50 **vernacular** adj.

**vernacularize (v.)**

⌐ regional, nonstandard

(of a language, dialect, terminology, etc.) native to a particular group, place, or period

## 01 **abridge** v.
**abridgement (n.), abridged (adj.)**
✎ trim, clip
to shorten a literary work without losing the central points

## 02 **accredit** v.
**accreditation (n.), accredited (adj.)**
✎ attribute; certify
to give credit for; to officially recognize that certain standards have been satisfied

## 03 **acrid** adj.
✎ pungent, harsh; sarcastic, bitter
having a sharp and awful taste or smell; very irritating or angry

## 04 **admonition** n.
**admonish (v.)**
✎ advice, caution
a warning to correct someone's behavior or fault

## 05 **albeit** conj.
✎ though, even though
although

## 06 **alignment** n.
**align (v.)**
✎ sequence; position
an arrangement of things in a line; a condition of cooperation or alliance

## 07 **allegiance** n.
✎ faithfulness, fidelity
loyalty to a cause, nation, or ruler

## 08 **apiculture** n.

apiculturist (n.), apicultural (adj.)

⚷ beekeeping

the raising of bees on a large scale

## 09 **assailant** n.

assail (v.), assailable (adj.)

⚷ assaulter, mugger

a person who attacks violently

## 10 **bereave** v.

bereaved (adj.), bereavement (n.)

⚷ rob; sadden

to take away; to leave someone in a state of emptiness, especially by the death of a loved one

## 11 **burlesque** n.

⚷ parody, mockery

a humorously exaggerated imitation of something (as in literature, theater, or drama)

## 12 **combustion** n.

combust (v.), combustive (adj.)

⚷ ignition; commotion

the act, instance, or process of burning, or a chemical process that creates heat or light; intense agitation or excitement

## 13 **commercial** adj./n.

commerce (n.), commercialize (v.)

⚷ corporate; marketable, monetary; endorsement

relating to trade or businesses; planned or created to have mass appeal, or functioning mainly to make profit; an advertisement of any form

## 14 **compunction** n.

compunctious (adj.)

⚷ remorse, qualm

an uneasy feeling arising from a sense of guilt or regret

## 15 **conservatory** n.

conservatoire (alt.)

greenhouse; academy

a glass room or house for displaying plants; a school for music or other fine arts

---

## 16 **contrivance** n.

contrive (v.), contrived (adj.)

gadget, tactic

a device made or planned for a certain purpose, such as a mechanical tool or a sophisticated scheme

---

## 17 **crestfallen** adj.

disheartened, dispirited

sad or depressed after experiencing disappointment; having a head hanging or bending downward

---

## 18 **cudgel** n./v.

club; ponder

a short, thick, and heavy stick used as a weapon; to think hard or exercise one's brain

---

## 19 **debonair** adj.

gentlemanly, confident; easy-going, casual

(of a man) stylish and charming; having a carefree mannerism

---

## 20 **defamation** n.

defame (v.), defamatory (adj.)

slander, character assassination

the act of injuring the good reputation of a person

---

## 21 **defecate** v.

defecation (n.), defecator (n.)

excrete; expel

to discharge waste from the bowels; to remove or become free from things that are considered impure or corrupt

## 22 **denounce** v.

**denouncement** (n.), **denunciation** (n.)

accuse, condemn; terminate, pull out of

to speak out against or criticize publicly or formally; to announce formally the ending of a treaty, pact, armistice, etc.

## 23 **deployment** n.

**deploy** (v.), **deployable** (adj.)

grouping, implementation; stationing, positioning

the act of arranging, classifying, or putting something into use; the distribution, arrangement, or extension of military forces

## 24 **derisive** adj.

**deride** (v.), **derision** (n.)

mocking, taunting

expressing or deserving ridicule

## 25 **desperado** n.

criminal, outlaw

a reckless person characterized by readiness to commit crime or violence

## 26 **doppelganger** n.

double, look-alike

someone who is nearly exact in appearance as someone else

## 27 **estranged** adj.

**estrangement** (n.)

alienated; separated

no longer close or having lost former affection; (of a husband or wife) no longer living together

## 28 **excise** n./v.

**excised** (adj.), **excision** (n.)

duty; fee; cut away, scratch out

a tax levied within a country (such as for tobacco, liquor, etc.); a payment for a license or privilege; to remove (surgically, from a text, etc.)

## 29 **fleck** n.

**flecked (adj.)**

speck; particle

a tiny patch of light or color; a tiny flake

## 30 **forlorn** adj.

cheerless, neglected; hopeless, discouraged

feeling sad, deserted, or lonely; not likely to succeed, or without hope

## 31 **geriatric** adj.

**geriatrics (n.)**

senior, aged; outmoded, old-fashioned

of or relating to the elderly; old, out-of-date, or obsolete

## 32 **heathen** n.

**heathenish (adj.)**

nonbeliever, infidel; barbarian, brute

anyone who is not a Christian (or Jew or Muslim); a savage or an uncultured person

## 33 **heteromorphic** adj.

**heteromorphism (n.)**

irregular, atypical

differing or deviating from the standard or normal form, or having or showing different forms in different stages of development in life

## 34 **ignominious** adj.

**ignominy (n.)**

humiliating, detestable

bringing or deserving disgrace, dishonor, or shame

## 35 **indentured** adj.

**indenture (n./v.)**

obligated, pledged

bound by contract or official agreement

## 36 **insatiable** adj.

**insatiability (n.)**

⬧ unquenchable, unappeasable

not capable of being satisfied, or extremely greedy

---

## 37 **intransigence** n.

**intransigent (adj./n.)**

⬧ hardheadedness, stubbornness

unwillingness to agree or change one's views or attitude

---

## 38 **kindred** n./adj.

⬧ kin, cousin; related, connected

family, relatives, or relations; of similar or like nature or kind

---

## 39 **nebulous** adj.

⬧ uncertain, imprecise; shapeless, blurry

ambiguous or ill-defined (as in ideas, concepts, etc.); like a cloud, or having no definite physical form or shape

---

## 40 **pandemic** n./adj.

⬧ outbreak; prevalent

a disease affecting a wide geographic area; widespread or universal

---

## 41 **pandemonium** n.

⬧ uproar, chaos

a loud or confused state or activity

---

## 42 **peripheral** adj./n.

**periphery (n.)**

⬧ outer, surrounding; lesser, minor; auxiliary

on the edge or boundary of something; only secondary, or unimportant; a device not part of the main computer (as in printer, keyboard, etc.)

### 43 **phlegm** n.

mucous secretion; self-control

thick mucus produced in the respiratory passage and released from the throat; bold calmness or indifferent coldness

---

### 44 **pittance** n.

scrap, next to nothing

a small amount or allowance of money, wage, food, etc.

---

### 45 **prate** v.

chatter, babble

to talk long and foolishly

---

### 46 **preamble** n.

**preambular (adj.)**

foreword, preface; preliminary, prelude

an introductory statement or remark, especially one to a formal document or written law; an introductory fact, event, circumstance, etc.

---

### 47 **sycophant** n.

**sycophancy (n.), sycophantic (adj.)**

flatterer, fawner

one who seeks favor or advantage by praising wealthy or powerful people

---

### 48 **tepid** adj.

**tepidity (n.)**

lukewarm; indifferent

slightly or moderately warm; having or showing little enthusiasm or passion

---

### 49 **veneer** n.

**veneering (n.)**

coating, overlay; show, guise

a thin layer or covering of fine or expensive material; a display or appearance that is attractive but superficial

## 50 **veracity** n.

**veracious (adj.)**

honesty, integrity; accuracy, precision

devotion to speaking or stating the truth; accordance with the facts or truth

# List 34

---

### 01 **abrasion** n.

**abrade (v.), abrasive (adj.)**

erosion, corrosion; cut, injury

the act of wearing away by friction; a wound caused by scraping

---

### 02 **accost** v.

confront, call to

to approach and speak to someone boldly with a demand or request

---

### 03 **amass** v.

collect, hoard

to gather together, pile up, or form into a mass over time

---

### 04 **askew** adj.

tilted, slanting

not straight, level, or in line

---

### 05 **atrocity** n.

**atrocious (adj.)**

brutality, horror

an act of extreme cruelty

---

### 06 **authenticate** v.

**authentication (n.)**

verify, confirm

to prove or determine something to be true or genuine

---

### 07 **barrage** n.

bombardment; torrent

a concentrated attack with heavy guns; something that appears rapidly and repeatedly in great amount

---

## 08 **bower** n./v.

alcove, summerhouse; hook; envelop, shroud

a leafy shade or shelter in a garden, or a cottage in the woods; a ship's bow anchor; to shade or enclose

---

## 09 **cauldron** n.

caldron (alt.)

hotspot; vessel

a situation or place marked by instability, danger, or intense emotions; a big metal pot for boiling or cooking

---

## 10 **chagrin** n.

chagrined (adj.)

dismay, annoyance

distress caused by humiliation or mistakes made

---

## 11 **chastise** v.

chastisement (n.)

criticize; lash

to scold severely; to punish by beating or whipping

---

## 12 **citadel** n.

stronghold, shelter

a fortress that acts as a command center or place of safety and typically rests high above a city

---

## 13 **compulsion** n.

compel (v.)

craving; coercion

an irresistible desire to do something; a force that urges

---

## 14 **conciliatory** adj.

conciliate (v.), conciliation (n.), conciliator (n.)

pacifying, peacemaking

tending or willing to put an end to a disagreement or hostility

Part 1

vocabulary

## 15 conglomerate n./adj.

**conglomeration (n.)**

group; composite; assorted

a large, diversified corporation; a cluster or mixture; (made up of separate parts) collected into a compact form or mass

## 16 consort n.

husband, wife; cooperation; escort

a spouse or a companion; an associate, association, or an agreement or pact; a ship or vessel that accompanies another

## 17 contiguous adj.

**contiguity (n.)**

adjacent, bordering; uninterrupted, consecutive

being in direct contact; connecting in unbroken sequence or near in time

## 18 contort v.

**contortion (n.)**

distort, deform

to twist violently or bend out of shape

## 19 covet v.

**covetous (adj.)**

desire, long for

to want to have something with eagerness (especially that belonging to someone else)

## 20 deleterious adj.

damaging, dangerous

causing harm, mostly in an unexpected way

## 21 depository n.

**depositary (alt.)**

storehouse, vault; trustee, keeper

a place where things are stored for protection or preservation; a person who is entrusted with something

## 22 **encumber** v.

encumbrance (n.)

burden, impede

to weigh down or restrict

## 23 **eschew** v.

eschewal (n.)

keep clear of, shun

to abstain from or avoid

## 24 **fissure** n.

crevice; difference

a narrow opening, line, or crack; a disagreement in ideas, views, etc.

## 25 **foist** v.

pass off, impose

to offer or force upon something useless or fake as necessary or worthy

## 26 **fraught** adj.

full of, packed; agitating, disturbing

filled, loaded, or furnished with; causing distress or anxiety

## 27 **furlough** n.

break, discharge

a leave of absence (especially for soldiers or government employees), or a temporary layoff from work or release from prison

## 28 **grandeur** n.

splendor, glory

the state of being impressive or magnificent

## 29 **hiatus** n.

gap, interruption

a break in a process, sequence, or time; having two vowel sounds without an intervening consonant

## 30  **hitherto** adv.

↗ so far, thus far

up to or until this (or that) time

---

## 31  **inchoate** adj.

**inchoation (n.)**

↗ undeveloped, immature; chaotic, unclear

just begun or not yet fully formed; disordered, confused, or incoherent

---

## 32  **ingratiate** v.

**ingratiation (n.), ingratiating (adj.)**

↗ charm, gain favor

to get on the good side of someone through flattery

---

## 33  **latent** adj./n.

**latency (n.)**

↗ potential; undeveloped; mark

existing but not yet obvious or active (as in talent, power, etc.); lying dormant (as in cocoons, buds, virus, etc.); a hardly visible fingerprint

---

## 34  **ludicrous** adj.

↗ absurd, idiotic

so ridiculous or exaggerated as to cause amusement or laughter

---

## 35  **miscreant** n.

↗ villain, wrongdoer

a criminal or evil person

---

## 36  **misdemeanor** n.

**misdemeanant (n.)**

↗ misdeed, violation

a minor wrongdoing, offense, or crime

---

## 37 **nexus** n.

bond; network; core

a connection or link between people or things; a connected series or group; a center or focus of something

---

## 38 **obfuscate** v.

**obfuscation (n.)**

blur, bewilder

to make obscure, unclear, or more confusing

---

## 39 **overshadow** v.

outweigh; darken

to appear or be more important, impressive, or successful than someone or something by comparison; to cast a shadow over

---

## 40 **panacea** n.

remedy, cure-all

a solution or cure for all ills or difficulties

---

## 41 **perigee** n.

the point in an orbit about Earth (or any planet) that is the nearest distance from it

---

## 42 **plaudit** n.

approval, acclaim; ovation

an enthusiastic praise; a round of applause

---

## 43 **poignant** adj.

**poignancy (n.)**

moving, stirring; piercing; pungent

emotionally touching, or evoking painful feelings; sharp, biting, or to the point; sharp or pervasive in smell

---

## 44 **premonition** n.

**premonitory (adj.)**

forewarning; presentiment

a notice or warning in advance; a feeling that something (especially something bad) is about to happen

---

### 45 **rancor** n.

**rancorous (adj.)**

spite, resentment

deep-seated hatred or bitterness

---

### 46 **reparation** n.

amends; restoration

the act of making up (or something to make up) for an injury, damage, or past wrong; a repairing of something

---

### 47 **retroactive** adj.

**retroactivity (n.)**

retrospective, ex post facto

taking effect from some specific date in the past

---

### 48 **risqué** adj.

improper, naughty

daringly suggestive, or very close to being indecent

---

### 49 **staid** adj.

steady, unadventurous

calm, serious, and not impulsive

---

### 50 **vis-à-vis** prep./n.

in relation to; opposite; as compared with; equivalent; chat

with regard to; face to face with; in comparison with; a counterpart; a private conversation between two individuals

---

vocabulary

# List 35

✐ = Synonyms, related words

## 01 **abut** v.

**abutment (n.)**

✐ touch, be next to

to have a mutual boundary or border

## 02 **accomplice** n.

✐ collaborator, co-conspirator

a person who assists in committing a crime

## 03 **acrimonious** adj.

**acrimony (n.)**

✐ scathing, biting

sharp or angry in language or tone

## 04 **adduce** v.

✐ cite, present

to bring forward or offer as evidence

## 05 **aggrandize** v.

**aggrandizement (n.)**

✐ boost, enlarge

to increase the power, wealth, or reputation

## 06 **alienate** v.

**alienation (n.), alienable (adj.)**

✐ break off, detach

to isolate, turn away, or set apart

## 07 **amiss** adj./adv.

✐ flawed; inappropriately

out of place or order; wrongly

Part 1

vocabulary

## 08 **articulate** adj.

**articulation (n.), articulately (adv.)**

 eloquent; jointed

being able to express oneself clearly and effectively; having segments connected by joints

---

## 09 **avid** adj.

**avidity (n.), avidly (adv.)**

 eager, passionate

having intense enthusiasm, sometimes to the point of being greedy

---

## 10 **batten** v./n.

 feed on, prosper; bolt, clamp

to grow fat or improve in condition at the expense of others; a strip of wood or piece of steel to hold something in place

---

## 11 **besiege** v.

 encircle; appeal; agonize

to surround, as with a huge crowd or armed forces; to overwhelm with requests or petitions; to cause a person to worry

---

## 12 **blithe** adj.

 thoughtless, casual; cheerful, carefree

showing a lack of concern or consideration; showing a happy and lighthearted mood or temper

---

## 13 **circulatory** adj.

**circulation (n.)**

 circular

relating to the body system that moves blood around; going around

---

## 14 **civic** adj.

**civics (n.)**

 municipal, public

relating to a town or city, citizens, or citizenship

---

## 15 collusion n.

collude (v.), collusive (adj.)

conspiracy, scheme

a secret agreement or cooperation, especially to engage in an illegal activity

## 16 commemorate v.

commemoration (n.), commemorative (adj./n.)

honor, pay tribute to

to maintain the memory of someone or something, or to do so through a celebration, observation, or ceremony

## 17 credence n.

credent (adj.)

confidence; credentials

acceptance of a claim as true; supporting material that provides confidence; a table on which bread and wine rest before Christian religious services

## 18 culprit n.

suspect, offender; trigger, root

a person accused or guilty of a crime or misdeed; the cause of a problem or difficulty

## 19 despot n.

despotic (adj.), despotism (n.)

tyrant, dictator

a ruler exercising absolute power, or a person who exercises power in a cruel and oppressive way

## 20 diabolical adj.

diabolic (alt.)

vicious, vile; satanic, demonic

extremely cruel or wicked; relating to or concerning the devil

## 21 dilatory adj.

stalling, putting off; tardy, sluggish

intentionally causing delay, wasting time, or gaining time; slow to act or in doing something

vocabulary

## 22 **foible** n.

fault, shortcoming

a minor weakness or small flaw in someone's character or behavior; the weaker part (between the middle and the point) of a sword blade

---

## 23 **fraternize** v.

**fraternization (n.)**

bond, consort

to have friendly relations with someone, especially with one considered an enemy

---

## 24 **fraudulent** adj.

**fraudulence (n.)**

dishonest, false

acting with, based on, or obtained by deceit

---

## 25 **gumption** n.

common sense, prudence

boldness and resourcefulness

---

## 26 **homely** adj.

**homeliness (n.)**

simple; unattractive

not elaborate, elegant, or complex; plain or not good-looking in appearance

---

## 27 **husbandry** n.

farming; conservation

the science or practice of agriculture; careful and prudent management of resources

---

## 28 **impertinent** adj.

**impertinence (n.)**

impolite, unmannerly; unrelated, immaterial

characterized by insolence or rudeness; not relevant or appropriate

---

## 29 **inane** adj.

blank, devoid; pointless, foolish

empty or vacant; having little or no sense or meaning

---

## 30 **incarnate** adj.

**incarnation (n.)**

*materialized; personified; rosy*

given a bodily (especially a human) form; being a living example of; pinkish, red, or flesh-colored

---

## 31 **incense** n./v.

*spice; aroma; compliment; enrage*

substance or perfume that produces smoke or fragrance when burned; any pleasant scent; a praise or flattery; to cause anger or indignation

---

## 32 **inception** n.

**inceptive (adj.)**

*beginning, origin*

the start or creation of something

---

## 33 **indefatigable** adj.

**indefatigability (n.)**

*determined*

persistent and untiring

---

## 34 **infinitesimal** adj.

*tiny, minute*

exceedingly or immeasurably small; of or relating to a value approaching zero

---

## 35 **inopportune** adj.

*unexpected; improper*

happening at an inconvenient time; unsuitable for a specific situation

---

## 36 **interlocutor** n.

**interlocution (n.), interlocutory (adj.)**

*conversationalist, speaker*

one taking part in a dialogue or discussion

## 37 **irk** v.

**irksome (adj.)**

bother, vex

to irritate or annoy

---

## 38 **jargon** n.

**jargonistic (adj.), jargonize (v.)**

specialized language; gibberish; jargoon

a technical terminology used in specific work, profession, etc.; a mixed, unfamiliar, or incoherent speech or writing; a variety of mineral zircon

---

## 39 **jovial** adj.

**joviality (n.)**

jolly, friendly

cheerful or full of good humor

---

## 40 **menacing** adj.

**menace (n.)**

threatening, frightening

suggesting imminent harm or danger

---

## 41 **mogul** n.

magnate, tycoon; hump, pile

a rich, important, or powerful person; a bump or mound on a ski slope

---

## 42 **multinational** n./adj.

**multinationalism (n.)**

conglomerate, group; international, global

a large corporation operating in multiple countries; of, relating to, or involving (individuals of) several countries

---

## 43 **pallid** adj.

white, wan; dull, unimaginative

pale or lacking color; insipid or lacking liveliness

---

## 44 **polemic** n.
**polemical (adj.)**

disputation; criticism

(one who engages in) a controversial discussion; a strong attack on another's principles or opinions

## 45 **precept** n.

commandment, doctrine; writ, warrant

a general rule or direction intended to regulate conduct or thought; a written order issued by legal authority

## 46 **proclamation** n.
**proclaim (v.)**

declaration, statement

an official public announcement

## 47 **progenitor** n.

forefather; founder

a parent or ancestor in the direct line, or a biological ancestor of a species; the originator or precursor of something

## 48 **quandary** n.

dilemma, predicament

a state of uncertainty or doubt

## 49 **recalcitrant** adj.
**recalcitrance (n.)**

defiant, disobedient

unwilling to cooperate or obey authority

## 50 **sybarite** n.
**sybaritic (adj.)**

sensualist, libertine

one devoted to luxury and sensual pleasures

# List 36

## 01 **accentuate** v.

**accentuation (n.), accentual (adj.)**

✎ highlight, stress

to make more noticeable or emphasize

## 02 **allegedly** adv.

**allege (v.), alleged (adj.), allegation (n.)**

✎ supposedly, presumably

according to some claim without proof

## 03 **aloof** adj.

**aloofness (n.)**

✎ detached, remote

physically or emotionally distant, or not friendly

## 04 **amputate** v.

**amputation (n.), amputee (n.)**

✎ sever, cut off

to remove by surgery a part of the body, especially an arm or leg

## 05 **apposite** adj.

✎ relevant, appropriate

suitable to the situation or circumstance

## 06 **attenuate** v.

**attenuation (n.)**

✎ lessen, diminish; thin

to reduce or weaken the force, effect, value, amount, etc.; to make slender

## 07 **auburn** adj.

⌐ coppery, chestnut

of a reddish-brown color

---

## 08 **austerity** n.

**austere (adj.)**

⌐ self-discipline; humbleness

a stern or serious quality; a plain or simple quality

---

## 09 **brunt** n.

⌐ shock; bulk

a negative effect resulting from a blow or attack; the worst or the most difficult part of something

---

## 10 **bustling** adj.

**bustle (v./n.)**

⌐ lively, thriving

very busy or full of energy or activity

---

## 11 **camaraderie** n.

**comradery (alt.), comrade (n.)**

⌐ companionship, solidarity

a feeling or spirit of good friendship or trust among fellow members in a group

---

## 12 **careen** v.

⌐ hurtle; tip, waver; heave

to move swiftly and uncontrollably; to lean or tilt while moving or sway from side to side; to lean a ship on one side for maintenance

---

## 13 **cartographer** n.

**cartography (n.), cartographic (adj.)**

⌐ mapmaker

a person who draws or makes maps or charts

vocabulary

## 14 **conformity** n.

conform (v.), conformist (n.), conformism (n.)

obedience, observance; resemblance, likeness

the act of complying to standards, rules, or regulations; similarity in form or character

---

## 15 **confound** v.

surprise; go against; beat; embarrass; combine

to cause confusion; to contradict or prove something wrong; to defeat or destroy; to shame someone; to blend with or mix up something

---

## 16 **consortium** n.

consortia (pl.)

alliance, coalition

a partnership (usually businesses forming a temporary pact); the legal right of a spouse to a relationship provided by marriage

---

## 17 **conspiracy** n.

conspire (v.), conspirator (n.)

setup, ring, plot

(the act of making or a group that engages in) a secret plan that is mostly unlawful or harmful

---

## 18 **contentious** adj.

contention (n.)

controversial; aggressive

causing or likely to create a disagreement or dispute; tending to clash or always prepared to argue

---

## 19 **correlation** n.

correlate (v.)

relationship, association

a mutual connection between two or more things being compared

---

## 20 **coterie** n.

circle, clique

an exclusive, intimate group of individuals unified by shared interests

## 21 **deficit** n.

*shortage, loss

the amount by which something (especially a sum of money or a score in sports) is less than the necessary or desired amount

---

## 22 **depravity** n.

**depraved (adj.)**

*wickedness, corruption

a morally corrupt act or practice

---

## 23 **derelict** adj./n.

**dereliction (n.)**

*run-down, deserted; vagrant, bum

in a very bad condition because of disuse and neglect; a poor person without a home or job; a part of land exposed or left dry by receding water

---

## 24 **deterrent** adj.

**deter (v.), deterrence (n.)**

*precautionary, oppressive

preventing or serving to discourage something from happening, especially to discourage an attack or use of nuclear weapons

---

## 25 **devout** adj.

*pious; dedicated; genuine

having deep religious commitment; very serious about a belief or hobby; earnestly sincere

---

## 26 **elapse** v.

*go by, progress

to pass or slip by (regarding time)

---

## 27 **entourage** n.

*staff, retinue

a group of attendants or followers, usually accompanying an important person

---

## 28 **estuary** n.
**estuarine (adj.)**
inlet, mouth
a water passage where ocean tides and river join

## 29 **eulogize** v.
**eulogy (n.), eulogistic (adj.)**
commend, extol
to praise highly in writing or speech

## 30 **flail** v./n.
flap; strike
to wave or swing fiercely or violently; to beat or whip; a threshing tool or weapon

## 31 **fledgling** n.
chick; beginner, newcomer
a young bird; a person who is young or inexperienced, or something that is new or underdeveloped

## 32 **germinate** v.
**germination (n.)**
bud, shoot; emerge, arise
(of a seed) to begin to sprout or grow; to begin growing or developing

## 33 **granule** n.
**granular (adj.)**
speck, bit
a tiny grain or particle; a small bright spot on the sun's photosphere that lasts only briefly

## 34 **inanimate** adj.
lifeless, motionless; limp, listless
not having life, consciousness, or the ability to move; dull or spiritless

## 35 **inchmeal** adv.

bit by bit, slowly
gradually or little by little

---

## 36 **ingrate** n.

thankless person, self-seeker
an ungrateful person

---

## 37 **inscrutable** adj.

**inscrutability (n.)**
puzzling, mysterious
difficult or impossible to understand or interpret

---

## 38 **institutionalize** v.

**institutionalization (n.)**
standardize, systematize; hospitalize
to incorporate into or establish as a convention or normal practice; to commit someone to treatment or confinement in a facility

---

## 39 **kiln** n.

oven, furnace
a heated enclosure or chamber used for baking, burning, or drying

---

## 40 **magistrate** n.

civil officer; justice of the peace
an official authorized to supervise the law; a minor judiciary official with limited powers

---

## 41 **midwife** n./v.

**midwifery (n.)**
childbirth assistant; prompt
a person (typically a woman or trained nurse) who helps women in childbirth; to aid in
producing or bringing into being

---

## 42 **multifaceted** adj.

varied, versatile
having complex or multiple sides or aspects

---

vocabulary

### 43 **mundane** adj.

worldly, earthly; everyday, plain

of the world, as opposed to heavenly or spiritual; ordinary or commonplace

---

### 44 **overt** adj.

undisguised, apparent

not secret, or open to view

---

### 45 **parsimonious** adj.

**parsimony (n.)**

miserly, penny-pinching

very unwilling to spend money or use resources

---

### 46 **peruse** v.

**perusal (n.)**

study, scrutinize; skim, glance through

to read or examine thoroughly or carefully; to read or look over quickly or casually

---

### 47 **polytechnic** adj./n.

(a school) relating or devoted to various vocational, technical, or scientific subjects

---

### 48 **quorum** n.

the minimum number of members required to conduct business

---

### 49 **unequivocal** adj.

clear, straightforward; unquestionable, undeniable

unambiguous or unmistakable; not disputable

---

### 50 **whittle** v.

carve, model; erode, diminish

to cut off chips from or shape into an object out of wood with a knife; to reduce, remove, or eliminate slowly or gradually

---

# vocabulary
**Part 2**

# List 1

### 01 **amphibious** adj.
capable of living or functioning both on land and in water

### 02 **caricature** n.
a drawing of someone in which certain features are exaggerated

### 03 **coagulate** v.
to thicken into a semisolid or solid state

### 04 **conduction** n.
the conveying or transmission of fluid, heat, electricity, waves, etc., through a channel or medium

### 05 **congruent** adj.
harmonious or in agreement; (in geometry, of figures) having identical form

### 06 **contradiction** n.
a person, thing, statement, situation, etc., that is different or opposite to another

### 07 **corruption** n.
dishonest or unlawful behavior; departure from what is pure, original, or correct

### 08 **curtsy** n.
an act of greeting or respect mainly performed by women and involving a lowering of the body and bending of the knees

### 09 **deformity** n.
a physical, moral, or aesthetic disfigurement, defect, or flaw

### 10 **demented** adj.
mad or insane

## 11 **digress** v.
to move away from the main subject of attention

## 12 **disinfectant** n.
an agent or substance that destroys germs, viruses, bacteria, etc.

## 13 **domain** n.
a territory owned or controlled by a person, organization, or government; a sphere or field of knowledge, activity, or influence

## 14 **domesticity** n.
(devotion to or affection for) home or family life

## 15 **encampment** n.
a temporary shelter or accommodations, especially one set up or utilized by nomads or the military

## 16 **enfeeble** v.
to make weak

## 17 **entwine** v.
to twist together or around

## 18 **grid** n.
a network of straight lines crossing over each other to form squares; a system for distributing electricity; starting positions of cars in auto racing

## 19 **illuminant** adj.
giving off light

## 20 **impartial** adj.
unbiased, unprejudiced, or fair and just

## 21 **impersonate** v.
to pretend to be or imitate another person (to deceive) or character (to entertain)

## 22 implement v./n.

to carry out or put into effect; a tool or piece of equipment

## 23 infamy n.

a wicked act or event known widely and publicly

## 24 installation n.

a military or industrial base or establishment; a work of art exhibited in multiple components within a gallery

## 25 jeopardize v.

to expose to danger, risk, or failure

## 26 jolt v.

to jerk or shake suddenly and roughly; to surprise or shock

## 27 legible adj.

clear enough to be read, understood, or discovered

## 28 machinery n.

the organization, system, or structure by which something functions; the working parts of a machine, or machines in general

## 29 meander v.

to take or follow a winding course; to wander casually without having a specific destination

## 30 metropolitan adj.

denoting, relating to, or characteristic of a large city and its surrounding communities or the mother country of a colony

## 31 mutilation n.

the act of cutting off a limb or causing serious damage to the body of a person or animal; the act of ruining or spoiling the beauty or essence of

## 32 obsolete adj.

no longer useful, in use, or produced; old-fashioned or out of style; (in biology) indistinct or less developed

## 33 **prevail** v.

to overcome, finish first, or be victorious; to be current, widespread, or in existence; to convince, urge, or persuade

## 34 **projection** n.

a forecast or estimate; a thing that sticks out; the display of an image upon a screen; the transferring of one's own emotions to another

## 35 **pronounced** adj.

very distinct or noticeable

## 36 **provision** n.

food, drink, or other supplies prepared or collected for later use; a condition or requirement specified in a law or agreement

## 37 **rue** v.

to be sorry or feel apologetic about; to feel regret or sorrow

## 38 **skeptical** adj.

having or expressing doubt

## 39 **solicitor** n.

a lawyer; a legal officer of a town or city; a person who tries to persuade people to purchase, donate, contribute, etc.

## 40 **spartan** adj.

lacking in or avoidance of luxury; brave and highly disciplined

## 41 **sporadic** adj.

occurring irregularly, randomly, or occasionally

## 42 **stringent** adj.

strict or precise with regard to regulations, standards, or conditions

## 43 **subsequent** adj.

following in order, time, or place

## 44 **taxing** adj.

difficult or demanding, mentally or physically

## 45 **topography** n.

the precise, detailed description of the physical shape of an area; a graphic representation of the natural and man-made features on a map

## 46 **transcend** v.

to go beyond the limits of; to excel, surpass, or be superior to; to be beyond the material existence

## 47 **trivial** adj.

of little value, significance, or importance

## 48 **unintelligible** adj.

unable or impossible to be understood

## 49 **versatile** adj.

competent in many different things; having many uses or functions; movable in many directions

## 50 **virulent** adj.

deadly, or highly dangerous, poisonous, or infectious; bitterly resentful or hostile

# List 2

## 01 **amenity** n.
an attractive characteristic or feature of a place, climate, etc.; something that adds to comfort or ease of living; politeness, civility, or courtesy

## 02 **apprehend** v.
to capture or arrest; to comprehend or understand

## 03 **artillery** n.
large, cannon-like guns, or a military unit that uses such weapons

## 04 **bewilderment** n.
a feeling or the state of being confused or perplexed

## 05 **buccaneer** n.
a pirate; someone (especially in business or politics) who is daring, reckless, and devious

## 06 **charitable** adj.
generous in giving to the needy; kind, lenient, or merciful

## 07 **commodity** n.
a material or product that can be bought and sold; anything useful or valuable

## 08 **conjugate** v.
(in grammar) to alter the form of a word to indicate gender, tense, mood, etc.; to unite or join together

## 09 **decrypt** v.
to break a deliberately coded or distorted message, transmission, or signal

## 10 **deduce** v.
to reach an answer or conclusion by reasoning

## 11 **devastate** v.
to damage, ruin, or destroy; to make helpless or overwhelm with shock or grief

## 12 **disillusion** v.
to cause to lose belief or faith

## 13 **dissertation** n.
a long, formal essay on a subject, especially one completed for a doctorate

## 14 **divest** v.
to take away power or possession from someone or a specific quality of something; to rid of something no longer wanted or needed

## 15 **equilibrium** n.
a state in which conflicting interests or opposing forces achieve equality; a state of emotional, intellectual, or physical balance

## 16 **foment** v.
to stir up trouble, disorder, rebellion, etc.; to treat with warm cloth or medicated lotions

## 17 **glee** n.
great pleasure or delight; an unaccompanied part-song, usually for men's voices

## 18 **groundbreaking** adj.
introducing new or positive ideas or methods; of or relating to the ceremony celebrating a construction project

## 19 **hemorrhage** n.
profuse or heavy bleeding; a rapid, unmanageable loss of something in large amounts

## 20 **illusory** adj.
based on something unreal, imagined, or nonexistent

## 21 **indifferent** adj.
unmoved or uninterested; neutral or unbiased; neither too much nor too little, good nor bad, right nor wrong, etc.

## 22 **intuitive** adj.
based on feeling or instinct instead of conscious thought or reasoning

## 23 **knickknack** n.
a small article of little value, especially a trinket or ornament

## 24 **legacy** n.
money or property left to a person in a will; something inherited from a predecessor, ancestor, or the past

## 25 **materialistic** adj.
overly concerned with worldly possessions or wealth

## 26 **odious** adj.
disgusting, repulsive, or offensive

## 27 **postulate** v.
to suggest (an idea, theory, etc.) as a basis for argument or reasoning; to nominate or appoint to an office related to the Christian church

## 28 **predicament** n.
a difficult, awkward, or unpleasant situation or condition

## 29 **propel** v.
to cause to move forward or in a certain direction; to cause to engage in a particular activity

## 30 **reconcile** v.
to settle a difference between or restore friendship with; to make compatible, consistent, or harmonious; to cause to accept or submit

## 31 **reformation** n.
the act, process, or movement intended to make drastic changes to improve social, political, or religious practices or institutions

## 32 **reimburse** v.
to pay or give back money that has been spent or for damages or losses

### 33 **sally** v.

to rush forth to attack from a defensive position; to set out on a venture or make a side trip

---

### 34 **secular** adj.

worldly, as opposed to spiritual; having no connection with religion; happening once in an age or a century; continuing for a long time

---

### 35 **solace** n.

comfort in time of sorrow, grief, or loneliness; a source of comfort, relief, or consolation

---

### 36 **squall** n.

a sudden storm, usually with rain, snow, or sleet; a loud, harsh cry or scream; a brief commotion or disturbance

---

### 37 **stark** adj.

complete or absolute; sharp, distinct, or obvious; bleak or barren; fierce or severe; stiff or rigid; bare or naked

---

### 38 **subdue** v.

to defeat or bring under control by force; to repress or bring under control (feelings, emotions, etc.); to tone down or make less intense

---

### 39 **subsistence** n.

the minimum (food, money, etc.) required to stay alive; a source or way by which one maintains life; real being or existence

---

### 40 **sullen** adj.

sulky, bad-tempered, or resentfully silent; gloomy or depressing; somber or dull (sound, color, etc.); slow or sluggish

---

### 41 **synchronous** adj.

occurring together, or happening or existing at the same time; having the same phase, rate, or period between movements

---

### 42 **testimony** n.

a statement made under oath; an external or visible sign; an open declaration or acknowledgment; an account of first-hand or religious experience

---

vocabulary

### 43 **transmute** v.

to alter from one nature, species, substance, etc., into another

---

### 44 **travesty** n.

a farcical, inferior, or distorted imitation or representation of something

---

### 45 **unorthodox** adj.

different from what is considered normal or generally accepted

---

### 46 **uproarious** adj.

wild, disorderly, or very noisy; extremely funny or amusing

---

### 47 **vapid** adj.

dull, uninteresting, or uninspiring; flavorless or tasteless

---

### 48 **venous** adj.

of, relating to, or having veins; full of veins

---

### 49 **ventilate** v.

to circulate air; to replace or provide with fresh air; to investigate or discuss (a complaint, issue, question, etc.) in public

---

### 50 **warrant** v.

to require, necessitate, or call for; to guarantee or be sure of something; to authorize or give official permission

## List 3

### 01 **bereft** adj.
not having or no longer having something; suffering the loss of a loved one

### 02 **buffet** v.
to strike with the hand; to pound or beat against (as by waves, wind, etc.); to cause trouble or suffering to

### 03 **clamp** v.
to fasten together; to hold or grip tightly; to impose or exercise tight control over

### 04 **confer** v.
to grant or bestow a gift, title, degree, honor, right, etc.; to exchange opinions or seek advice

### 05 **defiance** n.
the act of resisting or disobeying boldly or openly

### 06 **delinquent** adj.
characterized by a tendency to engage in immoral or unlawful acts; failing in paying a debt

### 07 **dissolution** n.
the termination of an assembly, partnership, or organization; death or decay

### 08 **docile** adj.
submissive, obedient, or ready to accept control

### 09 **enactment** n.
the process of passing a law, or a law that has been passed; a process of playing or acting out a role

### 10 **ennoble** v.
to dignify or make honorable; to elevate to the rank of nobility

vocabulary

## 11 **enthrall** v.

to charm, fascinate, or capture the attention of; to enslave or reduce to slavery

## 12 **exodus** n.

a departure of a large group

## 13 **forswear** v.

to promise or agree to give up; to swear falsely

## 14 **illustrious** adj.

famous, distinguished, or admired because of honorable qualities or past achievements

## 15 **imbue** v.

to inspire, influence, or fill with a certain feeling or quality; to fill with color or dye

## 16 **impel** v.

to urge a person to do something; to propel, drive forward, or set in motion

## 17 **imperil** v.

to place in or expose to danger

## 18 **impermissible** adj.

inadequate or imperfect to be allowed

## 19 **intoxicate** v.

to stupefy or make drunk; to excite, thrill, or exhilarate; to poison

## 20 **loiter** v.

to stand about in an area without specific purpose; to walk slowly and with frequent stops; to spend time lazily and idly

## 21 **mediate** v.

to intervene between conflicting parties to settle or resolve their differences; to act as in-between mechanism or agent

## 22 **muffle** v.

to cover or wrap up for protection, warmth, or hiding; to mute or deaden a sound; to suppress, prevent, or keep down

---

## 23 **nascent** adj.

being born, or just coming into existence; starting to grow, form, or develop

---

## 24 **nicety** n.

precision, accuracy, or attention to small details; a detailed aspect of politeness or proper social behavior; something elegant, fine, or civilized

---

## 25 **par** n.

an equal value, status, or level; the average or normal amount, state, or condition; an accepted standard

---

## 26 **precinct** n.

a territorial division that defines a district for election, law enforcement, etc.; a boundary, or a space enclosed by walls

---

## 27 **proficient** adj.

highly skilled, practiced, or competent

---

## 28 **protrusion** n.

something that bulges or sticks out

---

## 29 **purport** v.

to claim, profess, or pretend to be or do something; to intend, plan, or propose

---

## 30 **rectify** v.

to adjust, correct, or set right

---

## 31 **refractory** adj.

difficult to manage or control; resistant to treatment; able to withstand heat; immune to infection; not responding to stimulus

---

## 32 **replicate** v.

to repeat, reproduce, or make a copy of

---

### 33 **rudimentary** adj.
basic, introductory, or elementary; crude, primitive, or unsophisticated

### 34 **scornful** adj.
full of contempt or disrespect

### 35 **scoundrel** n.
a dishonest, wicked, or unprincipled person

### 36 **sojourn** n.
a short or temporary stay

### 37 **somber** adj.
depressing, gloomy, or melancholy; serious, earnest, or grave; dull or dark in color or brightness

### 38 **spawn** v.
(of an aquatic animal) to produce, release, or deposit eggs; to produce offspring, especially in large numbers; to generate, give rise to, or bring forth

### 39 **starboard** n.
the right side of a ship or aircraft when facing forward

### 40 **stereotypical** adj.
relating to a fixed or oversimplified conception of a particular type of person or thing; commonplace or boring because of overuse

### 41 **stipend** n.
a fixed sum of money paid as a salary, pension, or allowance

### 42 **subversion** n.
the attempt to weaken or overthrow an established system or government

### 43 **synopsis** n.
a summary, outline, or abstract

### 44 **terrestrial** adj.

of or relating to the planet Earth; of or relating to ground or land as opposed to water or air; relating to worldly concerns or matters

### 45 **trepidation** n.

fear, anxiety, or feeling of uncertainty about something that one is about to do or experience

### 46 **uncompromising** adj.

unwilling to change or make concessions

### 47 **vascular** adj.

relating to veins or vessels, especially blood vessels

### 48 **vilify** v.

to write or speak harshly or abusively, and often unfairly, about someone or something

### 49 **vulgar** adj.

lacking sophistication, culture, or taste ; indecent, obscene, or offensive in language; common, popular, or generally accepted

### 50 **wade** v.

to walk through something (water, sand, tall grass, etc.) that hinders movement; to proceed with difficulty (such as a task, project, etc.)

Part 2

# List 4

---

### 01 **anarchism** n.
the political belief that laws or the government should be abolished

---

### 02 **anecdote** n.
a short story about an entertaining or interesting event

---

### 03 **anthropology** n.
the study of humans, especially their characteristics, customs, cultures, social relations, etc.

---

### 04 **artifact** n.
an object that was made or shaped by the people of the past

---

### 05 **avow** v.
to declare, admit, or assert openly

---

### 06 **cohabitation** n.
the act, state, or condition of living or existing together

---

### 07 **condensation** n.
water droplets that form on a cold surface in humid air; the conversion of vapor to liquid; a shorten version of a work

---

### 08 **convertible** adj.
capable of being changed or exchanged

---

### 09 **convoy** v.
to escort or accompany, especially in order to keep safe

---

### 10 **decimate** v.
to kill or destroy a large part of; to remove or kill one-tenth of a group

---

## 11 **default** n.

failure to fulfill an agreement, duty, obligation, etc.; an automatic selection made or given in the absence of a specified alternative

## 12 **demise** n.

death; the end of something; the transfer of an estate; the transfer of sovereignty to a successor

## 13 **diffusion** n.

the scattering (as in light) or spreading (as in news) of something

## 14 **disfigure** v.

to ruin or spoil the shape, appearance, or attractiveness of

## 15 **elasticity** n.

the capability of a body or substance to return to its normal shape after deformation; ability to adapt

## 16 **exalt** v.

to praise highly; to raise in rank, status, wealth, etc.; to intensify the activity or effect of

## 17 **fanatical** adj.

overly or unreasonably devoted toward a cause; extremely interested or enthusiastic about something

## 18 **fathom** v.

to understand or make sense of; to measure the depth of

## 19 **feral** adj.

of or relating to a wild animal; having the characteristics of a wild beast (as in being unruly, fierce, savage, etc.)

## 20 **fictitious** adj.

imaginary or made up; false, fake, or pretended

## 21 **foliage** n.

the leaves of plants or trees; a bundle of flowers, leaves, and branches

## 22 **haphazardly** adv.

in a random, disorganized, or disorderly manner

## 23 **haughty** adj.

arrogantly superior or proud

## 24 **hospitable** adj.

having a favorable, pleasant, or livable environment; open-minded or receptive; friendly, generous, or welcoming to guests

## 25 **hydraulic** adj.

relating to or operated by the movement of water; hardening under water

## 26 **illustrate** v.

to explain or make clear; to use examples for easier understanding; to provide with pictures, diagrams, or other visual features

## 27 **indiscernible** adj.

impossible to recognize or distinguish clearly

## 28 **inexhaustible** adj.

without end or limit; incapable of becoming tired or weary

## 29 **lassitude** n.

a lack of energy or interest

## 30 **lustrous** adj.

shining brightly; illustrious or radiant (as in character or reputation)

## 31 **melee** n.

a noisy, confused fight or struggle; a confused mixture or mass of people

## 32 **plummet** v.

to drop or fall swiftly and straight down; to decrease sharply and quickly

## 33 **purgatory** n.

any place or situation of temporary suffering, punishment, or misery

## 34 **realignment** n.

the act of changing, restoring, or regrouping a system, structure, organization, etc.

## 35 **refutation** n.

the act of proving that something is wrong, false, or untrue

## 36 **reminiscent** adj.

tending to remind a person of something from the past; suggestive of something by resemblance; absorbed in remembering past events or times

## 37 **reproach** v.

to criticize or express disappointment in someone for not meeting up to expectations

## 38 **respiratory** adj.

relating to breathing

## 39 **resurgent** adj.

rising again after a period of being less popular, important, or active

## 40 **scathe** v.

to harm or injure; to burn or scorch; to criticize or condemn severely

## 41 **scuffle** n.

a brief, confused fight at close quarters; the sound of shuffling, or the act of moving in a shuffling manner

## 42 **sear** v.

to wither or dry up; to burn, scorch, or injure with a sudden, intense heat; to mark or brand with a hot instrument or into memory

## 43 **sordid** adj.

dishonest, corrupt, or vile; dirty, filthy, or unpleasant

## 44 **spate** n.

a sudden rush or outburst; a large number or amount; a sudden flood or heavy rain

vocabulary

## 45 **surmise** v.

to form an idea or opinion without having conclusive or concrete evidence

## 46 **thrash** v.

to beat severely (with a whip or stick); to defeat overwhelmingly; to move about violently; to separate the grain from the husks by beating

## 47 **undulate** v.

to move in wavy or flowing manner, or to have a wavy form, surface, or edge

## 48 **utopian** adj.

of, relating to, or having the nature of a perfect society; ideal but not realistic or practical

## 49 **vale** n.

a valley; farewell

## 50 **vibrant** adj.

full of life, spirit, or enthusiasm; trembling or pulsating; vivid or bright in color; (of sound) resounding or resonating

# List 5

### 01 **bogus** adj.
not real, true, or genuine

### 02 **compromise** v.
to settle by mutual agreement; to reveal or expose; to weaken or cause to become vulnerable or ineffective

### 03 **congregate** v.
to gather into a crowd or unite into a single mass

### 04 **cuisine** n.
a certain way of cooking or preparing food, especially one associated with a particular region or country

### 05 **disarray** n.
a disorderly or untidy condition; the state of being dressed insufficiently or carelessly

### 06 **disciplinary** adj.
of or having to do with behaving in a controlled way, exercising self-control, or imposing punishment; of or relating to a specific field of study

### 07 **dispossess** v.
to take away land or other possessions

### 08 **disruptive** adj.
tending to interrupt or prevent the normal course or usual operation of

### 09 **dour** adj.
harsh, stubborn, or cheerless in appearance or manner

### 10 **enervate** v.
to reduce or lessen the moral, mental, or physical strength or vigor of

## 11  **entrepreneur** n.

a person who sets up, manages, and takes on risks associated with operating a business or enterprise

## 12  **evict** v.

to remove or expel a tenant from a property by legal process

## 13  **execute** v.

to perform, carry out, or put into effect; to put to death

## 14  **facile** adj.

easy or achieved without much effort; smooth, confident, or fluent; superficial, shallow, or too simplistic

## 15  **formidable** adj.

causing dread or fear; difficult to overcome; inspiring awe or respect

## 16  **fugitive** n.

a person who tries to escape danger, persecution, or law enforcement; something that does not last long or is difficult to find

## 17  **impeccable** adj.

not capable of sinning; perfect, or without flaws or errors

## 18  **insurgence** n.

a rebellion, uprising, or revolt; a large increase

## 19  **literate** adj.

able to read and write; well-read, or knowledgeable or versed in literature; expressed clearly; having competence or adequate ability

## 20  **murky** adj.

dim, dark, or gloomy; foggy or misty (as in heaviness of air); dirty, dark, or not clear (as in liquid); questionable, vague, or suspicious

## 21  **nosedive** n.

a downward headlong plunge of an aircraft or any flying object; a sudden fall or drop

## 22 **oblivious** adj.

not aware of or caring about what is happening; uninformed about something; forgetful or lacking memory

## 23 **pestilence** n.

a deadly and infectious epidemic disease; anything dangerous or harmful

## 24 **proponent** n.

one who actively supports a theory, plan, cause, etc.; one who offers or makes a plan, idea, or proposal

## 25 **quaint** adj.

having unusual or old-fashioned attractiveness, appeal, or charm

## 26 **quarantine** n.

a state, period, or place of isolation to contain a contagious disease; a period of forty days

## 27 **quibble** n.

a small complaint or criticism about something minor; an evasion of or shift from the main point

## 28 **quiver** n.

the act of trembling or shaking; a case for carrying arrows

## 29 **ravine** n.

a deep, narrow, and steep-sided gorge or valley

## 30 **realm** n.

a territory ruled by a king or a queen; a field, discipline, or sphere of knowledge, activity, or influence

## 31 **render** v.

to give or provide; to make or cause to become; to surrender; to translate, depict, or interpret; to declare or deliver a verdict, judgment, etc.

## 32 **repression** n.

the act or process of using force to subdue or control a group of people; the act or process of holding back an emotion, thought, etc.

## 33 **reprove** v.

to scold or express disapproval

## 34 **repugnant** adj.

distasteful, disgusting, or offensive; contradictory to or inconsistent with

## 35 **sanction** n.

an official or authorized approval for an action; a coercive measure intended to enforce a treaty or international law

## 36 **scriptural** adj.

of, relating to, or based on a sacred writing, especially the Bible

## 37 **static** adj.

lacking in movement or change

## 38 **stunt** v.

to hinder or prevent from developing, progressing, or growing; to perform a spectacular, dangerous, or difficult feat

## 39 **suitor** n.

a man who seeks to marry a particular woman; one seeking to acquire a business; one who petitions or request; one who sues at law

## 40 **sully** v.

to damage the purity, sacredness, or reputation of

## 41 **sustenance** n.

food or nourishment; means of support or source of income

## 42 **talisman** n.

an object thought to bring good luck or provide protection against evil; something that apparently has magical powers

## 43 **tarnish** v.

to stain, or to dull or lose the glow or brightness of; to damage the reputation or good image of

## 44 **teeter** v.

to move unsteadily; to be indecisive; to be close to a negative situation

## 45 **trite** adj.

boring or unoriginal because of being used so many times

## 46 **unadulterated** adj.

not mixed or having anything added; complete, absolute, or total

## 47 **underhanded** adj.

dishonest, deceitful, or sly

## 48 **understatement** n.

a statement of something as being less important, serious, or intense than it actually is

## 49 **underworld** n.

the world of organized crime; the world of the dead

## 50 **ungainly** adj.

clumsy or ungraceful in movement; unattractive or awkward in appearance; hard to handle or manage

vocabulary

# List 6

### 01 **affluence** n.
abundance or the state of having great wealth

### 02 **anonymity** n.
the state of being unknown or having unknown origin, identity, or authorship; the state of lacking interesting or outstanding characteristics

### 03 **antipathy** n.
a strong or deep-seated dislike; an object of disgust or aversion

### 04 **apparatus** n.
the materials or tools needed for a specific purpose; a functional structure within a system or organization

### 05 **arable** adj.
(of land) suitable for producing crops

### 06 **archipelago** n.
a group of islands; a sea containing many scattered islands

### 07 **charismatic** adj.
having a unique or special quality that attracts or inspires people

### 08 **compression** n.
the act, process, or state of being pressed or squeezed together to reduce in size or volume

### 09 **concurrent** adj.
existing or occurring at the same time or place; moving toward or intersecting in a point; acting in conjunction; having equal authority

### 10 **damper** n.
someone or something that reduces, discourages, or inhibits

## 11 **decomposition** n.

the act of separating into parts; the process of decaying or rotting

---

## 12 **discount** v.

to deduct an amount from the usual price or cost; to set aside, disregard, or lessen the importance of something

---

## 13 **dismissive** adj.

showing or indicating that something is unworthy of attention or consideration

---

## 14 **eccentric** adj.

unconventional, odd, or not quite normal (as in person or behavior); away from the (or having a different) center; having an elliptical path

---

## 15 **embark** v.

to go aboard a craft or vehicle; to begin, engage, or invest

---

## 16 **empathetic** adj.

of or characterized by the ability to understand and share another person's feelings

---

## 17 **exploitation** n.

the act of benefiting from others by taking advantage of their efforts or from utilizing resources; the act of depriving one's right to something

---

## 18 **frivolous** adj.

having little or no importance, value, or serious purpose; not serious, mature, or thoughtful

---

## 19 **incompatibility** n.

inability of (two) people or things to coexist, live together, or be used in combination

---

## 20 **inlet** n.

a narrow water passage extending into land from a lake, river, ocean, etc.; a way or means of entering

---

## 21 **inscription** n.

a writing carved on a coin, plaque, tomb, etc.; a message or dedication written in a book or work of art

---

## 22 **intercede** v.

to plead, ask, or make a request on someone else's behalf; to mediate in a dispute

---

## 23 **irrelevant** adj.

not connected, related, or applicable

---

## 24 **irreparable** adj.

not capable of being repaired, remedied, or cured

---

## 25 **lavish** adj.

abundant, generous, or luxurious

---

## 26 **loom** v.

to appear in an impressive, frightening, or shadowy form; (of an occurrence) to seem unpleasantly close

---

## 27 **monosyllabic** adj.

using few words or saying very little; consisting of one syllable

---

## 28 **outcry** n.

a strong anger, disapproval, or protest by the public or media; a loud shout or uproar

---

## 29 **prim** adj.

too formal, moral, or proper; neat, clean, or orderly

---

## 30 **promissory** adj.

specifying the fulfilling of the requirements in an insurance or other business contract or agreement; relating to a promise

---

## 31 **pseudonym** n.

a fictitious name, as in stage or pen name used by celebrities and authors

---

## 32 **pyre** n.

a funeral pile, or any heap of material to be burned

---

## 33 **recession** n.

a temporary economic decline or slowdown; the act of withdrawing or receding

## 34 **reiterate** v.

to say or do something again in order to clarify or emphasize

## 35 **renaissance** n.

a revival or rebirth, or a period or movement of renewed interest

## 36 **replete** adj.

filled with or having plenty of something; full to bursting or stuffed with food

## 37 **retribution** n.

the act of punishing or taking revenge for a crime, sin, or wrongdoing

## 38 **revelry** n.

noisy and lively partying

## 39 **reverberate** v.

to resound or echo repeatedly; to reflect, deflect, or rebound; to have a powerful effect on

## 40 **snowball** v.

to grow rapidly and uncontrollably in size or intensity

## 41 **subsidiary** n.

a company owned or controlled by a parent or holding company

## 42 **succulent** adj.

(of food) juicy, moist, or tender; (of plants) having fleshy leaves or stems that store moisture

## 43 **syntax** n.

the arrangement of words to form phrases, clauses, or sentences; an orderly or harmonious arrangement of parts of something

## 44 **technicality** n.

a small, formal point or detail in a rule or law; something particular to a specific field, profession, etc.

---

## 45 **tectonic** adj.

of or relating to the structure of the Earth's crust; having a significant effect or impact; of or relating to building, construction, or architecture

---

## 46 **traverse** v.

to travel over or across; to move back and forth over or along; to oppose or go against; to survey or examine

---

## 47 **tribunal** n.

a court of justice; the seat or bench of a judge; any seat that decides or judges

---

## 48 **unsettling** adj.

causing worry, uneasiness, or uncertainty

---

## 49 **unwarranted** adj.

not appropriate or necessary; lacking justification or official support

---

## 50 **vacuous** adj.

empty or void; lacking purpose or meaningful content; having or showing a lack of thought, ideas, or intelligence; idle or inactive

---

vocabulary

# List 7

---

## 01 **abash** v.
to cause someone to feel embarrassed or ashamed

---

## 02 **apprentice** n.
a person learning a trade from an established craftsman; a beginner in a field

---

## 03 **arcane** adj.
understood by only a few people; hidden, mysterious, or secret

---

## 04 **archaeology** n.
the study of past human life, culture, and history through excavating and analyzing ancient sites and artifacts

---

## 05 **arson** n.
the crime of intentionally setting fire to a property

---

## 06 **assassination** n.
the murder of a prominent person carried out suddenly or secretly

---

## 07 **atlas** n.
a book or collection of maps, charts, or graphs; the topmost vertebra of the neck; a supporting column in the figure of a man

---

## 08 **autobiography** n.
a self-written story or account of an individual's own life

---

## 09 **concession** n.
something granted or acknowledged; a right to do business or preferential rate given by an authority or organization

---

## 10 **cunning** adj.
skillful or ingenious; shrewd or devious; cute or attractive

---

Part 2

vocabulary

## 11 **disembark** v.

to leave a ship and go ashore; to leave a craft or vehicle

## 12 **disservice** n.

an unhelpful, harmful, or unkind act

## 13 **distraught** adj.

extremely troubled, nervous, or agitated; crazed or mentally unsound

## 14 **distribution** n.

the act or process of sharing among many; the act or process of delivering or spreading out; the process by which consumers obtain goods

## 15 **enlighten** v.

to give spiritual insight, knowledge, or understanding; to instruct or explain a certain subject or situation carefully

## 16 **foyer** n.

a hall or lobby of a theater, hotel, etc.

## 17 **garish** adj.

overly or disturbingly bright or showy

## 18 **hamper** v.

to restrict, limit, or interfere

## 19 **impediment** n.

anything than hinders, restrains, or obstructs; a disability, especially one that affects speech

## 20 **matrix** n.

numbers arranged into rows and columns; an environment in which something originates or takes form; a mold to cast or shape something

## 21 **prelude** n.

an introduction to something more important or to the main event; a piece of music introducing an opera

## 22 **prologue** n.

a foreword or introductory section or speech; a preceding event, situation, or development

## 23 **proverbial** adj.

widely known, or commonly referred to or spoken of

## 24 **rebuff** v.

to reject, refuse, or turn down in a sudden or harsh manner

## 25 **regent** n.

a person ruling a kingdom in place of a monarch who is ill, too young, or absent; a member of the governing board of a college

## 26 **regime** n.

a form of government; the administration in power; the ruling period of a person or system

## 27 **rendition** n.

a performance or interpretation of an artwork, musical work, etc.; translation; the handing over of a suspect to another country

## 28 **reprieve** n.

the suspension, postponement, or cancellation of a punishment; a temporary relief from pain, harm, or trouble

## 29 **rescind** v.

to repeal, cancel, or take back an order, agreement, law, etc.

## 30 **residue** n.

a remaining part, remnant, or leftovers

## 31 **resolution** n.

a formal decision by a group; a firm determination or willpower; the answer or solution to a problem; the sharpness and clarity of an image

## 32 **retention** n.

the act of remembering or ability to remember; the act of continuing to possess or control someone or something

## 33 **rummage** v.

to search or investigate thoroughly; to look for something hastily or haphazardly

## 34 **sanctity** n.

the state or quality of being, or anything considered, holy or sacred

## 35 **scant** adj.

barely enough or hardly any

## 36 **sobriety** n.

the state of not being drunk or addicted to alcohol; the state or quality of being thoughtful, serious, or calm; modesty in tone, color, or style

## 37 **spectral** adj.

of, relating to, or suggesting a ghost; of, relating to, or caused by a spectrum

## 38 **spurn** v.

to reject or refuse with contempt or scorn

## 39 **squabble** v.

to argue noisily about a petty or unimportant matter

## 40 **strife** n.

a bitter conflict, struggle, or contention

## 41 **subjugate** v.

to take completely control or impose obedience by force

## 42 **suppression** n.

the act of bringing under control by authority, keeping from public knowledge, or excluding from consciousness

### 43 **tacit** adj.

implied or understood without being directly or openly expressed

### 44 **tangible** adj.

capable of being touched, felt, or understood

### 45 **tranquilize** v.

to calm, sedate, or make unconscious by the use of a drug

### 46 **tributary** n.

a river or stream flowing into a larger body of water; a ruler or nation that makes payment to another ruler or nation in submission or for protection

### 47 **unanimous** adj.

in complete agreement or of one mind; having the consent of all involved

### 48 **untimely** adj.

happening before the expected, normal, or natural time; not suitable or appropriate for a particular situation

### 49 **vigilance** n.

the act or state of being on the lookout for possible danger

### 50 **whereupon** conj.

at which, upon which, or immediately after which

# List 8

### 01 **appease** v.
to calm or pacify by accepting the demands of or making concessions to; to relieve or quell a thirst, hunger, feeling of guilt, etc.

### 02 **aspiration** n.
a strong desire or ambition that one hopes to achieve

### 03 **balm** n.
a healing or soothing ointment; a pleasant, spicy fragrance; any of various aromatic mint plants

### 04 **braggart** n.
someone who boasts loudly, arrogantly, or exaggeratedly

### 05 **camouflage** n.
the method, behavior, or ability designed to deceive or escape notice by blending in with the surroundings

### 06 **composure** n.
the state of being calm and in control of one's mind or manner

### 07 **confederacy** n.
an alliance formed by a common purpose or to achieve a common goal

### 08 **decamp** v.
to depart or run away suddenly or secretly; to break up or leave a camp

### 09 **despicable** adj.
extremely unpleasant or deserving hatred

### 10 **dismal** adj.
depressing or gloomy; bad, disgraceful, or inadequate

## 11 **divergent** adj.

moving, developing, or extending in different directions; differing from a standard; different in interests, viewpoints, ideals, etc.

## 12 **dub** v.

to give a nickname or title; to make smooth; to confer knighthood; to do something poorly; to add sound; to make a copy of

## 13 **edgy** adj.

tense, irritable, or apprehensive; trendy, innovative, or daring

## 14 **eloquent** adj.

persuasive and articulate in expression; clearly expressive or revealing

## 15 **enmity** n.

a very deep or strong hatred or hostility

## 16 **epoch** n.

an event or period of time characterized by notable or memorable events; the beginning of a new or distinctive period or development

## 17 **erudite** adj.

having or showing exceptional academic knowledge

## 18 **forfeit** v.

to lose or be forced to lose a right, privilege, property, etc.

## 19 **frenzy** n.

a momentary rage or madness; a violent mental agitation; a state of unrestrained excitement or disorderly behavior

## 20 **grievance** n.

a feeling of being treated unfairly, or resentment over something believed to be unjust; a formal statement of a complaint

## 21 **impending** adj.

drawing near or about to happen

vocabulary

## 22 **insomnia** n.

a sleeping disorder characterized by the inability to sleep

## 23 **inundate** v.

to flood; to overwhelm with a large number or amount of people or things to be dealt with

## 24 **irony** n.

an expression actually meaning the opposite of the literal meaning, or a condition or result opposite to what was expected

## 25 **poach** v.

to cook in gently boiling liquid; to hunt or fish illegally; to trespass on or take something unfairly or illegally; to trample or soften by stamping

## 26 **prickle** v.

to experience a stinging or tingling sensation, physically or emotionally

## 27 **pseudo** adj.

not real, authentic, or genuine

## 28 **quack** n.

a fraudulent, untrained, or incompetent practitioner of medicine; a person who pretends to have knowledge or skill in a particular subject

## 29 **rampant** adj.

increasing or occurring frequently or widely; violent and unrestrained

## 30 **reenactment** n.

the acting out of an earlier, past, or historic event; the act of bringing into effect a past law

## 31 **reverence** n.

a feeling of (or act of showing) awe or deep respect

## 32 **rogue** n.

a dishonest, deceitful, or unreliable person; a playful, mischievous person; an animal living apart from the herd; an inferior variation or specimen

## 33 **saturate** v.

to cause to become completely soaked or penetrated; to cause to be filled to the point where no more can be added

---

## 34 **scour** v.

to clean or polish by rubbing hard with a rough material; to remove impurities; to search thoroughly; to move rapidly or swiftly over something

---

## 35 **scourge** n.

a source or cause of great trouble, suffering, or widespread destruction; a whip, or any instrument, used to inflict pain or punishment

---

## 36 **singe** v.

to burn slightly or lightly

---

## 37 **skirmish** n.

a minor or brief battle in war; a minor or unimportant dispute

---

## 38 **specimen** n.

an individual or part that represents a whole, group, or class; a sample (of blood, urine, etc.) used for medical testing

---

## 39 **stratum** n.

one section of several horizontal layers of something; a level or class made up of people with equal social or economic status

---

## 40 **succinct** adj.

concise, brief, or to the point

---

## 41 **superfluous** adj.

extra, excess, or surplus; unnecessary, or not required, needed, or relevant

---

## 42 **syndicate** n.

a group of people or organizations working together for a common goal; a group engaged in organized crime; a group of media companies

---

### 43 **testament** n.

something that acts as a proof or evidence; an expression of firmly held belief or conviction; a will

---

### 44 **turnabout** n.

a change, shift, or reversal of policy, opinion, character, etc.; the act of turning to face the other way

---

### 45 **unsavory** adj.

morally disreputable or offensive; unpleasant to smell or taste; having no flavor

---

### 46 **unscrupulous** adj.

not fair, honest, or morally correct

---

### 47 **utter** v./adj.

to say something or use the voice to make a sound; to put into circulation, especially counterfeit money; total or absolute

---

### 48 **variability** n.

the fact or quality of being likely to change

---

### 49 **venture** v.

to go somewhere potentially dangerous; to risk or gamble; to say something at the risk of criticism or rejection

---

### 50 **zeal** n.

great enthusiasm or eagerness in working for a cause or pursuit of a goal

---

# List 9

### 01 **abase** v.
to put someone down so as to cause pain or hurt feelings

### 02 **appall** v.
to shock, horrify, or dismay

### 03 **blaze** v.
to burn or shine intensely; to make a path or route; to fire quickly and successively; to be filled with brightness and magnificence

### 04 **candor** n.
honesty or openness in expression; brightness or brilliance

### 05 **capacious** adj.
having a lot of room or space

### 06 **commitment** n.
dedication to a cause or something pledged; an obligation or responsibility

### 07 **condolence** n.
an expression of comfort or sympathy offered to someone who is suffering or grieving with the death of a loved one

### 08 **conjure** v.
to summon a supernatural being with a magic spell; to imagine or bring to mind; to devise or plan

### 09 **contaminate** v.
to stain, infect, or make inferior or unfit

### 10 **convulsion** n.
a sudden, violent movement of the body, social or political disturbance, or earthquake

## 11 **declamation** n.

the act or art of speaking in a loud, rhetorical manner

## 12 **deplete** v.

to reduce, empty, or use up

## 13 **diction** n.

the choice of words or phrases used in speech or writing; the style or manner of vocal expression in speaking or singing

## 14 **displacement** n.

the act or process of removing something from its usual place or people from their original homes

## 15 **dubious** adj.

hesitant or unsure; suspicious, untrustworthy, or questionable

## 16 **finery** n.

a showy or expensive ornament, especially clothes or jewels; a hearth or furnace where wrought iron is made

## 17 **gimmick** n.

any clever gadget or means intended to deceive or mystify; a trick or device that draws attention

## 18 **herald** v.

to be a sign of something that is approaching or going to happen; to publicize; to greet with excitement or enthusiasm

## 19 **illiterate** adj.

unable to read and write; having or showing a lack of knowledge in a particular field; not following the approved standards of speaking or writing

## 20 **impale** v.

to pierce with a pointed instrument; to punish, torture, or kill by fixing on a stake; to make helpless

## 21 **implausible** adj.

difficult to believe or not likely to be true

## 22 **inconsequential** adj.

not important, relevant, or logical

## 23 **intolerance** n.

unwillingness to accept behavior or opinions different from one's own; exceptional sensitivity or allergy to certain food or medicine

## 24 **muddle** v.

to bring into an untidy, disordered, or confused state; to stupefy or confuse the mind; to make (water) murky or muddy; to stir or mix

## 25 **perturb** v.

to cause to be worried or upset; to cause confusion or disorder

## 26 **portly** adj.

stout, plump, or somewhat fat; having a stately or dignified manner or appearance

## 27 **predominant** adj.

most noticeable, frequent, or important; possessing superior power or influence over others

## 28 **proportionate** adj.

having a relative number, size, or amount to something else

## 29 **ravage** v.

to damage, destroy, or harm

## 30 **rejuvenate** v.

to make someone or something feel or look young, new, or fresh again

## 31 **remnant** n.

a small part or trace of a larger thing or group still remaining

## 32 **reprehensible** adj.
deserving harsh criticism or condemnation

## 33 **respectively** adv.
in the order mentioned, given, or named

## 34 **resuscitate** v.
to restore or regain consciousness; to make something active or successful again

## 35 **rife** adj.
extensive, widespread, or commonly occurring

## 36 **rupture** n.
a forcible or sudden breaking, tearing, or bursting apart of something; a break in friendly relations

## 37 **sanitation** n.
the science, practice, or policy of promoting, managing, or achieving hygienic conditions

## 38 **sarcasm** n.
an ironic language or expression meant to convey insult or humor

## 39 **scythe** n.
a tool for cutting grass or crops, with a long curving blade and handle

## 40 **stigma** n.
a mark of shame; a negative belief about something; the upper tip of the flower that receives pollen; a specific or visible mark or sign of a disease

## 41 **subservient** adj.
obedient or submissive; secondary or less important; helpful or useful in an inferior capacity; serving to promote a specific result or end

## 42 **taint** v.
to contaminate, damage, or corrupt, morally or physically

### 43 **tapestry** n.

a heavy woven fabric with decorative pictures or designs; something that is complex, detailed, or made up of different elements

---

### 44 **tinge** n.

a slight tint or coloring; a slight trace, hint, or suggestion

---

### 45 **toilsome** adj.

requiring or involving hard work

---

### 46 **totter** v.

to walk unsteadily; to shake or tremble as if about to fall; to be on the verge of failure

---

### 47 **trajectory** n.

the curved path that an object follows as it moves; a course of development

---

### 48 **variegated** adj.

exhibiting irregular patches or markings of different colors; having or including many different types

---

### 49 **warren** n.

a group of connecting underground tunnels in which rabbits live; a crowded or maze-like building or district

---

### 50 **wrest** v.

to turn, twist, or pull away violently; to take, seize, or remove by force

---

Part 2

# List 10

## 01 **analogy** n.
a comparison or resemblance between two things

## 02 **bibliography** n.
a list of references used by an author; a list of works of an author or publisher

## 03 **cardiovascular** adj.
pertaining to the heart and blood vessels

## 04 **commodious** adj.
spacious and comfortable

## 05 **conclusive** adj.
leaving no doubt in proving a case; achieving a decisive result or winning by a huge margin

## 06 **consumption** n.
the use or using up of something

## 07 **deft** adj.
quick and skillful in movement or action; clever or efficient

## 08 **demobilize** v.
to disband troops; to release a person from military service

## 09 **domestication** n.
the process of taming animals or cultivating plants for human use

## 10 **escapade** n.
an exciting, dangerous, or adventurous act or experience

## 11 **ferment** v.

to undergo the process of a chemical breakdown, especially one involved in making alcoholic beverages; to excite, stir up, or give rise to

## 12 **gist** n.

the main point; the essential ground for a legal action

## 13 **impeach** v.

to bring a charge or case against a public official; to call into question or raise doubts about

## 14 **intermission** n.

a pause, recess, or rest; a break between parts of an activity, such as at a play, concert, seminar, etc.

## 15 **lair** n.

a place where a wild animal rests or lives; a secret place for hiding

## 16 **leverage** n.

the ability, influence, or advantage used to arrive at a desired outcome

## 17 **meritocracy** n.

a system in which status or power to rule is determined by talent; an elite or ruling class of educated or talented people

## 18 **mimic** v.

to simulate, or to imitate in order to amuse, entertain, or ridicule

## 19 **nullify** v.

to make legally void or declare invalid; to neutralize, negate, or cancel out

## 20 **obscurity** n.

the state of being largely unknown; something unclear or hard to understand; the absence or lack of light

## 21 **opaque** adj.

not shining, clear, or transparent; hard to understand; unintelligent or dull-witted

## 22  **plausible** adj.

seemingly or possibly true, reasonable, or honest

## 23  **port** n.

the left side of a ship or aircraft when facing forward; a type of sweet wine typically high in alcohol content and dark red in color

## 24  **predecessor** n.

one who held a certain position before the present holder; a thing that has been replaced or followed by the current one

## 25  **primeval** adj.

ancient, earliest, or primitive

## 26  **primordial** adj.

basic, instinctive, or inborn

## 27  **prospector** n.

one who searches an area for valuable metals or minerals

## 28  **recluse** n.

a person who leads a life of seclusion

## 29  **reprisal** n.

an act of vengeance or retaliation

## 30  **repudiate** v.

to refuse to accept, acknowledge, or be associated with

## 31  **rivulet** n.

a small stream

## 32  **satiate** v.

to satisfy fully, completely, or to excess

## 33 **scribe** n.

one who copied manuscripts or documents before the invention of printing; a public clerk; a writer or journalist

## 34 **scrutiny** n.

a critical or thorough examination, study, or inspection; a close, continuous watch or surveillance

## 35 **sedate** adj.

calm, composed, or dignified; quiet and unexciting

## 36 **septic** adj.

causing or relating to infection, toxin, or harmful bacteria; of or relating to sewage disposal or drainage system with a waste treatment tank

## 37 **snide** adj.

slyly or indirectly mocking, insulting, or malicious; tricky, dishonest, or deceptive

## 38 **strut** v.

to walk erectly with an air of superiority; to display proudly or show off; to swell or bulge; to provide with a brace or support bar

## 39 **substantiate** v.

to prove or verify; to give a concrete or visible substance, form, or body to something

## 40 **substantive** adj.

of considerable amount or number; involving important or practical matters; real, actual, or firm rather than apparent; totally independent

## 41 **susceptible** adj.

defenseless against or vulnerable to (infection, damage, etc.); easily influenced or affected emotionally

## 42 **template** n.

a mold used to create the shape of the piece being made; a model to be used for copying; a preset pattern or format

### 43 **unabashed** adj.

not ashamed, unsettled, or embarrassed; not disguised or concealed (as in feelings, facts, behavior, etc.)

---

### 44 **vanguard** n.

the forefront or individuals leading a movement in an academic field, politics, etc.; the part of an army leading an attack

---

### 45 **vested** adj.

absolutely fixed or established as a benefit or right

---

### 46 **vie** v.

to compete to gain superiority or win a competition

---

### 47 **wield** v.

to hold, use, or handle a weapon, tool, etc.; to exert or exercise power, influence, or authority

---

### 48 **wobble** v.

to move clumsily from side to side or with a rocking motion; to be or become unsure

---

### 49 **yardstick** n.

a standard for comparison, or a rule by which to judge or measure

---

### 50 **zany** adj.

strangely or unusually comical, amusing, or funny

---

# List 11

---

### 01 **arsenal** n.
a collection of or place where weapons are kept or made

---

### 02 **awe** n.
a feeling of both fear and respect

---

### 03 **blandish** v.
to persuade by using flattery

---

### 04 **byzantine** adj.
extremely complicated, complex, or convoluted

---

### 05 **detached** adj.
not interested, or having or showing no bias; not attached or connected physically

---

### 06 **deteriorate** v.
to become or make inferior or progressively worse

---

### 07 **dispel** v.
to scatter and make disappear; to get rid of

---

### 08 **enterprise** n.
a project or undertaking, especially one that requires courage or risk; a company or business organization

---

### 09 **haggard** adj.
looking exhausted or fatigued; wild or untamed

---

### 10 **hallmark** n.
a characteristic or typical quality, trait, or feature; a stamp or mark on an item to indicate its origin, authenticity, purity, etc.

---

## 11 **hypocritical** adj.

behaving in a way that contradicts one's claimed or stated belief

## 12 **immunity** n.

resistance to a particular disease, infection, or toxin; exemption or protection from a specified duty, penalty, or legal prosecution

## 13 **impoverished** adj.

reduced to poverty; exhausted or deprived of strength, richness, or fertility

## 14 **insulate** v.

to separate or isolate; to protect or cover with a non-conducting material so as to stop the loss of heat, sound, electricity, etc.

## 15 **invoke** v.

to refer to something as an authority in order to validate one's argument or action; to summon (a spirit); to ask or beg for; to cause or bring about

## 16 **legitimacy** n.

the quality or state of being acceptable, valid, or legal

## 17 **momentous** adj.

of great significance or importance

## 18 **muster** v.

to bring or gather together, or to call up or to arms

## 19 **mutinous** adj.

openly showing the desire or will to resist or rebel against authority

## 20 **pompous** adj.

pretentious, arrogant, or self-important

## 21 **prejudice** n.

predetermined opinion or judgment not based on reason or experience

## 22  priory n.

a religious house or community, such as a convent or monastery

## 23  prop v.

to hold up or hold in place with; to lean against something; to strengthen or make able to withstand

## 24  punctual adj.

on time or prompt

## 25  regression n.

a return to a simpler, previous, or less developed state; a progressive decline or gradual loss

## 26  reincarnation n.

the rebirth of a soul in a different body or form; a new version of something

## 27  reprimand v.

to criticize or rebuke harshly, especially formally or officially

## 28  reservoir n.

a lake used for collecting and storing water; a source, supply, or store of something; a part of something in which fluid is held

## 29  retort v.

to answer back in a sharp or witty manner

## 30  revulsion n.

a sense of strong disgust, shock, or hatred; an abrupt change of feeling

## 31  row n.

a serious or noisy dispute, quarrel, or disagreement; a loud noise or disturbance

## 32  ruse n.

an action intended to trick or deceive

## 33 **sage** n.

a person respected for having profound wisdom or sound judgment; a plant belonging to the genus Salvia

## 34 **salvage** v.

to save, rescue, or recover from a disaster or danger (such as shipwreck, fire, capture, etc.)

## 35 **severance** n.

the act or process of ending a relationship or cutting off ties; payment given to an employee upon leaving the company

## 36 **sham** n.

something made, meant, or intended to deceive; a person pretending to be someone else; a decorative pillow cover

## 37 **stupendous** adj.

amazingly large or great; astonishing, marvelous, or overwhelming

## 38 **tempest** n.

a severe wind or violent storm; a violent disturbance or commotion

## 39 **treachery** n.

an act of betrayal, disloyalty, or treason

## 40 **tycoon** n.

a businessperson of great power, wealth, and influence

## 41 **unbecoming** adj.

not attractive, proper, or suitable, as in clothing or color; not appropriate or fitting to one's position, character, or condition

## 42 **unprecedented** adj.

never done, known, or happened before

## 43 **unsullied** adj.

not spoiled, stained, or tarnished

### 44 **upstart** n.

a person who has suddenly gained success and behaves arrogantly

---

### 45 **validate** v.

to make legal or give official confirmation to; to show to be real, true, or correct

---

### 46 **valor** n.

great courage or bravery, especially when facing danger or in battle

---

### 47 **waft** n.

a light breeze; something (such as a scent, music, etc.) flowing through the air

---

### 48 **wrangle** v.

to engage in a long dispute, argument, or controversy; to control or take care of horses, cattle, or other livestock

---

### 49 **writhe** v.

to twist and turn, especially in pain; to suffer from extreme emotional discomfort or pain

---

### 50 **wry** adj.

bent or twisted; cleverly, ironically, or dryly humorous

---

# List 12

### 01 **abate** v.
to reduce in amount, size, or value

### 02 **alias** n./adv.
a false name or identity; otherwise known as

### 03 **arduous** adj.
difficult to achieve; requiring or involving great labor; hard or exhausting to climb

### 04 **battalion** n.
a military unit with a headquarters and two or more companies; a large group of people pursuing a common goal

### 05 **blemish** n.
a visible or apparent flaw or imperfection

### 06 **cognizant** adj.
being aware or having understanding of something

### 07 **controversial** adj.
of, relating to, or giving rise to disagreement, argument, or debate

### 08 **convection** n.
the movement within a liquid or gas caused by differences in temperature in different parts, or the transfer of heat by this motion

### 09 **convolute** v.
to coil or twist; to make needlessly complex or difficult

### 10 **degradation** n.
the act or process of declining or decaying physically, morally, or intellectually

vocabulary

## 11 **depiction** n.
a representation of someone or something, in words or illustrations

## 12 **disabuse** v.
to set right, free from, or rid of an incorrect or mistaken idea or belief

## 13 **dissipate** v.
to break up or cause to spread thin and vanish; to waste or use up unwisely

## 14 **dormant** adj.
asleep, still, or temporarily not active

## 15 **edifice** n.
a building or large structure; a complex, abstract structure or system of beliefs

## 16 **enkindle** v.
arouse, excite, or inspire; to set on fire

## 17 **excursion** n.
a brief trip or journey; a digression from the main or proper subject or course

## 18 **expatriate** n.
a person living in a foreign country

## 19 **fervor** n.
strong and passionate feeling for or believe in something; intense heat

## 20 **imperative** adj.
extremely important or urgent; expressing a command or authority

## 21 **incorporate** v.
to include, admit, or merge; to form into a legally organized group or company; to embody or give physical form to

### 22 **intimidate** v.
to threaten or frighten in order to persuade someone

### 23 **juncture** n.
a particular point or crucial moment in time; a joint, connection, or meeting point

### 24 **legislate** v.
to make or pass a law

### 25 **leniency** n.
the quality of being less severe in judgment or punishment than expected

### 26 **maritime** adj.
in, near, or bordering on the sea; of or relating to navigation, military activity, or commerce on the sea

### 27 **mutter** v.
to say something in a low or indistinct tone; to grumble or complain; to make a low, rumbling sound

### 28 **potency** n.
the power and influence of a person, idea, etc.; the strength of a drug, poison, etc.; the ability or capacity to perform or achieve something

### 29 **primal** adj.
the most important; original or primitive

### 30 **probe** v.
to physically examine with a slender or pointed instrument; to study, survey, or explore; to conduct an investigate into (a case, crime, etc.)

### 31 **prod** v.
to poke with a pointed object; to persuade, encourage, or urge on

### 32 **prominent** adj.
famous, important, or popular; readily noticeable or distinct; protruding, bulging, or sticking out

### 33 **protean** adj.

tending to change frequently; capable of doing many different things

---

### 34 **qualm** n.

a feeling of guilt or uncertainty, especially in matters of conscience; a sudden feeling of fear or doubt; a sudden feeling of sickness or nausea

---

### 35 **requisite** n.

something required or necessary for achieving a particular goal or purpose

---

### 36 **revoke** v.

to take back, cancel, or make void a permit, license, will, etc.

---

### 37 **scapegoat** n.

a person blamed or punished for the errors or wrongdoings of others

---

### 38 **shrivel** v.

to wrinkle and become smaller, especially from lack of water; to become insignificant, helpless, or steady less

---

### 39 **sortie** v.

a movement into enemy position or territory for a brief attack

---

### 40 **squatter** n.

a person who illegally lives in an unoccupied place or settles on public land without legal title

---

### 41 **terse** adj.

to the point, or not using many words; direct and concise to the point of being un-friendly or rude

---

### 42 **thoroughbred** n.

a purebred animal; a person who is cultured, educated, or comes from a family of high social standing

---

### 43 **till** v.

to prepare a piece of land for raising crops

---

## 44 **tractable** adj.

easy to control or deal with

---

## 45 **tutelage** n.

the act of protecting or guarding; the act or process of training, educating, or guiding

---

## 46 **undermine** v.

to weaken the power or effectiveness of, especially secretly; to wear away the foundation of (a wall, rock formation, etc.); to dig beneath

---

## 47 **underscore** v.

to stress or emphasize; to draw a line under a word or words

---

## 48 **vacillate** v.

to be indecisive or keep changing in mind; to move or sway unsteadily; to fluctuate or move back and forth

---

## 49 **voluminous** adj.

full, large, or bulky; (of writing) lengthy and detailed; having written many books

---

## 50 **wherewith** conj.

with which or by means of which

---

# List 13

### 01 **antibody** n.
a protein produced by the body to neutralize a toxin or other foreign substance

### 02 **beacon** n.
a light, fire, or radio used as a signal, guidance, or warning; a source of inspiration

### 03 **bestow** v.
to give, present, or provide; to devote, apply, or put to use

### 04 **bilateral** adj.
having or relating to (or involving or affecting) two groups or nations

### 05 **bombard** v.
to attack with bombs or artillery; to press or assail continuously with questions, suggestions, information, etc.

### 06 **carnivore** n.
an animal that feeds mainly or only on meat

### 07 **complacency** n.
the state of being very satisfied with oneself or how things are and thus not seeing the need to change them

### 08 **compliant** adj.
willing, ready, or tending to agree; agreeing or compatible with rules, requirements, or specifications

### 09 **decipher** v.
to decode a secret message; to understand or interpret the meaning of an illegible or ancient writing, literary work, etc.

### 10 **detectable** adj.
able to be discovered, noticed, or identified

## 11 **disputatious** adj.
inclined to dispute, debate, or cause argument; provoking or characterized by controversy

## 12 **douse** v.
to drench or throw liquid over; to extinguish a fire or light

## 13 **embolden** v.
to give courage or confidence to; to format a printed text in bold typeface

## 14 **exhaustive** adj.
leaving nothing out, or very thorough or comprehensive

## 15 **exposition** n.
a detailed and comprehensive explanation of an idea, fact, or theory; a large public show, fair, or exhibition

## 16 **fidelity** n.
faithfulness, loyalty, or devotion; exactness, or the degree of accuracy

## 17 **functionary** n.
a person who carries out official duties

## 18 **imbibe** v.
to drink (as in water or alcoholic beverage); to take in (as in knowledge or scenery); to absorb (as in moisture or light)

## 19 **implication** n.
a hint or suggestion; a likely result, effect, or consequence; the act or state of being connected or involved

## 20 **indulge** v.
to give in to a temptation; to satisfy or fulfill (a goal, interest, etc.); to pamper, spoil, or humor oneself or someone

## 21 **intangible** adj.
unable to be felt or touched; having an abstract quality; of or relating to business assets that are not physical but have monetary value

## 22 **lineage** n.
direct descent or people descended from a common ancestor

## 23 **listless** adj.
lacking energy, spirit, or enthusiasm

## 24 **maul** v.
to injure or bruise badly; to handle roughly

## 25 **microcosm** n.
a smaller version or representation of an activity, society, or the world

## 26 **practitioner** n.
one who is actively involved in a discipline, art, or profession, especially medicine

## 27 **prototype** n.
the first, original, or preliminary model; someone or something that serves a typical or perfect example

## 28 **quip** n.
a clever, witty, or sarcastic remark; something odd or strange

## 29 **quirk** n.
a peculiar trait, habit, or behavior; a sudden twist or turn

## 30 **rabid** adj.
furious, raging, or extremely violent; exceedingly fanatical or unreasonable in expression, opinion, or support of; affected with rabies

## 31 **reactionary** n.
a person who is opposed to social or political change or reform

## 32 **recitation** n.
the act of repeating from memory or reading aloud before an audience; a small class taken in association with a larger lecture course

### 33 **reclamation** n.

the process of recovering or changing wasteland or flooded land into one that can be utilized for farming or other useful activities

### 34 **recuperate** v.

to recover or regain former health, state, or condition; to get back something taken or lost

### 35 **saccharine** adj.

of, relating to, or containing sugar; extremely or excessively sweet; overly sentimental or romantic

### 36 **salutary** adj.

producing helpful or beneficial result; promoting health

### 37 **senile** adj.

of, relating to, or characteristic of old age; showing deterioration in mind or conscious mental activities

### 38 **soluble** adj.

able to be dissolved; capable of being solved or explained

### 39 **sovereign** adj.

possessing supreme rank or authority; of or relating to a ruler or royalty; independent or self-governing; excellent or exceptional in quality

### 40 **supplant** v.

to take the place of another by force, treachery, or reason of superiority

### 41 **tactile** adj.

tangible, or perceptible by touch; of or relating to the sense of touch

### 42 **tattered** adj.

torn, broken down, or in poor condition

### 43 **transfusion** n.

the transfer of fluid into a vein or artery, especially blood; the act or instance of diffusing, infusing, or permeating through something

### 44 **ultimatum** n.

a final demand, condition, or warning

---

### 45 **unveil** v.

to show, introduce, or announce to the public or for the first time; to remove a covering from

---

### 46 **venerate** v.

to regard or treat with great respect

---

### 47 **vista** n.

a large, scenic view of an area; a mental view of a series of past events or future possibilities

---

### 48 **vitality** n.

energy, strength, or liveliness; the capacity to continue developing or living

---

### 49 **vouch** v.

to confirm, back up, or give personal assurance

---

### 50 **weighty** adj.

important, serious, or critical; burdensome, worrisome, or oppressive; powerful, respectable, or influential; having much weight

Part 2

# List 14

## 01 **amnesty** n.
an act granting pardon for an offense by an authority or government

## 02 **brawl** n.
a rough, noisy, or violent fight or quarrel

## 03 **cache** n.
a hidden, secure place for keeping or storing things, or anything stored in such a place

## 04 **charlatan** n.
one who pretends to possess a certain skill, expertise, or knowledge

## 05 **choreograph** v.
to compose, arrange, or direct the steps or movements of a ballet, dance, figure skating, etc.; to plan or control an operation, event, etc.

## 06 **dehydrate** v.
to lose water from the body; to remove water (as from food) for the purpose of preserving and storing

## 07 **demean** v.
to degrade or lower in status, reputation, character, etc.; to manage or conduct oneself in a particular manner

## 08 **deplorable** adj.
deserving condemnation; miserable or terrible in quality; regrettable or lamentable

## 09 **disrepute** n.
a state of being held in low esteem or disgrace

## 10 **dissolute** adj.
lacking restraint or morals

## 11 **divulgence** n.

the act of making something private or secret known

## 12 **enshrine** v.

to enclose something sacred or precious in a holy or revered place; to cherish, preserve, or hold as sacred

## 13 **eradicate** v.

to uproot, wipe out, or destroy completely

## 14 **ethos** n.

the set of beliefs or attitudes associated with a particular person, group, or organization

## 15 **extremity** n.

the furthest point, part, or section; an extreme degree, condition, or state; a hand or foot; a limb (such as a leg, arm, wing, etc.)

## 16 **fleeting** adj.

passing swiftly, short-lived, or temporary

## 17 **flotsam** n.

the wreckage of a ship; remains or debris

## 18 **gravitate** v.

to be attracted to or tend to move toward someone or something

## 19 **grimace** n.

a distortion of the face to express disgust, pain, disapproval, etc.

## 20 **guru** n.

a popular or influential teacher, leader, or expert; a religious or spiritual teacher in Hinduism

## 21 **hindrance** n.

someone or something that acts as an obstacle, resistance, or obstruction to someone or something else

## 22 **instill** v.

to put in or cause to enter drop by drop; to gradually put (an idea, attitude, principle, etc.) into someone's mind

## 23 **jest** v.

to make a funny, joking, or mocking remark

## 24 **lactic** adj.

of, relating to, or obtained from milk

## 25 **lissome** adj.

moving with graceful flexibility and agility

## 26 **mull** v.

to consider or think about at length; to grind, crush, or powder; to heat and add spices and sweetening to ale, wine, cider, etc.

## 27 **oblique** adj.

slanting, sloping, or inclined; evasive, indirect, or devious; having unequal sides (as in leaves)

## 28 **offhand** adj./adv.

casual, unconcerned, or cool, especially in an unfriendly or offensive manner; without planning or preparation

## 29 **offset** v.

to counteract, make up for, or balance or cancel out; to place out of line or alignment

## 30 **oppression** n.

cruel or unjust control, treatment, or exercise of power; physical or mental stress or depression

## 31 **profanity** n.

the quality or state of treating something sacred with abuse or contempt; the use of abusive, obscene, or foul language

## 32 **provincial** adj.

narrow in mind or outlook; lacking in sophistication, culture, or refinement; relating to an administrative division of or region within a country

## 33 **provocative** adj.

causing argument, thought, excitement, or lustful desires

## 34 **quota** n.

a fixed, proportional, or limited share, quantity, or number of something or people

## 35 **resignation** n.

the act of accepting or submitting to something inevitable; an act of giving a formal notice to leave or give up a job or position

## 36 **rhetoric** n.

the command or art of using effective language; exaggerated language designed to impress but lacking in sincerity or honesty

## 37 **rustic** adj.

relating to or typical of the countryside; uncultured, backward, or unsophisticated; made of untrimmed timber or branches

## 38 **seclusion** n.

the state of being away, or the act of keeping someone away, from others

## 39 **semblance** n.

outward appearance, form, or aspect; similarity or likeness; an image or representation; false show or appearance

## 40 **sinister** adj.

harmful, evil, or dishonest; indicating ill omen or approaching danger

## 41 **sublime** adj.

noble or grand in thought or expression; inspiring admiration or awe (because of beauty, excellence, etc.); complete or total (in a negative sense)

## 42 **synthetic** adj.

not natural, genuine, or real

vocabulary

### 43 **tact** n.

the ability to say or do the appropriate thing in order to avoid offending others

### 44 **tenacious** adj.

persistent, determined, or stubborn; having the capacity of retaining, especially knowledge; clinging or holding firmly to an object or substance

### 45 **to and fro** adv.

back and forth, or from place to place

### 46 **tranquil** adj.

calm, quiet, or peaceful

### 47 **unilateral** adj.

done by or affecting only one party without the agreement of the others; affecting or occurring on only one side of the body

### 48 **vogue** n.

the popular style or fashion at a certain time

### 49 **wane** v.

to diminish in intensity, strength, or brightness; to decrease gradually in power, wealth, or influence; to come to an end

### 50 **wily** adj.

crafty, cunning, or sly

# List 15

---

### 01 **abide** v.
to follow or accept a rule or a decision without resisting

---

### 02 **aggression** n.
a hostile or destructive attitude, behavior, or habit

---

### 03 **antecedent** n.
something that precedes another, especially the cause or condition of the latter

---

### 04 **bolster** v.
to support, encourage, or strengthen

---

### 05 **confidential** adj.
meant to be kept secret or private; entrusted with private or secret affairs or information

---

### 06 **context** n.
the background or situation in which a particular event happens; words near a specific word and that help to clarify or determine its meaning

---

### 07 **debase** v.
to reduce or lower in status, character, quality, value, etc.

---

### 08 **detention** n.
the act of keeping someone in custody; a punishment requiring a student to stay after school

---

### 09 **disciple** n.
a follower of the thoughts, teachings, or doctrines of another

---

### 10 **elusive** adj.
difficult to find or capture; difficult to gain or achieve; difficult to understand or remember

---

## 11 **emphatic** adj.

expressed, spoken, or done with force and clarity

---

## 12 **erratic** adj.

having irregular or random course, pattern, or movement; deviating from what is considered normal or customary

---

## 13 **evoke** v.

to call or bring (a memory, feeling, etc.) to mind; to arouse or bring out a reaction or response; to summon a spirit, deity, magical creature, etc.

---

## 14 **frolic** v.

to have fun, or to run about in an excited or carefree way

---

## 15 **frugal** adj.

not spending unnecessarily or wastefully; not expensive or luxurious

---

## 16 **gaffe** n.

an embarrassing mistake, error, or blunder

---

## 17 **genesis** n.

the source, origin, or beginning of something

---

## 18 **hygiene** n.

the science of promotion or maintenance of health; cleanliness

---

## 19 **illegitimate** adj.

born to parents who are not married to each other; illegal or unlawful; not logical; not in line with accepted usage

---

## 20 **invariable** adj.

never changing, or not capable of change

---

## 21 **kinetic** adj.

of, relating to, or characterized by motion

---

## 22 **makeshift** adj.

serving as a substitute until a better option is available

---

## 23 **medial** adj.

of a mean or average; being in or extending toward the middle

---

## 24 **membrane** n.

a thin layer of tissue acting as lining or boundary in an organism; any thin, pliable material serving as a filter, partition, covering, etc.

---

## 25 **obliterate** v.

to remove completely from memory, recognition, or existence; to blot out or make indistinct

---

## 26 **parched** adj.

dry or dried out, especially due to extreme heat and no rainwater; very thirsty

---

## 27 **pastoral** adj.

of, portraying, or relating to shepherds, livestock raising, or rural life; peaceful, blissful, or picturesque; relating to spiritual guidance

---

## 28 **peevish** adj.

moody, childishly irritable, or easily annoyed

---

## 29 **precarious** adj.

unstable, or not securely fixed or in position; dependent on chance, uncertain conditions, or the will of another person

---

## 30 **primp** v.

to improve one's appearance by making minor changes to hair, clothes, makeup, etc., in a careful or fussy manner

---

## 31 **recant** v.

to withdraw (especially publicly or formally) a statement, opinion, or belief formerly expressed

## 32 **recoil** v.

to flinch or pull back in fear or disgust; to spring back upon release; (of a gun) to kick back upon firing

## 33 **regal** adj.

of, relating to, or fit for a king or queen; dignified, stately, or majestic

## 34 **rehabilitate** v.

to restore or return someone or something to former state, condition, or quality (such as health, reputation, environment, etc.)

## 35 **retract** v.

to draw back in or pull back inside; to take back or go back on something one has said or written

## 36 **salutation** n.

an expression made as a greeting; the phrase of greeting used at the beginning of a letter

## 37 **sanctuary** n.

a holy place; a place of refuge, safety, or protection; a nature reserve or reservation for animals

## 38 **segregation** n.

the enforced practice of separating people of different sexes, races, religions, etc.

## 39 **sentinel** n.

a person who guards or keeps watch

## 40 **shackle** n.

something, especially a metal ring, that fastens wrists or ankles together; anything that prevents free action or freedom of expression

## 41 **spoils** n.

valuables taken forcibly, especially in war; the benefits of public office regarded as property of a successful party; waste material of an excavation

## 42 **spontaneity** n.
the quality or state of being natural rather than forced or planned

## 43 **tinker** v.
to make an awkward or casual attempt to repair or adjust something; to experiment with

## 44 **totalitarian** adj.
of or relating to a system of government or state in which an autocratic authority has complete control

## 45 **transpire** v.
to happen, occur, or take place; to become known or be revealed; to give off vapor, as through the pores of the skin or leaves

## 46 **turbulence** n.
great turmoil, conflict, or disorder; violent or irregular movement of air or water

## 47 **unravel** v.
to undo something that is twisted, tangled, or woven; to explain, clear up, or find an answer to

## 48 **versed** adj.
skilled in or knowledgeable about

## 49 **vexation** n.
a feeling of annoyance, frustration, or distress; the source of worry or trouble

## 50 **witticism** n.
a clever remark or joke

## 01 **amnesia** n.
a loss of memory

## 02 **animosity** n.
a strong dislike or hostility

## 03 **antiseptic** adj.
preventing decay or infection; extremely clean or orderly; cold and impersonal; free from life's problems

## 04 **condone** v.
to overlook or allow something that is considered immoral or offensive to continue

## 05 **confinement** n.
the act or state of being restricted or restrained; childbirth

## 06 **constrict** v.
to make narrower; to squeeze or compress; to limit, inhibit, or stop

## 07 **customize** v.
to build or modify to suit personal or individual tastes or specifications

## 08 **dystopia** n.
an imagined society or world, one that is dehumanized, totalitarian, post-apocalyptic, etc.

## 09 **enshroud** v.
to cover completely

## 10 **enumerate** v.
to mention or name one by one or in order; to count, or to establish or determine the number or amount of

## 11 **facilitate** v.

to make easy or easier, or to help cause something to take place

## 12 **flora** n.

(a list of) plants of a particular area or period

## 13 **fluctuate** v.

to shift back and forth or rise and fall; to change or vary continually and irregularly

## 14 **furbish** v.

to brighten by rubbing or polishing; to restore or renovate

## 15 **hearth** n.

the floor or area in front of a fireplace; the lowest part of a furnace on which molten metal is deposited; home or family life; a creative hub

## 16 **iconic** adj.

widely recognized, known, or acknowledged

## 17 **interpretation** n.

the act of explaining something in understandable terms; a stylistic adaptation or representation of a creative or artistic work

## 18 **lecherous** adj.

given to or characterized by lustful desire

## 19 **lurch** v.

to make a sudden, uncontrolled movement

## 20 **morose** adj.

gloomy, sullen, or miserable and ill-tempered

## 21 **pessimistic** adj.

tending to think negatively or expecting the worst in all things

## 22 **pious** adj.

very religious; showing loyalty or reverence for someone or something; deserving praise; insincere, self-righteous, or hypocritical

## 23 **posit** v.

to set firmly or in place; to assume as fact; to suggest as a reason or explanation

## 24 **proceedings** n.

legal action; a written record of a meeting

## 25 **querulous** adj.

habitually complaining; having or showing a complaint in attitude or expression

## 26 **rebuke** v.

to scold or criticize sharply

## 27 **relegate** v.

to banish or exile; to assign to a lower or unimportant position, rank, or division

## 28 **relinquish** v.

to give up or yield a title, power, or right; to release or let go physically

## 29 **resonate** v.

to influence or appeal to someone emotionally or in a meaningful way; to vibrate and produce a full, strong sound

## 30 **resounding** adj.

complete, unquestionable, or emphatic; having or producing deep, clear, and echoing sound

## 31 **savory** adj.

pleasing to the sense of taste or smell; salty or spicy; pleasant, satisfying, or attractive; respectable or morally acceptable

## 32 **sedentary** adj.

tending to do or require much sitting; somewhat still or inactive; living, remaining, or fixed in one location

## 33 **seethe** v.

to be in a state of intense, unexpressed anger; to soak in liquid; to boil, or to cook by boiling; to foam or bubble as if boiling

---

## 34 **serenity** n.

the state or quality of being calm, serene, or peaceful; a royal title (as in His, Her, or Your)

---

## 35 **solicit** v.

to ask for or make a petition to; to attempt to urge someone to buy; to lure, tempt, or entice someone into doing something immoral or evil

---

## 36 **soothsayer** n.

a person who predicts the future

---

## 37 **steadfast** adj.

firmly established or fixed in place; firmly loyal, resolute, or unwavering

---

## 38 **stoic** adj.

able to endure pain or hardship without showing signs of distress

---

## 39 **streamline** v.

to design or construct so as to minimize resistance to movement through water or air; to simplify, organize, or make more efficient; to modernize

---

## 40 **symmetrical** adj.

having two same halves; well-proportioned or well-balanced

---

## 41 **synthesis** n.

the production or formation of something by combining

---

## 42 **tangent** n.

a sudden change of course; a line touching the edge of a curve

---

## 43 **temperament** n.

an individual's basic nature or usual manner; a tendency to become irritated, angry, or excited

---

Part 2

## 44 **tomfoolery** n.

foolish, playful, or silly behavior

## 45 **torrid** adj.

intensely hot and dry; eager, passionate, or full of strong emotions

## 46 **transcript** n.

a written, typed, or printed copy; a legal or official copy, especially that of one's educational record

## 47 **transpose** v.

to change the sequence or position of; to write or play music in a different key; to translate, transform, or transfer

## 48 **variant** n.

a different or alternative form or version

## 49 **vendetta** n.

a blood feud, or a bitter fight between two factions or groups; a prolonged effort to cause harm to a particular person or group

## 50 **verbose** adj.

using or containing more words than necessary

## 01 **amble** v.

to move or walk at a leisurely pace

## 02 **anesthetic** adj.

relating to or capable of reducing pain

## 03 **animate** v.

to bring to life; to make lively or spirited; to inspire or motivate to action

## 04 **antiquity** n.

ancient times, or the quality of being old or ancient; the people, relics, cultures, etc., of the ancient past

## 05 **buffer** n.

someone or something that acts as a shield or barrier against harm or annoyance

## 06 **caption** n.

a title or short explanation or comment added to an illustration, cartoon, article, etc.; a subtitle added in a television show or film

## 07 **conclave** n.

a (gathering or place for) private or secret meeting

## 08 **cosmopolitan** adj.

affecting, found in, or composed of people from many parts of the world; having worldly sophistication

## 09 **determinate** adj.

having fixed or exact limits; definitive, conclusive, or settled

## 10 **disdain** n./v.

a feeling of dislike or contempt; to treat as inferior or unworthy

## 11 **disjunctive** adj.

separated or lacking connection

## 12 **evenhanded** adj.

fair, just, or impartial

## 13 **exterminate** v.

to kill off or eliminate completely, especially pests

## 14 **fester** v.

to become infected and form pus; to rot or decay; to intensify or worsen (a problem, negative emotion, or ill feeling)

## 15 **fickle** adj.

changing often, or quick to change one's mind

## 16 **filament** n.

a fine fiber, wire, or threadlike object; the slender stalk of a flower stamen

## 17 **forestall** v.

to prevent something from happening by taking early action

## 18 **genial** adj.

cheerful and friendly; pleasantly warm and mild; relating to the chin

## 19 **inadmissible** adj.

not to be allowed or granted, especially that cannot be accepted as valid evidence in court

## 20 **inexplicable** adj.

unable to be explained or accounted for

## 21 **jetsam** n.

objects thrown overboard from a ship in an emergency

## 22 **lurk** v.

to lie in wait to spring an ambush; to remain hidden; to move secretly; to read an internet discussion forum without contributing comments

## 23 **miscellaneous** adj.

consisting of diverse or various things; having various qualities, traits, or abilities

## 24 **mutable** adj.

capable of change, or prone to change frequently

## 25 **perilous** adj.

dangerous or risky, or exposed to danger or risk

## 26 **pithy** adj.

concise and effective or expressive in the use of words

## 27 **profile** n.

the outermost shape or view of something; the side view of a person's face; a short description of a person or thing

## 28 **pun** n.

a play on a word or phrase with multiple meanings or that suggests another with the same or similar sound but different meaning

## 29 **rationalize** v.

to describe or attempt to justify something so as to make it seem appropriate, appealing, or excusable

## 30 **renunciation** n.

the act of rejecting, resigning, or abandoning by formal declaration; the act of giving up a practice, habit, or way of living

## 31 **repentance** n.

a feeling of genuine regret or remorse for wrongdoing or sins committed

## 32 **repository** n.

a place or container for safe storage; a place or area filled with a natural resource; a source or storage of knowledge or information; a burial vault

vocabulary

## 33 **rile** v.
to annoy, anger, or irritate; to make muddy or murky by stirring up

## 34 **salient** adj.
most important, relevant, or noteworthy; noticeable or standing out above others; pointing or projecting outward

## 35 **satire** n.
the use of humor, exaggeration, or irony in order to expose or criticize a foolish or wicked idea or behavior

## 36 **slander** n.
a false statement intended to damage a person's reputation

## 37 **snarl** v.
to growl aggressively with bared teeth; to speak angrily or rudely; to become tangled or knotted; to make extremely confused or complicated

## 38 **steppe** n.
a large, flat grassy plain with very few or no trees

## 39 **straggler** n.
one who falls behind or becomes separated from a group; one who moves about without any settled course or destination

## 40 **subscribe** v.
to sign on a legal document; to pay to receive a publication or service regularly; to support, agree with, or consent to

## 41 **supersede** v.
to remove or take the position or place of

## 42 **tantalize** v.
to tease or bait with something that is desirable but unobtainable

## 43 **transfigure** v.
to change the form or appearance of; to transform into a more glorious, beautiful, or advanced state

## 44 **tyranny** n.

oppressive power, government, or rule; a cruel, unreasonable, or unjust act or use of power; a harsh or severe condition

## 45 **unaccountable** adj.

beyond understanding or comprehension; not required to explain or be responsible for a decision or action

## 46 **undertone** n.

a hint or suggestion, or an underlying meaning or feeling; a toned-down color or sound

## 47 **untapped** adj.

not yet used or exploited

## 48 **uproot** v.

to force someone to leave home or country; to destroy or remove completely; to pull out of the ground

## 49 **vice** n.

wickedness or moral corruption; a bad habit; crimes involving prostitution, drugs, gambling, etc.

## 50 **vigilante** n.

a person who catches or punishes criminals without legal authority

# List 18

### 01 **aptitude** n.
a natural talent, ability, or tendency to do something or learn quickly

### 02 **borough** n.
a town, or an administrative unit or district

### 03 **boycott** v.
to abstain from buying, using, or participating in something as a means to voice a protest

### 04 **candid** adj.
honest or straightforward; fair or just; natural or spontaneous without posing or rehearsing (as in photography)

### 05 **compatibility** n.
a state of being able to exist together without conflict

### 06 **connotation** n.
an idea or notion that a word suggests in addition to its main meaning

### 07 **contemplate** v.
to look at or examine carefully; to think about, consider, or meditate

### 08 **counterfeit** n.
an imitation made in order to deceive or cheat; the quality of making a pretense or not being sincere

### 09 **dialect** n.
a form of a language spoken in a particular region, community, or social group

### 10 **disclose** v.
to make known (a secret, information, etc.); to expose or allow to be viewed

## 11 **disquieting** adj.

causing worry, anxiety, or fear

## 12 **divinity** n.

a god or deity, or the quality or state of being heavenly or godlike; the study of religion or religious faith

## 13 **duplex** adj.

double, or having two main parts, aspects, or elements; able to operate or move in opposite directions (in telecommunication) at the same time

## 14 **edify** v.

to instruct in a way that improves one's morals or intellect

## 15 **emulate** v.

to copy or imitate; to match or excel, often by imitating someone or something one admires

## 16 **enclave** n.

a distinct cultural, social, or territorial unit or group that is surrounded by another

## 17 **exasperate** v.

to frustrate, irritate, or anger

## 18 **fauna** n.

animal life, or (a list of) animals characteristic of a particular environment, region, or time period

## 19 **forgery** n.

something falsely made, or the act or crime of producing something false or fake; an act of (or something made by) forming metal into shape

## 20 **gallant** adj.

showy in dress or manner; brave, heroic, or courageous; grand, imposing, or stately; gentlemanly, polite, or attentive, especially to women

## 21 **hypothetical** adj.

based on conjectural or speculative idea; imagined as an example

vocabulary

## 22 **impart** v.

to give, convey, or bestow; to tell, disclose, or make known

---

## 23 **improvise** v.

to perform (music, play, drama, etc.) without planning in advance; to make something quickly from whatever material is available

---

## 24 **indiscreet** adj.

not careful in keeping secrets, or lacking wisdom or judgment in speech or action

---

## 25 **inestimable** adj.

incapable of being calculated or computed; too valuable or outstanding to be appropriately appreciated or measured

---

## 26 **infestation** n.

the state of being swarmed by parasites, insects, pests, etc.; the presence of something troublesome existing in an abnormally large number

---

## 27 **inherent** adj.

existing in a person or thing as a natural quality, attribute, or right

---

## 28 **inhibition** n.

the act of restraining, forbidding, or holding something in check

---

## 29 **judicious** adj.

having or showing sound judgment or good sense

---

## 30 **meticulous** adj.

characterized by extreme or precise attention to details

---

## 31 **postscript** n.

a remark added to a completed letter; additional details that provide further information to a completed story or account

---

## 32 **purge** v.

to cleanse of guilt, impurities, or unwanted feeling, or to rid of undesirable individuals, qualities, or elements

---

### 33 **retrospect** n.
a looking back on past events or times

### 34 **roil** v.
to make (a liquid) thick or opaque by stirring up the sediment; to move in a violent, unsteady manner; to make someone irritated or angry

### 35 **sagacious** adj.
having or showing an ability to understand or make wise judgments

### 36 **saline** adj.
containing or resembling salt

### 37 **scatterplot** n.
a graph in which plotted points show correlation between two variables or sets of data

### 38 **servitude** n.
the state of being a slave or subject to a powerful person

### 39 **sinuous** adj.
full of curves and turns; graceful, agile, or supple; complex or intricate; devious or morally crooked

### 40 **slothful** adj.
lazy, or tending to avoid movement or effort

### 41 **taper** v.
to become gradually thinner or smaller toward one end; to reduce gradually in number, degree, size, etc.

### 42 **therapeutic** adj.
having or producing a positive effect on the mind or body; of or relating to the treatment of illness or disease

### 43 **thwart** v.
to prevent from happening or succeeding

## 44 **ubiquitous** adj.

being or seeming to be present or found everywhere at the same time

## 45 **unassuming** adj.

not pretentious, self-assertive, or arrogant

## 46 **vagrant** n.

one who wanders from place to place and lives by begging for food or money

## 47 **vandalism** n.

the act of deliberately damaging public or private property

## 48 **vanquish** v.

to defeat, subdue, or conquer completely; to suppress or overcome fear, passion, etc.

## 49 **volatile** adj.

likely to change suddenly and unpredictably; evaporating easily or quickly; easily angered or aroused

## 50 **wholesome** adj.

helpful or useful in keeping body healthy; promoting moral or mental well-being

# List 19

### 01 **antiquated** adj.
aged, obsolete, or no longer useful or in use

### 02 **brevity** n.
concise or brief use of words in expressing one's thoughts; shortness of time or duration

### 03 **catastrophe** n.
a tragic or destructive natural event; a complete and absolute failure; the final, resolving part of a drama or play

### 04 **deadlock** n.
a standstill resulting from the opposition of equal forces

### 05 **decry** v.
to express disapproval openly or publicly; to lower the value of something (such as money, coin, etc.) officially or by proclamation

### 06 **dilemma** n.
a situation or circumstance in which a choice must be made between undesirable alternatives; any serious or difficult problem or situation

### 07 **distensible** adj.
able to extend, stretch out, or expand

### 08 **dominion** n.
supremacy, power, or control over something; the territory or country of a ruler or government

### 09 **entail** v.
to involve or imply as a necessary part or consequence; to restrict the inheritance of property to a particular line or descendants

## 10 **excruciating** adj.
extremely painful or agonizing

## 11 **extravagant** adj.
wasteful in managing money or resources; very expensive or costly; going beyond necessity or reason; excessively showy or elaborate

## 12 **fabricate** v.
to invent or make up, especially to deceive; to make, build, or manufacture by assembling standardized components

## 13 **factious** adj.
producing or tending to cause division or dissension

## 14 **fortify** v.
to strengthen or make stronger; to enhance the defenses by strengthening with military works; to support or confirm

## 15 **frigid** adj.
extremely cold; unenthusiastic, impersonal, or too stiff in style or behavior

## 16 **futility** n.
a useless or pointless act, or the state or quality of being useless

## 17 **glimmer** n.
a dim or flickering light or sparkle; a faint idea or hint

## 18 **incomprehensible** adj.
impossible to understand

## 19 **infamous** adj.
widely known for some bad reputation; wicked, dishonorable, or shameful; deprived of rights as a result of conviction of a crime

## 20 **menial** adj.
of or relating to work requiring little skill or considered low in status; relating or appropriate to a servant

## 21 **overbearing** adj.

unpleasantly bossy, demanding, or dictatorial; snobbish or arrogantly superior; of greatest importance or significance

## 22 **pigmentation** n.

the natural coloring of plants or animals; unusual or distinctive coloring of a person's skin

## 23 **piteous** adj.

causing feelings of sympathy or compassion

## 24 **platoon** n.

a military unit consisting of two or more squads; a group of people sharing a common activity or characteristic

## 25 **portrayal** n.

a representation or depiction of someone or something; an instance of an actor performing a part

## 26 **reciprocate** v.

to give and take; to respond by returning in kind; to move backwards and forwards

## 27 **relapse** v.

to fall back into a former state or condition after a brief improvement (such as illness, bad habit, etc.)

## 28 **revelation** n.

the act of disclosing or making something known; an interesting or surprising fact or experience; an explanation or revealing of divine truth

## 29 **robust** adj.

strong and healthy; sturdy, or strongly constructed; rough, forceful, or coarse; having a strong, full, or rich flavor

## 30 **saunter** v.

to walk in a slow, leisurely manner

### 31 **scavenge** v.

to search through waste for useful items; to search for or feed on rotting flesh of dead animals; to expel burned gases; to purify molten metal

### 32 **seer** n.

a person who foretells the future

### 33 **seismograph** n.

an instrument for detecting, recording, and measuring the intensity, direction, or duration of earthquakes

### 34 **simulate** v.

to imitate, reproduce, or replicate; to fake or pretend; to produce a model of something with a computer

### 35 **stagnant** adj.

not developing, growing, or active; having no current, flow, or motion; foul, stale, or decaying from lack of movement

### 36 **stupefy** v.

to shock, astonish, or astound; to dull the senses or ability to think

### 37 **subsidy** n.

financial assistance, support, or benefit

### 38 **succumb** v.

to yield or give in to pressure, desire, or overpowering strength; to die as a result of (illness, injury, old age, etc.)

### 39 **sumptuous** adj.

costly, luxurious, or splendid

### 40 **supremacist** n.

one who believes in or advocates the superiority of one particular group over all others

### 41 **surreal** adj.

bizarre, unreal, or dreamlike

## 42 **symbiosis** n.

a mutually beneficial relationship between two different organisms; any cooperative relationship benefiting all involved

---

## 43 **synergy** n.

a mutual advantage or greater effectiveness resulting from a combined action, effort, or force

---

## 44 **temper** v.

to strengthen or harden (steel, glass, etc.); to bring to a proper or suitable state by mixing; to toughen through hardship; to tune an instrument

---

## 45 **tether** n.

a rope or chain fastened to an animal to restrict its movement; a line or cable to hold something in place; the limit of one's strength or abilities

---

## 46 **titter** v.

to laugh in a short, nervous, and somewhat restrained manner

---

## 47 **transcribe** v.

to put (ideas, data, speech, etc.) into written form; to make a full written version of (notes, shorthand, etc.)

---

## 48 **unrest** n.

a state of agitation, dissatisfaction, or confusion, typically expressed by protesting or rioting

---

## 49 **vagabond** n.

someone who moves from place to place without a fixed home or job

---

## 50 **zest** n.

keen enjoyment; a lively or exciting quality; the peel of a citrus fruit used as flavoring

---

Part 2

vocabulary

## List 20

### 01 **archaic** adj.
old-fashioned, outdated, or antiquated; (of words) no longer in common use but still used for specific purposes

### 02 **claustrophobia** n.
a fear of enclosed or confined spaces or places

### 03 **debris** n.
broken pieces or remains of something destroyed or discarded

### 04 **deface** v.
to spoil or damage the appearance of something; to weaken, devalue, or nullify

### 05 **degenerate** adj.
showing signs of deterioration or decline; morally depraved or corrupt

### 06 **dementia** n.
a mental disorder marked by a progressive decline in cognitive functions, such as judgment, memory, perception, language, etc.

### 07 **designate** v.
to name or appoint a person to an office, position, or a specific task; to specify, show, or point out; to call or refer to by a specific name or title

### 08 **dilute** v.
to make or become thinner or weaker by adding water; to diminish in strength, brilliance, value, etc.

### 09 **diminutive** adj.
extremely or notably tiny or small

### 10 **dismay** n.
distress or disappointment; a sudden loss of courage or confidence

## 11 **doctrine** n.

a set of religious or political beliefs or principles; a declaration of fundamental national policy

## 12 **encompass** v.

to include or contain; to encircle or surround; to accomplish or achieve

## 13 **extraction** n.

the action of pulling, tearing, or taking out something; one's ethnic origin or ancestry

## 14 **extraterrestrial** adj.

existing, occurring, or coming from outside the earth's atmosphere

## 15 **heritage** n.

property that is inherited; tradition, culture, language, etc., of a particular society; a birthright, or the status acquired by birth

## 16 **hysteria** n.

an outbreak of uncontrolled excitement, fear, or panic

## 17 **imperceptible** adj.

difficult or unable to distinguish, observe, or detect

## 18 **ingrained** adj.

deeply embedded (as in stain) or established (as in belief) and thus not easily removed or reformed

## 19 **perplex** v.

to confuse, puzzle, or baffle; to complicate or make something more difficult

## 20 **plight** n.

a difficult, dangerous, or unfortunate situation

## 21 **pragmatic** adj.

practical, sensible, or realistic

## 22 **prattle** v.
to chatter tediously or talk in a childish manner

## 23 **proximity** n.
closeness, or the quality or state of being near (as in time, space, etc.)

## 24 **pungent** adj.
having a sharp smell or taste; sharply critical, stinging, or sarcastic; having a stiff, sharp point; sharply or piercingly painful

## 25 **quell** v.
to crush or put down a disturbance, rebellion, etc.; to suppress or pacify a feeling of anger, grief, fear, etc.

## 26 **remorse** n.
a sense of regret or guilt felt over a wrong one has committed

## 27 **renegade** n.
a person who abandons or betrays a cause, religion, country, etc.; one who ignores laws, rules, or traditions

## 28 **reprobate** v.
to criticize or condemn strongly; to refuse or reject; to damn

## 29 **resilient** adj.
capable of recovering (from illness, hardship, etc.) quickly; able to get back to original state after being bent or twisted out of shape

## 30 **ruffian** n.
a brutal, violent, or lawless person

## 31 **sabotage** v.
to deliberately prevent, destroy, or damage

## 32 **scintillating** adj.
sparkling, shining, or glittering; brilliantly exciting, lively, or clever

## 33 **sentiment** n.

an opinion, attitude, or point of view; a nostalgic, romantic, or tender feeling, especially to the point of being overemotional

## 34 **shroud** v.

to conceal or cut off from view; to dress a corpse for burial

## 35 **silhouette** n.

a dark shape, outline, or figure seen against or fixed on a light background

## 36 **stagger** v.

to move or walk unsteadily; to astonish, amaze, or shock; to doubt or hesitate; to arrange or schedule alternately or in intervals

## 37 **stifle** v.

to restrain, prevent, or hold back; to kill by or die of suffocation; to become unable to breathe properly

## 38 **stolid** adj.

having or expressing little or no emotion

## 39 **suffuse** v.

to fill or spread over or through

## 40 **supple** adj.

flexible, pliant, or agile; easily influenced or adaptable to changes; smooth, soft, or rich (as in flavor, sound, fabric, etc.)

## 41 **surmount** v.

to overcome, deal with, or get over; to climb or get to the top of; to be placed on top of

## 42 **telltale** adj.

revealing or indicating something hidden or intended to be kept secret

## 43 **theology** n.

the study of religious faith, practice, or doctrines; a system of religious beliefs or theories

## 44 **torrent** n.

a violent, fast-moving flow (of water, lava, etc.); a sudden, seemingly uncontrollable rush (of words, email, etc.); a heavy rain

## 45 **trinket** n.

an ornament, toy, or any small object that has little value

## 46 **ulterior** adj.

beyond what is obvious, or intentionally concealed or hidden; situated beyond or on the farther side; coming later or in the future

## 47 **unmitigated** adj.

not eased, lessened, or diminished; absolute or definite, mostly to describe or emphasize something bad or unsuccessful

## 48 **upheaval** n.

a sudden, violent, or major change or disorder; a process in which a of part of the earth's surface rises up

## 49 **valedictory** adj.

serving as a formal way of saying goodbye

## 50 **vermin** n.

small insects or animals regarded as pests; an offensive or loathsome person

# vocabulary
### Part 3

### 01 **accept** v.
to agree to take something

### 02 **except** prep.
not counting

### 03 **aggravate** v.
to make worse

### 04 **agitate** v.
to stir or shake (a liquid); to upset, disturb, or excite

### 05 **irritate** v.
to cause pain or inflammation; to annoy someone

### 06 **anxious** adj.
worried, concerned, or uneasy

### 07 **eager** adj.
having an impatient desire for or to do something

### 08 **audible** adj.
capable of being heard

### 09 **auditory** adj.
relating to the sense or organs of hearing

### 10 **balk** v.
to resist or hesitate

### 11 **bulk** n.
a large size, mass, or quantity

Part 3

vocabulary

## 12 **biannual** adj.

happening twice a year

## 13 **biennial** adj.

happening every two years; lasting or living for two years

## 14 **bloc** n.

a coalition, alliance, or union

## 15 **block** n.

a chunk of hard material

## 16 **brake** n./v.

a device used to stop a moving vehicle; to make a moving vehicle stop

## 17 **break** n./v.

a rest, pause, or interruption; to shatter or separate into pieces

## 18 **canvas** n.

a coarse cloth used as a surface for oil painting or for making tents, sails, etc.

## 19 **canvass** v.

to campaign or solicit votes

## 20 **complement** n.

something that improve or completes

## 21 **compliment** n.

an expression of respect, praise, or admiration; something given for free or as service

## 22 **crevasse** n.

a large, deep opening or crack, especially in a glacier

## 23 **crevice** n.

a small, narrow split or gap, especially in a wall or rock

### 24 **custom** n.

a traditional observance, practice, or way of behaving

### 25 **costume** n.

the clothes worn for a particular purpose or by people of a particular place or historical period

### 26 **device** n.

a piece of equipment or hardware; a plan or scheme

### 27 **devise** v.

to come up with an idea, plan, or design

### 28 **gorilla** n.

a very large African ape

### 29 **guerilla** n.

a small group of independent soldiers engaging in surprise attacks

### 30 **historic** adj.

having (or likely to have) great or lasting fame, importance, or significance in history

### 31 **historical** adj.

concerning or belonging to the past or past events

### 32 **ingenious** adj.

clever, creative, or brilliant

### 33 **ingenuous** adj.

innocent, trusting, or simple

### 34 **loath** adj.

unwilling or reluctant to do something

### 35 **loathe** v.

to hate or despise

### 36 **marital** adj.

relating to marriage

### 37 **martial** adj.

relating to war, soldiers, or military life

### 38 **marshal** n./v.

an officer of the highest military rank (in some countries); a law officer; to assemble or gather together

### 39 **peak** v.

to reach a maximum or highest point

### 40 **peek** v.

to take a quick or secret look

### 41 **pique** v.

to stimulate curiosity or interest; to make angry or irritated

### 42 **premise** n.

a proposition in making an argument

### 43 **premises** n.

land or property

### 44 **quarry** n.

an animal being hunted down; a large, open pit for obtaining minerals

### 45 **query** n.

an inquiry or question

### 46 **sheath** n.

a case for the blade of a sword or knife; a covering that protects or insulates; a tight-fitting dress

### 47 **sheathe** v.

to put a sword or knife into its case; to enclose in a protective covering

## 48 **weather** n./v.

the condition of the atmosphere; to break down or wear away; to endure or deal with a difficult situation

## 49 **wether** n.

a castrated ram or goat

## 50 **whether** conj.

in any or either case that

# List 2

### 01 **affect** v.
to influence or have an impact on

### 02 **effect** n.
an outcome or result

### 03 **amenable** adj.
open to suggestion

### 04 **amiable** adj.
having a pleasant or friendly nature or personality

### 05 **amicable** adj.
having or showing the will or desire to maintain peace or good relationship (with the parties involved)

### 06 **apprehensible** adj.
capable of being understood

### 07 **apprehensive** adj.
anxious, uneasy, or worried

### 08 **assure** v.
to guarantee, promise, or tell someone with confidence

### 09 **ensure** v.
to make sure something will or will not happen

### 10 **insure** v.
to arrange for monetary compensation in case of loss, accident, or death

11 **bridal** adj.

relating to a bride or wedding

12 **bridle** n.

a set of straps with which to control a horse

13 **casual** adj.

relaxed, informal, or easygoing

14 **causal** adj.

being, relating to, or acting as a cause of something

15 **click** n.

a short, sharp sound or noise; the act of pressing a switch or mouse button

16 **clique** n.

a small, exclusive group of people

17 **clothes** n.

garments that people wear

18 **cloths** n.

pieces of woven fabric

19 **continual** adj.

coming and going or frequently recurring

20 **continuous** adj.

without interruption, break, or stopping

21 **definite** adj.

precise, specific, or clearly defined (as in not having doubts about something)

22 **definitive** adj.

official, final, or conclusive (as in an answer or decision that will not be changed)

### 23 **economic** adj.

relating to an economy or the study of economics

### 24 **economical** adj.

careful in spending or using money or resources; cheap, reasonable, or efficient

### 25 **eminent** adj.

famous, distinguished, or respected

### 26 **immanent** adj.

inherent, built-in, or existing within something

### 27 **imminent** adj.

fast approaching or about to happen

### 28 **farther** adv.

to a greater physical distance

### 29 **further** adv./adj./v.

to a greater figurative distance; additionally; more or additional; to promote or stimulate

### 30 **hangar** n.

a large building where aircraft are kept

### 31 **hanger** n.

a device used to hang things, especially clothes

### 32 **heroin** n.

a powerful, addictive drug made from morphine

### 33 **heroine** n.

a woman greatly admired by many; the main female character in a movie, book, etc.

### 34 **luminary** n.

a well-known or successful person or intellectual

### 35 **luminous** adj.

producing, filled with, or giving off light

### 36 **marinade** n./v.

a sauce in which meat or fish is soaked before cooking; to marinate (alternative spelling)

### 37 **marinate** v.

to soak meat or fish in a spiced sauce

### 38 **secession** n.

the act of breaking away from an organization or country to become independent

### 39 **succession** n.

the act of coming in sequence; the right to inherit or action of inheriting a title, position, property, etc.

### 40 **serf** n.

one who worked and lived on the land of a feudal lord

### 41 **surf** n./v.

waves breaking on a shoreline; to ride on waves on a board

### 42 **sleight** n.

a trick or scheme; skill or dexterity

### 43 **slight** adj./v.

small in quantity, degree, or extent; slender or delicate; to insult, ignore, or treat with disrespect

### 44 **taunt** v.

to mock, provoke, or make fun of someone

---

### 45 **taut** adj.

tightly stretched (as in rope); tense or stiff (as in muscles or facial expression); concise, tidy, or efficient

---

### 46 **tout** v.

to praise, recommend, or promote; to peddle or try to sell

---

### 47 **verses** n.

parts of a song or poem

---

### 48 **versus** prep.

against or in contrast to

---

### 49 **wet** adj.

covered in liquid

---

### 50 **whet** v.

to sharpen; to excite or stimulate

# List 3

---

### 01 **adverse** adj.
unfavorable or harmful

---

### 02 **averse** adj.
strongly disliking or opposed to something

---

### 03 **amoral** adj.
neither morally right or wrong, or not having the ability to distinguish between what is morally right or wrong

### 04 **immoral** adj.
corrupt, unethical, or morally wrong

---

### 05 **amused** adj.
pleasantly or delightfully entertained

### 06 **bemused** adj.
confused or puzzled

---

### 07 **auger** n.
a tool with a screw-like blade used for making holes

---

### 08 **augur** n.
a person who predicts the future

---

### 09 **berth** n.
a fixed bunk or bed; a docking site for ships; a place or position

---

### 10 **birth** n.
the act of being born

---

## 11 **carousal** n.

a loud, wild drinking party

## 12 **carousel** n.

a rotating machine that carries items, especially baggage; a merry-go-round

---

## 13 **choral** adj.

relating to a choir or chorus

## 14 **coral** n.

a stony substance made of the skeletons of marine creatures

## 15 **corral** n.

a pen for keeping livestock

---

## 16 **complacent** adj.

proud or pleased with oneself; happy with the way things are

## 17 **complaisant** adj.

eager or willing to please others

## 18 **complicit** adj.

participating in an illegal or questionable activity

---

## 19 **compose** v.

to form by combining (as in the parts making up a whole)

## 20 **comprise** v.

to contain or include (as in the whole having several parts)

---

## 21 **confidant** n.

a close friend, companion, or associate

## 22 **confident** adj.

sure of oneself or having optimism

## 23 **disinterested** adj.
not biased, partial, or prejudiced; indifferent

## 24 **uninterested** adj.
not interested

## 25 **entomology** n.
the study of insects

## 26 **etymology** n.
the study of the origins of words

## 27 **extant** adj.
still existing or surviving

## 28 **extent** n.
the size, range, or degree of something

## 29 **incredible** adj.
unimaginable or beyond belief

## 30 **incredulous** adj.
suspicious or unwilling to believe

## 31 **moral** adj./n.
relating to the principles or standards of right and wrong; a lesson learned from a story

## 32 **morale** n.
the amount of enthusiasm or confidence

## 33 **negligent** adj.
careless, irresponsible, or neglectful

## 34 **negligible** adj.
trivial, unimportant, or insignificant

## 35 **personal** adj.
relating to a particular person or person's private life

## 36 **personnel** n.
the employees of a particular organization or company

---

## 37 **pair** n.
a set of two

## 38 **pare** v.
to trim, peel, or cut off the skin or outer edges; to reduce expenses, costs, etc.

## 39 **pear** n.
a type of sweet fruit with brownish-green or yellowish color

---

## 40 **riffle** v./n.
to flip through (a book) or shuffle (cards); a shallow part of a stream that produces ripples

## 41 **rifle** v./n.
to ransack or steal; a gun with a long barrel

---

## 42 **suit** n./v.
a set of clothes; to be acceptable to; go well with

## 43 **suite** n.
a set of related things (such as connected rooms in a hotel); a group of attendants accompanying someone important

---

## 44 **vain** adj.
self-loving or conceited; failing to produce a desired result

## 45 **vane** n.
a flat or curved blade moved by wind or water

## 46 **vein** n.
a blood vessel; a style, mood, or tendency; a layer of a substance or water channel in rock or ice

---

vocabulary

## 47 **waiver** n.

the act of giving up a right, privilege, or claim

## 48 **waver** v.

to be indecisive between choices or opinions; to flicker, tremble, or move back and forth unsteadily

## 49 **wrath** n.

extreme anger or rage

## 50 **wraith** n.

a ghost or spirit

# List 4

**01 ambiguous** adj.

unclear, vague, or having more than one meaning

**02 ambivalent** adj.

undecided or having conflicting feelings

**03 appraise** v.

to evaluate or assess

**04 apprise** v.

to inform or notify

**05 assent** n.

an agreement or approval

**06 ascent** n.

the act of climbing up

**07 born** adj.

having started or brought into life

**08 borne** adj.

carried or transported by a particular thing

**09 congenial** adj.

pleasant or to one's liking; very friendly

**10 congenital** adj.

existing or present from birth

## 11 **decent** adj.

adequate or satisfactory; morally acceptable; kind or friendly

## 12 **descent** n.

a downward climb or slope; ancestry or lineage; a drop or decline in condition, status, morals, etc.; a raid or attack

## 13 **dissent** v.

to disagree or differ in opinion

## 14 **ephemeral** adj.

lasting for a very short period of time

## 15 **ethereal** adj.

spiritual, heavenly, or unearthly; very light and delicate

## 16 **fair** adj./n.

honest or just; light-colored; adequate or sufficient; lovely or beautiful; bright or sunny; a festival, market, or exhibition

## 17 **fare** n./v.

money paid for transportation; a range of food; to do or perform well or badly

## 18 **faze** v.

to shock, embarrass, or cause to hesitate

## 19 **phase** n.

a distinct stage or part of a cycle

## 20 **feat** n.

a remarkable or rare accomplishment

## 21 **fete** n.

a major celebration, festival, or event

## 22 **flaunt** v.
to show off

## 23 **flout** v.
to intentionally or openly ignore or refuse to obey (a law, rule, etc.)

## 24 **grisly** adj.
horrifying, shocking, or disgusting

## 25 **gristly** adj.
containing or full of gristle (a tough, stringy substance in meat)

## 26 **grizzly** n./adj.
a type of brown bear found in North America; grayish or gray-haired

## 27 **hail** v./n.
to greet or call out to someone; to acclaim or praise; to originate from; small pellets of frozen rain

## 28 **hale** adj./v.
strong and healthy; to force someone to go, especially to court; to drag or pull forcibly

## 29 **hoard** n.
a large sum of money or supply of valuable items kept hidden or in reserve

## 30 **horde** n.
a large crowd

## 31 **idle** adj.
not active

## 32 **idol** n.
an image or statue worshipped as a god; a person greatly admired by many

## 33 **idyll** n.
a short poem or piece of writing describing peaceful rural life

### 34 **pedal** n./adj.

a foot-controlled lever used to operate or play a machine, vehicle, instrument, etc.; relating to the foot

### 35 **peddle** v.

to travel to different places selling small goods; to sell illegal items

### 36 **petal** n.

any of the colorful outer parts of a flower

### 37 **perspective** n.

a point of view

### 38 **prospective** adj.

likely, expected, or about to be

### 39 **pray** v.

to address a higher being; to wish, hope, or ask for

### 40 **prey** n.

an animal hunted by a predator

### 41 **prophecy** n.

a prediction or forecast

### 42 **prophesy** v.

to predict or foretell

### 43 **rational** adj.

reasonable or logical

### 44 **rationale** n.

a reason, explanation, or justification for something

### 45 **stationary** adj.

not moving or changing

### 46 **stationery** n.

materials (such as paper, envelopes, etc.) used for writing

### 47 **straight** adj.

direct or unbending

### 48 **strait** n.

a narrow channel connecting two large bodies of water; a difficult situation

### 49 **yoke** n.

a wooden bar attaching the necks of a pair of working animals; oppression or en-slavement

### 50 **yolk** n.

the yellow part of an egg

# List 5

### 01 **allusion** n.
a hint or indirect reference

### 02 **illusion** n.
something that is not, but seems like it is, real

### 03 **alternate** adj.
every other

### 04 **alternative** adj.
available as a substitute or option

### 05 **carat** n.
a unit of weight for diamond and other precious stones

### 06 **caret** n.
a mark used in writing to show where an additional written material is to be inserted

### 07 **karat** n.
a unit to measure how pure gold is

### 08 **censor** v.
to delete parts that are considered sensitive or inappropriate

### 09 **censure** v.
to condemn or criticize severely, especially formally or officially

### 10 **comprehensible** adj.
easy to understand or able to be understood

### 11 **comprehensive** adj.
nearly or completely covering all elements

## 12 **contemptible** adj.

deserving contempt (referring to someone receiving contempt)

## 13 **contemptuous** adj.

feeling or expressing contempt (referring to someone showing contempt)

## 14 **correspondence** n.

communication by letters; correlation, connection, or similarity

## 15 **correspondents** n.

ones who communicate by letters; journalists or commentators

## 16 **depravation** n.

the act of making someone evil or morally wrong

## 17 **deprivation** n.

the lack of something that people need

## 18 **discriminant** n.

a distinguishing feature, agent, or characteristic

## 19 **discriminate** v.

to be able to tell the difference; to show prejudice or be biased

## 20 **discriminating** adj.

having good taste or judgment

## 21 **dual** adj.

having two kinds, parts, or aspects

## 22 **duel** n.

a fight, contest, or conflict between two people or opponents

## 23 **duo** n.

two people working or performing as partners

## 24 **epitaph** n.

a brief statement (especially one inscribed on a gravestone) written in memory of a deceased person

## 25 **epithet** n.

a description, title, or nickname of someone or something

## 26 **expedient** adj.

advantageous or convenient although may not be morally right or just

## 27 **expeditious** adj.

done in a swift and efficient manner

## 28 **explicit** adj.

clear, straightforward, or obvious

## 29 **implicit** adj.

implied, hinted, or not directly stated

## 30 **flair** n.

a special or natural ability

## 31 **flare** n.

an outburst of flame or light

## 32 **forbear** v./n.

to refrain or hold back from doing something; a forebear (alternative spelling)

## 33 **forebear** n.

an ancestor

## 34 **impetuous** adj.

done hastily without care or thought; moving violently or rapidly

## 35 **impetus** n.

the driving force that stimulates, increases, or encourages a process or activity

### 36 **patience** n.
tolerance or self-restraint

### 37 **patients** n.
people receiving medical treatment or care

### 38 **practicable** adj.
possible, doable, or feasible

### 39 **practical** adj.
actual, useful, or effective

### 40 **precede** v.
to come before in order, time, or position; to go before or ahead of

### 41 **proceed** v.
to move or go forward; to begin and continue to do something

### 42 **proceeds** n.
money or profit made from a sale, event, business venture, etc.

### 43 **premier** adj.
the best or most important

### 44 **premiere** n.
the first showing or performance of a film, play, musical, etc.

### 45 **prescribe** v.
to specify or order a drug for use by a patient; to require or set down as a rule

### 46 **proscribe** v.
to prohibit, forbid, or ban; to condemn or denounce

### 47 **regimen** n.

a systematic plan designed to maintain or improve health

### 48 **regiment** n.

an army unit made up of two or more battalions

### 49 **team** n.

a group of people formed to realize a common purpose

### 50 **teem** v.

to be full of or overflowing with; to pour down (as in rain); to empty or pour out

## 01 **adapt** v.

to adjust or make suitable

## 02 **adept** adj.

thoroughly skilled at something

## 03 **adopt** v.

to take someone else's child as one's own; to accept or start to use

## 04 **advice** n.

guidance or recommendation

## 05 **advise** v.

to offer suggestions or make recommendations

## 06 **ail** v.

to suffer or to be ill or troubled

## 07 **ale** n.

a type of alcoholic beverage

## 08 **broach** v.

to introduce or bring up a subject for discussion; to make a hole in order to draw liquid

## 09 **brooch** n.

a ornamental jewelry held by a pin

## 10 **canon** n.

a general rule, law, or principle

## 11 **cannon** n.

a big, heavy mounted gun

## 12 **cite** v.

to quote a book, author, etc.; to praise or commend

## 13 **site** n.

a place for a specific use or where something important happened

## 14 **coarse** adj.

having a rough texture; lacking in taste or refinement

## 15 **course** n.

a route, path, or direction; a part of a meal

## 16 **conscience** n.

a sense of right and wrong

## 17 **conscientious** adj.

diligent, careful, or thorough; relating to conscience

## 18 **conscious** adj.

wide awake; noticing or sensitive to something

## 19 **consul** n.

an official appointed to a foreign post

## 20 **council** n.

a group of people elected to govern; an advisory body

## 21 **counsel** n.

advice or guidance; a lawyer

## 22 **defuse** v.

to deactivate a bomb; to reduce or settle a tense or dangerous situation

## 23 **diffuse** v.

to scatter or spread out

### 24 **discreet** adj.

careful not to attract attention, cause embarrassment, or reveal a secret

### 25 **discrete** adj.

individually distinct or clearly separate

### 26 **envelop** v.

to cover or surround completely

### 27 **envelope** n.

an enclosing cover for a letter, document, card, etc.

### 28 **infernal** adj.

relating to hell or the world of the dead

### 29 **inferno** n.

a large, destructive fire; hell, or any place or situation resembling hell

### 30 **infirmary** n.

a place where sick or injured people are cared for

### 31 **infirmity** n.

physical, mental, or moral weakness

### 32 **mantel** n.

a decorative shelf above a fireplace

### 33 **mantle** n.

a loose, sleeveless robe or cloak; something that covers or conceals; the layer between the earth's crust and the core

### 34 **noisome** adj.

harmful to health; unpleasant, disgusting, or foul-smelling

### 35 **noisy** adj.

full of noise

## 36 **pendant** n.

a piece of jewelry hanging on a chain; any object hanging from something else

## 37 **pendent** adj.

dangling, suspended, or hanging down

## 38 **pistil** n.

the long central part of a flower composed of style, stigma, and ovary

## 39 **pistol** n.

a small gun

## 40 **prodigal** adj.

wasteful or extravagant

## 41 **prodigious** adj.

amazing, exciting, or wonderful; huge or enormous

## 42 **prodigy** n.

a child genius or young person with exceptional talent; a model or outstanding example of something

## 43 **tenant** n.

someone who pays rent to use or live in a place

## 44 **tenet** n.

a belief, principle, or doctrine

## 45 **veracious** adj.

true, correct, or accurate

## 46 **voracious** adj.

wanting or eating a lot of food; having an extremely greedy approach to some desire, activity, or pursuit

## 47 **wreak** v.
to destroy or damage

## 48 **wreck** v.
to inflict punishment or vengeance; to cause, result in, or bring about

## 49 **wreath** n.
a ring-shaped arrangement of flowers and leaves; a circular formation

## 50 **wreathe** v.
to encircle or surround

# List 7

**01 aisle** n.

a passage through rows of seats

**02 isle** n.

an island

**03 assume** v.

to think that something is true without reason or proof

**04 presume** v.

to think that something is true based on probability or reasonable evidence

**05 bare** adj./v.

naked or exposed; to remove, uncover, or reveal

**06 bear** v.

to carry or support; to endure or tolerate; to produce or give birth to

**07 bazaar** n.

a marketplace or fundraiser

**08 bizarre** adj.

very strange, odd, or unusual

**09 classic** adj.

of the highest quality; serving as a model or standard

**10 classical** adj.

customary or traditional; relating to the ancient Greek and Roman literature, art, etc.

## 11 **climactic** adj.

reaching or acting as the most important or exciting part of a story or event

## 12 **climatic** adj.

relating to climate

## 13 **compulsive** adj.

unable to control or stop doing something

## 14 **compulsory** adj.

required by a rule or law

## 15 **corporal** adj./n.

relating to or affecting the body; a military officer ranking below sergeant

## 16 **corporeal** adj.

relating to the physical world or material body, as distinct from or opposed to the spiritual

## 17 **demur** v.

to object, take exception, or show reluctance

## 18 **demure** adj.

modest, shy, or serious (usually describing a woman); not flashy, showy, or revealing

## 19 **eligible** adj.

qualified or allowed to do or be something

## 20 **illegible** adj.

unreadable because badly written or faded

## 21 **exercise** v.

to train, keep fit, or work out; to utilize, exert, or put into use

## 22 **exorcise** v.

to drive out an evil spirit

## 23 **forego** v.
to precede or go before; to forgo (alternative spelling)

## 24 **forgo** v.
to give up or do without

## 25 **incite** v.
to cause or stir up violent feeling or action

## 26 **insight** n.
the ability to gain a deep understanding of people, things, or situations

## 27 **medal** n.
a small metal object given as an award

## 28 **meddle** v.
to interfere or become involved in other people's business

## 29 **metal** n.
a solid substance such as iron, steel, lead, etc.

## 30 **mettle** n.
the courage, strength, or spirit to press on in difficult situations

## 31 **mendacity** n.
untruthfulness or dishonesty

## 32 **mendicity** n.
the state of being or activities of a beggar

## 33 **muscle** n.
a tissue inside a body

## 34 **mussel** n.
a type of shellfish with a dark, elongated shell

### 35 **naval** adj.
relating to a navy

### 36 **navel** n.
a small, rounded cavity in the middle of one's stomach (a belly button)

### 37 **parameter** n.
a limit or rule controlling how something should be made or done

### 38 **perimeter** n.
the border or boundary of a surface or area

### 39 **peal** v.
to chime or ring loudly

### 40 **peel** v.
to strip off the skin, covering, or outer layer

### 41 **purposely** adv.
intentionally or deliberately

### 42 **purposefully** adv.
with determination

### 43 **restive** adj.
impatient, restless, or nervous

### 44 **restful** adj.
peaceful, quiet, or relaxing

### 45 **wary** adj.
cautious, alert, or careful

### 46 **weary** adj.
tired or exhausted; having lost interest or patience

### 47 **whither** adv./conj.

to what place or situation; to which or whatever place or condition

### 48 **wither** v.

to shrivel or dry up; to weaken, decline, or become helpless

### 49 **wishful** adj.

having a wish

### 50 **wistful** adj.

regretful, sad, or longing

# List 8

### 01 **aid** v.
to help or assist

### 02 **aide** n.
a person who helps or assists

### 03 **altar** n.
a table used for religious ceremonies

### 04 **alter** v.
to change, modify, or adjust

### 05 **bail** n.
a sum of money given to release a prisoner until the trial

### 06 **bale** n.
a bundle, load, or pack

### 07 **breath** n.
the act of breathing

### 08 **breathe** v.
to inhale and exhale air

### 09 **capital** n.
a country's seat of government; money, property, or assets

### 10 **capitol** n.
a building in which lawmakers meet

## 11 **chord** n.

a group of musical notes played simultaneously

## 12 **cord** n.

a string, rope, or wire

## 13 **coddle** v.

to treat with great or too much care

## 14 **cuddle** v.

to hold tight or hug affectionately

## 15 **collaborate** v.

to work together

## 16 **corroborate** v.

to support, confirm, or make more certain

## 17 **elicit** v.

to draw out (especially a response or information) from a person

## 18 **illicit** adj.

against the law; not morally acceptable

## 19 **faint** v./adj.

to lose consciousness; lacking strength or courage; not clear or distinct

## 20 **feint** v.

to make a pretended attack

## 21 **foreword** n.

an introductory section of a book

## 22 **forward** adv./adj.

toward the front; facing toward the front; relating to the future

### 23 **imaginary** adj.

fictional, unreal, or make-believe

### 24 **imaginative** adj.

creative, original, or inventive

### 25 **imprudent** adj.

not showing care or good judgment

### 26 **impudent** adj.

rude, disrespectful, or ill-mannered

### 27 **inflammable** adj.

capable of burning or being set on fire; easily angered or provoked

### 28 **inflammatory** adj.

relating to a part of the body becoming reddened or swollen; intended to arouse anger or disorder

### 29 **palate** n.

the roof of the mouth; the sense of taste; an intellectual taste or liking

### 30 **palette** n.

a flat board on which a painter mixes colors; a particular range of colors used by a painter

### 31 **pallet** n.

a portable platform used for stacking, storing, or transporting items; a straw mattress; a hard makeshift bed

### 32 **pellet** n.

a small, usually round-shaped medicine, food, etc.; a small, rounded object used as a bullet

### 33 **peremptory** adj.

demanding prompt obedience or attention; not open to challenge or debate

### 34 **preemptory** adj.

relating to action taken to prevent something from happening

### 35 **perpetrate** v.
to perform or commit an illegal or immoral act

### 36 **perpetuate** v.
to cause something to last or continue indefinitely

### 37 **persecute** v.
to abuse or oppress unfairly or cruelly

### 38 **prosecute** v.
to bring legal action against a person accused of a crime

### 39 **pole** n.
a stick or rod; the northern and southern points of the earth's axis

### 40 **poll** n.
the process of or place for voting, or the record of votes

### 41 **precedence** n.
the fact of being a priority or more important than something or someone else

### 42 **precedent** n.
a past case that may serve as an example to justify a decision; an established custom

### 43 **principal** n./adj.
the person in charge; the money or capital originally invested; first or most important

### 44 **principle** n.
a fundamental truth, moral rule, or law of nature

### 45 **tortuous** adj.
having many twists, turns, or curves; confusing or complicated

### 46 **torturous** adj.
causing great pain or suffering

### 47 **urban** adj.

relating or belonging to a city

### 48 **urbane** adj.

sophisticated, fashionable, or cultured

### 49 **vassal** n.

one receiving land or protection from a feudal lord in return for pledging loyalty or doing military service

### 50 **vessel** n.

a large boat or ship; a bowl or container; a tube circulating blood or other body fluid

**vocabulary**
I n d e x

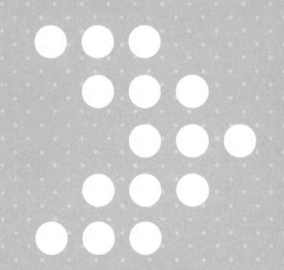

Index

Index

Index

Index

Index

Index

Index

# SAT CORE VOCAB 3000 plus

초 판 1쇄 인쇄 | 2019년 5월 28일
초 판 1쇄 발행 | 2019년 6월 7일

지은이 | KEITH KYUNG
펴낸이 | 조선우 • 펴낸곳 | 책읽는귀족

등록 | 2012년 2월 17일 제396-2012-000041호
주소 | 경기도 고양시 일산서구 대산로 123, 현대프라자 342호(주엽동, K일산비즈니스센터)

전화 | 031-944-6907 • 팩스 | 031-944-6908
홈페이지 | www.noblewithbooks.com
E-mail | idea444@naver.com

책임 편집 | 조선우
표지 & 본문 디자인 | twoesdesign

값 25,000원
ISBN 978-89-97863-99-0 (13740)

이 도서의 국립중앙도서관 출판예정도서목록(CIP)은
서지정보유통지원시스템 홈페이지(http://seoji.nl.go.kr)와
국가자료공동목록시스템(http://www.nl.go.kr/kolisnet)에서
이용하실 수 있습니다.
(CIP제어번호: CIP2019020576)